The Cross of Redemption

JAMES BALDWIN

The Cross of Redemption

UNCOLLECTED WRITINGS

Edited and with an Introduction by
RANDALL KENAN

PANTHEON BOOKS · NEW YORK

Library of Congress Cataloging-in-Publication Data
Baldwin, James, 1924–1987.
The cross of redemption : uncollected writings / James
Baldwin ; edited and with an introduction by Randall Kenan.
p. cm.
A collection of essays, speeches, letters, reviews, etc.
Includes bibliographical references.
ISBN 978-0-307-37882-8
I. Kenan, Randall. II. Title.
PS3552.A45C76 2010
818'.54—dc22
2009050897

www.pantheonbooks.com

Printed in the United States of America

First Edition

2 4 6 8 9 7 5 3 1

The Estate of James Baldwin would like to extend appreciation to Erroll McDonald, Randall Kenan, Lily Evans, Eileen Ahearn, Douglas Field, Rene Boatman, and Quentin Miller for bringing this collection to fruition.

CONTENTS

PROFILES

LETTERS

FOREWORDS AND AFTERWORDS

Introduction: Looking for James Baldwin

I

IMAGINE: It is 1947, late autumn. You are twenty-three years old. You are black. You are living in New York's Greenwich Village. You work at a small Caribbean restaurant on MacDougal Street called Calypso. You wait tables. You have worked laying railroad tracks in New Jersey. You hated the job. You hate segregated life and the indignities to which you were subjected on top of your hardscrabble existence. You cannot afford to go to college. You must earn money to send home to your large, impoverished family up in Harlem and to survive. People say you look about fifteen years old. You have interesting friends, paramount among them being the African-American painter Beauford Delaney, worldly and wise. He takes a special interest in you. He is your mentor. A surrogate father. (Your father died in 1943.) You will later write of Delaney, "He opened the unusual door" for you. Delaney introduces you to the writer Henry Miller. At the restaurant you meet Paul Robeson and Burt Lancaster and Eartha Kitt and C. L. R. James and so many others. You become good friends with a young, weird, wild, beautiful midwesterner enthralled by the possibilities of Method acting. His name is Marlon Brando. He is not your lover, but he will remain a lifelong friend.

In this exciting Manhattan Village you meet a lot of politically noisy, rambunctious, revolutionary, bohemian, fun-loving types, people who follow socialist ideals, Trotsky and the like, but also you meet musicians, singers, theater people of all stripes, public intellectuals, writers and editors at places like *The Nation*, the *Partisan Review*, the *New Leader*, *Commentary*, people like Randall Jarrell and Philip Rahv. You get a job as a messenger for a left-leaning newspaper, *PM*. The editor of the *New Leader*, Sol Levitas, takes a liking to you. He knows you've been working on a novel, *Crying Holy*—no, you've changed the name to *In My Father's House* by now. Levitas suggests you try your hand at writing book reviews. It will give you discipline, he says.

Your first review, of a collection of short stories by the Russian writer Maxim Gorky, is published in the April 12, 1947, issue of *The Nation*. You write that Gorky is "far from a careful writer and by no means a great one. He is almost always painfully verbose and frequently threatens to degenerate into simple propaganda." The review is somewhat brutal; yet you go on to praise Gorky for his "rare sympathy for people," and further, you chastise "present-day realistic novelists" for their lack of sympathy, for failing to see "the unpredictability and the occasional and amazing splendor of the human being." You end your first review, which has a somewhat sermonic tone, on the word "salvation."

IMAGINE: At twenty-three, so much of the James Baldwin the world will come to admire and heed and laud and consider as indispensable was already well formed.

Later that year, in November, in another review of Gorky, of his novel *Mother*, Baldwin writes:

> Art, to be sure, has its roots in the lives of human beings: the weakness, the strength, the absurdity. I doubt that it is limited to our comrades; since we have discovered that art does not belong to what was once the aristocracy, it does not therefore follow that it has become the exclusive property of the common man—which abstraction, by the way, I have yet to meet. Rather, since it is involved with all of us, it belongs to all of us, and this includes our foes, who are as desperate and as vicious and as blind as we are and who can only be as evil as we are ourselves.

He is now only twenty-four; yet the elevated diction, the preoccupation with societal ethics, the syntactical willingness to allow his thoughts to unfurl and take up space, majestically, as they precess toward his hermeneutical ends—looking back, it all feels rather like Athena bursting forth from her daddy's head, fully made.

Yet, though Baldwin was certainly precocious, he had earned his world vision and his eloquence, as he would go on to essentially document. Rather than springing forth from his stepfather's brow, he instead wrestled his very gift away from the disapproving Reverend David Baldwin, who saw nothing but ruination in young Jimmy's fascination with the secular world and with art. It was a fraught relationship, accompanied by severe discipline, harsh beatings, verbal abuse, but also tinged with what Baldwin himself would call love but locked up in a man who did not know how, or who was afraid, to show it.

By the time of his first publication James Baldwin was already onto his second, or even third, life.

II

But of course the fact that he could be such a powerful writer, against such powerful odds, at such a young age, seems to make sense, in retrospect.

His mother, Berdis Emma Jones, had come to New York from Maryland, a young woman. A failed relationship left her with a child. By the time James was three, in 1927, she had wed a Baptist minister turned Pentecostal, David Baldwin, originally from Louisiana. They would have eight children together.

Their life in Harlem, at the height of the Great Depression, was a constant struggle. David worked in factories, when he could find work; but he also continued preaching in storefront churches. Berdis worked cleaning houses and as a laundress. It fell to young James to help with his brothers and sisters.

The world of literature came knock-knock-knocking on James Baldwin's door early: Reading and rereading *Uncle Tom's Cabin* before he was ten. Discovering the novels of Charles Dickens at around the same time. The Schomburg Library on 135th Street, which he seemed to haunt when not baby-sitting his siblings. Frederick Douglass Junior High School, where he would study with Countee Cullen ("To make a poet black, and bid him sing!"), by then the author of two volumes of poetry. Surely, for Baldwin, already the idea of being a writer, for a black man, was a tangible, possible thing.

Then, 1938, simultaneously: Fireside Pentecostal Assembly and DeWitt Clinton High School. Through one door he was learning to "walk holy," thus becoming a young minister wielding the power of the Word from the pulpit with the sonorous cadences of the King James Bible and with the force of an Old Testament prophet; through the other door—at a school considered by many to have been among the best in the country—he was experiencing another other world of words, as a short-story writer, playwright, editor, critic.

To be sure, Baldwin gives us vivid portraits of the pressure cooker in which he stewed—not only in his virtuoso first novel, *Go Tell It on the Mountain* (1953), but later in literally scores of autobiographical essays, again and again, revisiting that existential struggle he faced, like Saint Augustine or John Donne, warring against visions of the sacred and the profane, fighting to become himself, to find himself. But even with those great testaments, which seem to make his emergence as a literary maven seem inevitable, to clothe his history in Myth, there yet remains an impenetrable mystery, still, surrounding James Baldwin, created in the quintessence of a disadvantaged childhood—almost like that of a character from the very Dickens novels he loved so much—rising up, phoenix-like, on the wings of a literary archangel.

One thinks of Aristotle's admonition that in a well-made play a probable impossibility is always preferable to an improbable possibility, such is the narrative conundrum that is James Arthur Baldwin. Not that it is improbable that a young black man should struggle out of such unforgiving circumstances to achieve literary fame and fortune—literally hundreds of young men and women have accomplished just that—but it is the staggering quality and sheer magnitude of Baldwin's achievements that beggar the imagination. Musical prodigies, though few and far between, are numerous and sundry; literary prodigies are rarely ever heard from, and the few who shine forth tend to burn out quite young.

Any new glimpse into the probable impossibility that is James Baldwin is a welcome treat and treasure.

III

As a companion volume to *James Baldwin: Collected Essays* (1998), the Library of America's edition of his collected nonfiction, these heretofore uncollected occasional writings give us a different lens through which to view Baldwin's artistry. A collection of snapshots. A sketchbook. An omnium-gatherum of those ideas he revisited most often. A GPS map of the geography of his mind's progress. It brings together an eclectic mix of reviews, essays, and public letters from 1947 to 1985 that charts his incredible passage.

The trajectory of James Baldwin's life has the quality of epic saga. He fled racially intolerant America for France in 1948. He had already become acquainted with Richard Wright, by far the most successful and famous black novelist in America at the time. Wright had intervened on Baldwin's behalf with his publisher, Harper and Row, to obtain an option for the unfinished first novel. But that novel would not come together. Now in war-scarred France Baldwin tried to try again, yet he quickly found himself in even worse circumstances than he had faced back in his homeland. No money, ill health, and, much to his chagrin, racist encounters with the French police led him to near despair. The famous American colony of intellectuals and artists and writers (now including Richard Wright) soon grew peevish with him. Fortunately for Baldwin, his young Swiss lover, Lucien Happersberger, with the help of his father, was able to spirit Baldwin away to an Alpine village, Loèche-les-Bains, which Baldwin would later write about with great affection in his essay "A Stranger in the Village." There he would regain his health, his optimism, his creative spark, and, to the gut-bucket blues of Bessie Smith, he would complete the novel now called *Go Tell It on the Mountain*. He was twenty-nine when Alfred A. Knopf published the book, to great acclaim. This was the story he had been struggling to tell, of a large family in a small Harlem apartment, of a loving mother, of an unreasonable minister father, of communing with the Holy Spirit, of becoming fascinated with the wide world.

His second novel seemed initially to hit a roadblock—a brief, lyrical novel written from the point of view of a white man in love with another white man, an Italian named Giovanni—which led Baldwin's publisher to abandon the now-too-controversial-to-handle young black writer. In the meantime, Beacon Press brought out a collection of his essays, often written to keep body and soul together while he completed his first novel. That collection, *Notes of a Native Son* (1955), drew even greater attention to James Baldwin, marking him as a skilled essayist and thinker and commentator on the racial scene. The volume contained seminal essays for which he would become known for decades to come, including the title essay, in which he artfully came to some reconciliation with his late stepfather and somehow spun that heartache with larger events dealing with race and politics and humanity. There was that style, part sermon, part nineteenth-century mandarin (Henry James, about whom he had written and felt a certain kinship as a fellow expatriate, now being a profound influence on his prose).

The next year saw the publication of the new novel, *Giovanni's Room*, which miraculously survived the firestorm of homophobia and firmly established Baldwin as a hot novelist of note, an important new voice.

Thus began over a decade of a rather heady and tumultuous life, dominated not only by tremendous literary production, but by a hands-on involvement in the struggle for civil rights for black folk, particularly in the South, and throughout America. He was commissioned by top-flight national magazines—*Esquire, Harper's, Playboy*—to go to North Carolina and Tennessee and Arkansas and Alabama and Mississippi and Georgia, foreign lands for him, to write about those increasingly heated battles. There was something about his background—this Northern child of Holy Roller Harlem, this American who had fled racist America for France only to encounter another racism, this gay man (the ultimate outsider)—that gave James Baldwin not only the insight, but a language and a moral vision inflected by the righteous rhythms of Protestantism, that made his writings like none other. The essays collected in *Nobody Knows My Name: More Notes of a Native Son* (1961) and later in the hugely successful *The Fire Next Time*, the 1963 account of the Nation of Islam that turned into a national sermon on race, all served to transform Baldwin into something more than a writer for the American public and the world at large—if the Reverend Martin Luther King Jr. was the civil rights movement's Moses, James Baldwin had become its Jeremiah, despite his protestations of speaking for no one but himself.

Of course Baldwin considered himself first and foremost a novelist. Nineteen sixty-two's *Another Country* represented a maturation that seemed to represent the fruition of all his literary ambitions. A dramatic exploration of love and race in its many manifestations—black man with white woman, white man with black woman, black man with white man—the book proved to be even more controversial than *Giovanni's Room*. It was banned in many states yet became one of the best-selling paperback novels of 1963.

Radio, television, far-flung speaking engagements, interviews galore, and a taste for the high life—Baldwin was now leading as hectic a life as any million-seller recording artist, perhaps even more so. The cover of *Time* magazine. A place on the rostrum at the 1963 March on Washington. This period was a lengthy crescendo that resonated throughout the 1960s.

But the 1960s were both halcyon and hell for Baldwin. More literary successes followed: a Broadway play, *Blues for Mister Charlie* (1964); a collection of short stories, *Going to Meet the Man* (1965); another best-selling novel, *Tell Me How Long the Train's Been Gone* (1968). And also a time for assassinations: Medgar Evers, Malcolm X, Martin Luther King Jr.—men he knew, men he considered friends. He even had a problematic relationship with Robert F. Kennedy. The weight of all this bloodshed, and a lifestyle that seemed to be spiraling out of control, led him to go into what looked more and more like an unofficial exile, first to Turkey and later to the south of France, where throughout the 1970s he held court in a three hundred-year-old farmhouse in Saint-Paul-de-Vence, rather like an oracle frequently visited by acolytes and pilgrims and admirers from far and wide.

IV

Here's the thing about James Baldwin's prose:

As noted earlier, from the start, he was audacious in his love for complex sentences; one might say even fearless in the way he deployed the English language. Faulkner, Virginia Woolf, Malcolm Lowry, among English-language writers, dared put so much demand on the language. To watch them create a sentence is often like watching a high-wire act. Death-defying sentences. Lush, romantic sentences. Sentences that dared to swallow the entire world. These writers were undaunted by outrageous complexity, clauses, dependent and independent, modified, interrupted, periodic. They trusted in the force of their meaning and their music (and the rules of good grammar) to carry the feat. But the aforementioned writers almost always saved their linguistic pyrotechnics for fiction: Baldwin unleashed his most baroque prose in his nonfiction, something that not only set him apart from his contemporaries, gave him a singular voice, but also allowed him to create thoughts of great nuance and shading and meaning. Reading a Baldwin sentence can feel like recreating thought itself. One has to take hands off the rudder and trust the river of thought as it flows. Here is a sentence from a 1967 review of Elia Kazan's novel *The Arrangement:*

> This is not the official version of American history, but that it very nearly sums it up can scarcely be doubted by anyone with the courage to look into the faces one encounters all over this land: who listens to the voices, hearing incessantly the buried uneasiness, the bewilderment, the unad-

mitted despair, hearing the arrogant, jaunty, fathomless, utterly astounding ignorance; a cultivated ignorance of all things public, and a terrified
ignorance of all things private; translating itself, visibly, hourly, into a
hatred of all that is strange or vivid—and what is vivid is always strange;
into a hatred, at last, of life.

I do not mean to suggest that Baldwin was totally given over to highly
complex prose, that he overindulged in ornate rhetoric. In fact this book
contains fewer rococo passages than in some of his better-known work.
(See *The Fire Next Time*.) Rather, I hope to underscore Baldwin's uncanny
mastery of the English language; how, like his contemporary Miles Davis
on the trumpet, his skill allowed him to go any place he wanted, with
deceptive ease. Like magic.

But above all—and this cannot be stressed strongly enough—meaning
was always utmost. Despite a highly evolved aesthetic sensibility, despite a
punishingly high level of artistic standards, Baldwin's goal was always to
communicate, not to show off. George Orwell would definitely approve of
his overall strategies. For him the medium was not the message; the message was always the message.

It is easy to say that Baldwin's main message was racial equality. Surely
the topic flows through his work more than it ebbs. Yet one makes a grave
mistake in pigeonholing James Baldwin's worldview so narrowly, for
throughout this miscellany, though racial topics and racial politics are often
the touchstone, his true themes are more in line with the early church
fathers, with Erasmus of Rotterdam, with the great Western philosophers,
with theologians like Reinhold Niebuhr and Dietrich Bonhoeffer and
James Cone. And though it is too broad—if not useless—to say his true
topic is humanity, it is useful to see how, no matter his topic, how often his
writing finds some ur-morality upon which to rest, how he always sees
matters through a lens of decency, how he writes with his heart as well as
with his head. Baldwin left the pulpit at sixteen, but he never stopped
preaching.

This book has been organized into Baldwin's essays, profiles, reviews, letters, introductions, and a short story.

The reviews show a writer of broad tastes; a writer always agile and
with a rapier wit, sometimes feeling a bit sharper than necessary, but
always hitting his mark. Aside from Gorky, he reviewed biographies, the

fiction of Erskine Caldwell, Catholic philosophy, a novel by Mississippi newspaperman Hodding Carter, and a late novel by James M. Cain, among others. There is a fascinating 1949 piece he wrote for *Commentary*, "Too Late, Too Late," in which he rounds up seven books about black Americans, including John Hope Franklin's classic *From Slavery to Freedom*. Baldwin is rather harsh on all of them—bewilderingly so:

> And the very moment these questions are asked, this long view—which is demanded most vociferously of Negroes—emerges as something less lofty; comes close, indeed, to being nothing more than a system of justification. The American need for justification is a good deal stronger than the American sense of time—which began, as we are inclined to believe, with the Stars and Stripes. Thus, not even Mr. Rose's careful and comprehensive study escapes the pit into which all of these books fall: they record the facts, but they cannot probe the immense, ambiguous, uncontrollable effect. The full story of white and black in this country is more vast and shattering than we would like to believe and, like an unhindered infection in the body, it has the power to make our whole organism sick.

Truth to tell, James Baldwin comes across in almost all his reviews as a pretty strict and unforgiving taskmaster. This revelation should come as no surprise to students of Baldwin, who notoriously excoriated *Native Son*—written by his chief patron, Richard Wright—an act that broke their friendship for the rest of their lives. And there was also the review of *Raintree County*, by Ross Lockridge Jr., which called the book phony, among other select qualifications. The author committed suicide shortly before the review was published; Baldwin qualified his original review by essentially saying the book was still no good.

Baldwin's letters, on the other hand, strike a more complex mélange of emotions. Indeed, his tone is often fiery, as in his 1970 open letter to activist Angela Davis, who had just been imprisoned. ("One might have hoped that, by this hour, the very sight of chains on black flesh, or the very sight of chains, would be so intolerable a sight for the American people, and so unbearable a memory, that they would themselves spontaneously rise up and strike off the manacles.") His tone is militant, as condemnatory toward the U.S.A. as ever; yet his tenderness toward Davis and her comrades elicits a forlorn sense of longing.

His 1968 essay "Black Power," written in response to activist Stokely

Carmichael's 1967 book of the same name, feels even more like a plea. In a 1967 letter to *Freedomways,* he takes issue with public calls for blacks to embrace anti-Semitism, saying that black folk have no use of such ancient evil.

An arresting sequence of letters, published together in *Harper's* in 1963, strikes yet another note, showing us a young James Baldwin on the road, from September 1961 to February 1962. Paris. Israel. Turkey. Switzerland. Here we see glimpses of a much more idealistic young man, an admixture of hope and light and wonder and concern for his loved ones, tempered by discomfort and a clear eye cast toward the injustice he encounters:

> "Oh, What a Beautiful City!" Well, that's the way Jerusalem makes one feel. I stood today in the upper room, the room where Christ and his disciples had the Last Supper, and I thought of Mahalia and Marian Anderson and "Go Down, Moses" and of my father and of that other song . . . And here I am, far from ready, in one of the homelands which has given me my identity and on my way to another.

The forewords and prefaces Baldwin writes are an interesting grab bag, written largely by his goodwill and affection and sense of fellowship toward fellow writers. A generosity of spirit. An odd kiss to a brother in the foreword to Bobby Seale's 1978 autobiography ("For it is that tremendous journey which Bobby's book is about: the act of assuming and becoming oneself"). A valentine to a book he recognized as an instant classic, Louise Meriwether's *Daddy Was a Number Runner,* about his own Harlem. But that tone differs in a brief but powerful preface to *The Negro in New York.* Somehow he links the Dutch to the Industrial Revolution and then to the plight of black folk in present-day Harlem—there is a wicked humor afoot in his anger, bracing and ruefully amusing.

As fascinating and piercing and blood-quickening and exciting as these shorter pieces are, James Baldwin truly shines in the longer form. It is thrilling to see so many of these largely forgotten pieces reintroduced into wider circulation. Many are positively breathtaking. Moreover, my earlier point about Baldwin's wide and diverse interests is here proven. He writes about literature; he writes about Turkey and Africa and Europe; he writes about music; he writes about the American language; he writes about theater and boxing and child rearing; and yes, he writes at great length about those matters with which he shall always be associated: race, the American empire, justice, and James Baldwin.

A standout piece is one he wrote in 1962, where he comes as close to writing a manifesto for his art as any place else ("As Much Truth As One Can Bear"). Here he takes to task his literary predecessors Faulkner, Fitzgerald, Hemingway, Dos Passos: "One must be willing—indeed, one must be anxious—to locate, precisely, that American morality of which we boast."

"Of the Sorrow Songs: The Cross of Redemption" is a lyric praise-song to great African-American song: "It is out of this, and much more than this, that black American music springs. This music begins on the auction block . . . Music is our witness, and our ally. The 'beat' is the confession which recognizes, changes, and conquers time."

Here, in this volume, are three companion pieces to "If Black English Isn't a Language, Then Tell Me, What Is?," the essay he wrote in 1979 and which is still widely read today. "Why I Stopped Hating Shakespeare," "On Language, Race, and the Black Writer," and "Black English: A Dishonest Argument" will surely be as equally well read and discussed.

Without exaggeration I must say the 1963 piece of reportage "The Fight: Patterson vs. Liston," about the fabled Chicago prizefight, is easily among the best writing Baldwin ever committed. And no one else could do proper justice to the great Sidney Poitier the way James Baldwin did in *Look* magazine in July of 1968.

Baldwin made no secret of his deep love for his good buddy the playwright Lorraine Hansberry, immortalized in his oft-reprinted reminiscence, "Sweet Lorraine." Here are two more paeans to the author of *A Raisin in the Sun*, one about that play's bedrock truths, and the other, his 1979 recounting of Attorney General Robert Kennedy's infamous 1963 meeting in New York with Baldwin, Hansberry, Lena Horne, Harry Belafonte, and a number of other black activists. This meeting turned into a shouting match recounted in the papers. Sixteen years later, Baldwin's tone is now wistful, yet piercing, a shot through the heart on many levels.

V

For years, for some reason, I always thought upon Baldwin's time during the 1970s as bitter and angry and unhappy. That was the popular narrative that attended him as the Nixon years waned into the Carter years and Ronald Reagan waxed onto the stage. Journalists often quoted the interviews that Baldwin gave in the late 1960s and early 1970s, at the height of the Vietnam War and in the wake of so much death and an American land-scape pockmarked with riot-ruined cities. Clearly his feelings had been injured by his rejection by youthful groups like the Black Panthers. He came off in the press as an aloof, wealthy old warrior who had left the bat-tlefield, his country forsaken, his ministry of love turned into one of bit-terness.

Henry Louis Gates Jr.'s memorable essay/interview simply called "An Interview with Josephine Baker and James Baldwin," written in 1973, did not see print until 1985, and it told a slightly different story. In truth, the piece does end with Baldwin predicting "apocalypse" for America. But again, this was 1973. However, the image one comes away with is one of Baldwin communing with the great Josephine Baker, who, oddly enough, had a much more sanguine attitude toward her faraway country. The two veterans reminisce and a young Skip Gates leaves with a renewed sense of the possible, not only for himself but for his hero, James Baldwin.

Baldwin would go on to write some of his best and some of his less good work: *Just Above My Head,* his last novel, and *The Devil Finds Work,* a funky combination of memoir and movie criticism, representing the best; *The Evidence of Things Not Seen,* his swan song, about the Atlanta child mur-ders, being among his least successful.

Yet life was rich, despite what the media would have led us to believe. Baldwin would begin teaching in the 1980s, in America, where he wound up influencing a number of young African-American women who would go on to important literary careers, one even winning a Pulitzer Prize.

As I have traveled the country in the last several months, back into the fall of 2008, talking to students about the work of James Baldwin and African America, I can always count on one question coming from young people for whom the civil rights movement is a collection of pictures in a textbook, and, if they are lucky, perhaps a few good films about heroic black folk singing "We Shall Overcome."

What, they ask, would James Baldwin think of Barack Obama?

Now I can tell them I think I know. In a 1961 speech for the Liberation Committee for Africa, Baldwin wrote:

Bobby Kennedy recently made me the soul-stirring promise that one day—thirty years, if I'm lucky—I can be President too. It never entered this boy's mind, I suppose—it has not entered the country's mind yet—that perhaps I wouldn't want to be. And in any case, what really exercises my mind is not this hypothetical day on which some other Negro "first" will become the first Negro President. What I am really curious about is just what kind of country he'll be President of.

And there's the rub. He goes on to say that in order for such a seemingly unimaginable event to occur, first the United States must be "revised"; that the then-so-called "Negro problem" would have to be first reinvented and reseen as the problem of the ruling classes ("The confusion in this country that we call the Negro problem has nothing to do with the Negroes"); that every switch must be flipped; and then and only then could he see a black man in the White House.

Whether or not America has actually undergone the total revision Baldwin outlines in his peroration, and throughout his works—now more accessible and complete to the eager reader with this timely volume—remains an open question. Yet I'm certain he'd acknowledge that the nearly fifty years between then and now have brought us closer to that Braver Newer World. Barack Obama may not be presiding over a color-blind, gender-equal, economically fair, same-sex-love-affirming, environmentally clean, disease-cleansed, morally upright America—I'm sure even Baldwin would eschew that ultimate possibility as a bit too utopian—but I'm sure he'd believe the possibilities for his country were looking up since he wrote, in 1961:

> What can we do? . . . I don't know how it will come about, but I know that no matter how it comes about, it will be bloody; it will be hard. I still believe that we can do with this country something that has not been done. We are misled here because we think of numbers. You don't need numbers; you need passion. And this is proven by the history of the world.

ESSAYS AND SPEECHES

Mass Culture and the Creative Artist:
Some Personal Notes

SOMEONE ONCE SAID TO ME that the people in general cannot bear very much reality. He meant by this that they prefer fantasy to a truthful re-creation of their experience. The Italians, for example, during the time that De Sica and Rossellini were revitalizing the Italian cinema industry, showed a marked preference for Rita Hayworth vehicles; the world in which she moved across the screen was like a fairy tale, whereas the world De Sica was describing was one with which they were only too familiar. (And it can be suggested perhaps that the Americans who stood in line for *Shoeshine* and *Open City* were also responding to images which they found exotic, to a reality by which they were not threatened. What passes for the appreciation of serious effort in this country is very often nothing more than an inability to take anything very seriously.)

Now, of course the people cannot bear very much reality, if by this one means their ability to respond to high intellectual or artistic endeavor. I have never in the least understood why they should be expected to. There is a division of labor in the world—as I see it—and the people have quite enough reality to bear, simply getting through their lives, raising their children, dealing with the eternal conundrums of birth, taxes, and death. They do not do this with all the wisdom, foresight, or charity one might wish;

nevertheless, this is what they are always doing and it is what the writer is always describing. There is literally nothing else to describe. This effort at description is itself extraordinarily arduous, and those who are driven to make this effort are by virtue of this fact somewhat removed from the people. It happens, by no means infrequently, that the people hound or stone them to death. They then build statues to them, which does not mean that the next artist will have it any easier.

I am not sure that the cultural level of the people is subject to a steady rise: in fact, quite unpredictable things happen when the bulk of the population attains what we think of as a high cultural level, e.g., pre–World War II Germany, or present-day Sweden. And this, I think, is because the effort of a Schoenberg or a Picasso (or a William Faulkner or an Albert Camus) has nothing to do, at bottom, with physical comfort, or indeed with comfort of any other kind. But the aim of the people who rise to this high cultural level—who rise, that is, into the middle class—is precisely comfort for the body and the mind. The artistic objects by which they are surrounded cannot possibly fulfill their original function of disturbing the peace—which is still the only method by which the mind can be improved—they bear witness instead to the attainment of a certain level of economic stability and a certain thin measure of sophistication. But art and ideas come out of the passion and torment of experience: it is impossible to have a real relationship to the first if one's aim is to be protected from the second.

We cannot possibly expect, and should not desire, that the great bulk of the populace embark on a mental and spiritual voyage for which very few people are equipped and which even fewer have survived. They have, after all, their indispensable work to do, even as you and I. What we are distressed about, and should be, when we speak of the state of mass culture in this country, is the overwhelming torpor and bewilderment of the people. The people who run the mass media are not all villains and they are not all cowards—though I agree, I must say, with Dwight Macdonald's forceful suggestion that many of them are not very bright. (Why should they be? They, too, have risen from the streets to a high level of cultural attainment. They, too, are positively afflicted by the world's highest standard of living and what is probably the world's most bewilderingly empty way of life.) But even those who are bright are handicapped by their audience: I am less appalled by the fact that *Gunsmoke* is produced than I am by the fact that so many people want to see it. In the same way, I must add, that a thrill of terror runs through me when I hear that the favorite author of our President is Zane Grey.

But one must make a living. The people who run the mass media and those who consume it are really in the same boat. They must continue to produce things they do not really admire, still less love, in order to continue buying things they do not really want, still less need. If we were dealing only with fintails, two-tone cars, or programs like *Gunsmoke*, the situation would not be so grave. The trouble is that serious things are handled (and received) with the same essential lack of seriousness.

For example: neither *The Bridge on the River Kwai* nor *The Defiant Ones*, two definitely superior movies, can really be called serious. They are extraordinarily interesting and deft: but their principal effort is to keep the audience at a safe remove from the experience which these films are not therefore really prepared to convey. The kind of madness sketched in *Kwai* is far more dangerous and widespread than the movie would have us believe. As for *The Defiant Ones*, its suggestion that Negroes and whites can learn to love each other if they are only chained together long enough runs so madly counter to the facts that it must be dismissed as one of the latest, and sickest, of the liberal fantasies, even if one does not quarrel with the notion that love on such terms is desirable. These movies are designed not to trouble, but to reassure; they do not reflect reality, they merely rearrange its elements into something we can bear. They also weaken our ability to deal with the world as it is, ourselves as we are.

What the mass culture really reflects (as is the case with a "serious" play like *J.B.*) is the American bewilderment in the face of the world we live in. We do not seem to want to know that we are *in* the world, that we are subject to the same catastrophes, vices, joys, and follies which have baffled and afflicted mankind for ages. And this has everything to do, of course, with what was expected of America: which expectation, so generally disappointed, reveals something we do not want to know about sad human nature, reveals something we do not want to know about the intricacies and inequities of any social structure, reveals, in sum, something we do not want to know about ourselves. The American way of life has failed—to make people happier or to make them better. We do not want to admit this, and we do not admit it. We persist in believing that the empty and criminal among our children are the result of some miscalculation in the formula (which can be corrected); that the bottomless and aimless hostility which makes our cities among the most dangerous in the world is created, and felt, by a handful of aberrants; that the lack, yawning everywhere in this country, of passionate conviction, of personal authority, proves only our rather appealing tendency to be gregarious and democratic. We are very cruelly trapped between what we would like to be and what we actually are. And we cannot possibly become what we would like to be until we are willing to ask ourselves just why the lives we lead on this continent are mainly so empty, so tame, and so ugly.

This is a job for the creative artist—who does not really have much to do with mass culture, no matter how many of us may be interviewed on TV. Perhaps life is not the black, unutterably beautiful, mysterious, and lonely thing the creative artist tends to think of it as being; but it is certainly not the sunlit playpen in which so many Americans lose first their identities and then their minds.

I feel very strongly, though, that this amorphous people are in desperate search for something which will help them to re-establish their connection with themselves, and with one another. This can only begin to happen as the truth begins to be told. We are in the middle of an immense metamorphosis here, a metamorphosis which will, it is devoutly to be hoped, rob us of our myths and give us our history, which will destroy our attitudes and give us back our personalities. The mass culture, in the meantime, can only reflect our chaos: and perhaps we had better remember that this chaos contains life—and a great transforming energy.

(1959)

A Word from Writer Directly to Reader

This is from the anthology *Fiction of the Fifties: A Decade of American Writing* (1959), edited by Herbert Gold, which included a story by Baldwin. The editor had asked the contributors: "In what way—if any—do you feel that the problem of writing from the Fifties has differed from the problems of writing in other times? Do you believe that this age makes special demands on you as a writer?"

.   .   .

I SUPPOSE THAT IT HAS always been difficult to be a writer. Writers tell us so; and so does the history of any given time or place and what one knows of the world's indifference. But I doubt that there could ever have been a time which demanded more of the writer than do these present days. The world has shrunk to the size of several ignorant armies; each of them vociferously demanding allegiance and many of them brutally imposing it. Nor is it easy for me, when I try to examine the world in which I live, to distinguish the right side from the wrong side. I share, for example, the ideals of the West—freedom, justice, brotherhood—but I cannot say that I have often seen these honored; and the people whose faces are set against us have never seen us honor them at all.

But finally for me the difficulty is to remain in touch with the private life. The private life, his own and that of others, is the writer's subject—his key and ours to his achievement. Nothing, I submit, is more difficult than deciphering what the citizens of this time and place actually feel and think. They do not know themselves; when they talk, they talk to the psychiatrist; on the theory, presumably, that the truth about them is ultimately unspeakable. This thoroughly infantile delusion has its effects: it is contagious. The writer trapped among a speechless people is in danger of becoming speechless himself. For then he has no mirror, no corroborations of his essential reality; and this means that he has no grasp of the reality of the people around him. What the times demand, and in an unprecedented fashion, is that one be—not seem—outrageous, independent, anarchical. That one be thoroughly disciplined—as a means of being spontaneous. That one resist at whatever cost the fearful pressures placed on one to lie about one's own experience. For in the same way that the writer scarcely ever had a more uneasy time, he has never been needed more.

(1959)

From *Nationalism, Colonialism, and the United States:*

One Minute to Twelve—A Forum

This talk was given on June 2, 1961, at a forum hosted by the Liberation Committee for Africa on nationalism and colonialism and United States foreign policy.

.   .   .

BOBBY KENNEDY recently made me the soul-stirring promise that one day—thirty years, if I'm lucky—I can be President too. It never entered this boy's mind, I suppose—it has not entered the country's mind yet—that perhaps I wouldn't want to be. And in any case, what really exercises my mind is not this hypothetical day on which some other Negro "first" will become the first Negro President. What I am really curious about is just what kind of country he'll be President of.

I can only speak about my own country, because I know this country; I think I know it pretty well. In this country now—and I have to preface everything I am going to say with this—all terms without exception must be revised. I dare anyone in this room or in the streets to define for me today a "literate" man, or an "educated" man, or to tell me precisely what you mean when you call someone an historian, to say nothing of a novelist. Now this may seem frivolous, but it is very important, because when all these terms have no meaning, then we have the populace that we have today, and we have the press that we have today, and impenetrable speeches from high places, from people who should know better, but who clearly don't.

Now one of these terms is "nationalism." Let us try to strip this term of all the rhetoric that now surrounds it. The term means, as I understand it, that a certain group of people, living in a certain place, has decided to take its political destinies into its own hands. I don't think it means anything more than that, and I know it doesn't mean anything less than that. I know the time has come for some extremely harsh words. And if I could make them harsher, and if this were another audience, if it were possible to penetrate the unconsciousness—because it is not simply wickedness, which would be easy to deal with, but the apathy, the sleep, the unwillingness to know what is going on, not only in Cuba, which is ninety miles away, not only in Mississippi, which is closer, but up the street in Harlem, which has been there quite some time. The white racist has ruled the world for a long time, and the crises we are undergoing now are involved with the fact that the habits of power are not only extremely hard to lose; they are as tenacious as some incurable disease. So that, for example, when I talk about "colonialism"—which is also a word that can be defined—it refers to European domination of what we now call underdeveloped countries. It also refers, no matter what the previous colonial powers may say, to the fact that these people entered those continents not to save them, not, no not, to bring the Cross of Christ or the Bible—though they did; that was a detail. And still less to inculcate into them a notion of political democracy. The truth is that they walked in and they stayed in, and they recklessly destroyed whatever was in their way, in order to make money. And this is what we call the rise of capitalism, which is a pre-phrase covering an eternity of crimes. If I try to point out to these people—and I'm not an African; I've never been to Africa; I'm talking only from my experience in this country and my experience of the West—if I point out that you cannot conceivably frighten an African by talking about the Kremlin, panic ensues, and I'm promptly called a Muslim.

Now God knows I am not, I really am not, trying to accuse anybody of anything, and when I talk the way I apparently talk, it does not mean that I am ready to go out and cut your head off, or dash your children's heads against a stone. What I'm trying to say to this country, to us, is that we must know this, we must realize this, that no other country in the world has been so fat and so sleek, and so safe, and so happy, and so irresponsible, and so dead for twenty years. For twenty years. No other country can afford to dream of a Plymouth and a wife and a house with a fence and the children growing up safely to go to college and to become executives, and then to marry and have the Plymouth and the house and so forth. A great many people do not live this way and cannot imagine it, and do not know that when we talk about "democracy," this is what we mean.

Now I submit that if Mr. [John F.] Kennedy is the President of this country, and it is his country, and if Senator Eastland* can be responsible in this country, and it is his country—well, it's my country too. And that means that it's your country too. I do not believe in the twentieth-century myth that we are all helpless, that it's out of our hands. It's only out of our hands if we don't want to pick it up. And the truth about us in this country is that we have evaded it for so long. The last cooling-off period relating to the Negro problem, as somebody put it, occurred during the Reconstruction, and we are paying for that now. It has escaped everybody's notice that it doesn't go back as far as the Civil War; it doesn't go back any further than 1900. Those laws that we are trying to overthrow in this country now are not much older than I am. Faulkner says they are folkways, and one would think they came from Rome. But they came out of Southern legislatures just before the First World War. And they are no older than that. Now, if they can be put there, they can be taken away. One of the great confusions, again, is the nonsense that we hear about states' rights. We hear this from people who have no concern with states' rights, and still less with freedom, but who simply want to perpetuate a system which is doomed. The truth is that whether I like it or not is absolutely irrelevant. It is over. The sun did set on the British Empire, and there won't be any more British gunboats down the Chinese rivers.

I am trying to explain that I, speaking now again as a black man, have been described by you for thousands of years. And maybe I loved being described by you. But time passed, and now, whether I like it or not, I can not only describe myself but, what is much more horrifying, I can describe

---

*Senator James Oliver Eastland (1904–1986) represented the state of Mississippi in the United States Senate briefly in 1941 and later from 1943 until 1978. He was a vocal opponent of civil rights legislation.

YOU! Now this is why, in this country which we call the leader of the West, there is such confusion. This panic is the real key, as Mr. Make pointed out, to what we call, in this country, anticommunism. The people who are running around throwing people in jail and ruining reputations and screaming about Communists wouldn't know one if he fell from the ceiling. And wouldn't care! What they are concerned about is propping up somehow the doctrine of white supremacy, so that they can seem to have given it up, but really still hold the power. Now this is not only obvious in American relations with South Africa in terms of economics. Nor is it only obvious in such things as the invasion of Cuba. It is obvious on a much more subtle level, and that is what attacks us here. It is something I call the new paternalism, which in a very curious way is foreshadowed by Mr. [Bobby] Kennedy's statement. The key to that statement, as I understand it, is that when Negroes have achieved the Americanism of the Irish, they will be allowed to get to Washington. Now, to tell the truth, I personally do not feel that what I would like to see come out of the last three hundred years is another Kennedy. I think the price was too high, and I insist that I believe we are better than that.

The confusion in this country that we call the Negro problem has nothing to do with the Negroes. And this is a fact. It has to do with the actual level of American life. And when I say this, I don't mean the life that we have in the headlines, and that is celebrated in rhetoric, which fools only us. I mean the lives, the actual private lives, being led here on this continent as we sit here, from coast to coast. It is astonishing that in a country so devoted to the individual, so many people should be afraid to speak. It is astonishing that in a country so wealthy, and with nothing to fear in principle, everyone should be so joyless, so that you scarcely meet anyone who hasn't just come from a psychiatrist, or isn't just running off to one.

I'm afraid we'll have to face such facts as these. And it's difficult in this country now. For example, it is difficult for me to take seriously the selling of Coca-Cola. You know I don't blame you for making money, but the selling of soap is not really an endeavor worthy of man. Especially when it is accompanied by TV jingles. What I am trying to point out is that people who think that this is important are unable to realize that something else is. The only hope this country has is to turn overnight into a revolutionary country, and I say "revolutionary" in the most serious sense of that word: to undermine the standards by which the middle-class American lives. And, by the way, there is nothing but a middle class in this country, because no worker thinks of himself as a worker. He is going to graduate UP when he has two Fords instead of one. Now, the only hope we have is to undermine these peculiar standards, and I will be pleased to know that the American middle class does not live by the standards it uses to victimize me. The social habits of, let us say, Scarsdale, are not more reprehensible than the social habits of Harlem. Or vice versa. But in Harlem you are a target, and in Scarsdale you are covered.

What are you covered by? This is another question we have to face sooner or later. We are covered by an outmoded Puritan God. Now you know, the Pilgrim fathers who came here with their God had never heard of Cubans; in fact, they had never heard of me. And this concept is not large enough, is not large enough, to embrace this peculiar country. It does not embrace me. If one only considers the difficulty I had to become a Christian when I thought I was, the impossibility for the African to become a Christian by imitating Europeans! And the impossibility of anyone in the world today, who wants to be free, becoming free by imitating us. And the world I'm talking about is most of the world.

What can we do? Well, I am tired. I personally am tired of the double-talk about Governor John Patterson's* freedom to beat me up. Now it is time to create new standards. It is impossible to take seriously a country which will allow a hillbilly to overturn the government of the United States, at the very same time that this very government puts in jail people who take the Fifth Amendment. And really, it is scarcely a question whether Carl Braden,[†] for example, or John Patterson more menaces the future of this democracy.

I don't know how it will come about, but I know that no matter how it comes about, it will be bloody; it will be hard. I still believe that we can do with this country something that has not been done. We are misled here because we think of numbers. You don't need numbers; you need passion. And this is proven by the history of the world.

The tragedy of this country now is that most of the people who say they care about it do not care. What they care about is their safety and their profits. What they care about is not rocking the boat. What they care about is the continuation of white supremacy, so that white liberals who

---

*John Malcolm Patterson (b. 1921) was governor of Alabama from 1959 to 1963, some of the most turbulent years of the civil rights movement in Alabama.

[†]Carl (1914–1975) and Anne (1924–2006) Braden were journalists and anti-segregation activists based in Kentucky. In 1958 Carl Braden refused to testify before the House Un-American Activities Committee and was sentenced to a year in prison. He served nine months, and was released in 1962 after Martin Luther King Jr. pushed for clemency in his case.

are with you in principle will move out when you move in. Now when this is challenged, bitter tears come to their eyes, and they say to you, "You sound as if you think white people don't have any decency." Well, this is much too simple. That is not the question. The question here is how long can Americans believe that the rest of the world, including me, will take the will for the deed. If the country means what it says, why is the question which ends every argument "Would you let your sister marry him?" Why would I want to marry her?

I'm trying to suggest that in this long and terrifying history, something has happened to the country far worse than what has happened to the Negroes. People are always consoling me by pointing out that if one thinks of this country as an enormous hall, well, everybody got here, and they had to stand in line, and you know that by and by, standing in line, I'll get to the banquet table too. Well, of course, I got here first, and I helped to cook the food. But leaving that question aside, it has not occurred to anyone yet that the people at the table are starving to death.

People talk about what we can do to aid Africa, and this is, again, a kind of new paternalism. I don't know what we can do to aid Africa or Latin America or Asia. But I do know what this source can do for us. They will survive with our help or without it. They are really our opportunity. We have been smothered, and really, let's not talk about the public life which mirrors it, but only consider, consider the private life. Consider what is happening in those streets today to our young. To all our young. How is it that this country can only produce so demoralized a generation? And this generation is imitating its elders. They are doing what they have seen their elders do. And what their elders have been doing since they have been on earth is taking nothing seriously. Now there are some things which must be taken seriously. The nation that doesn't take them seriously, the person who doesn't take them seriously, can only perish.

Now I'm here too. I am an American too. I would like to see this peculiar dialogue ended. I really would like to see Governor John Patterson, or the governor of Mississippi, told what to do and put in jail if he doesn't do it. There is a great captive Negro population here, which is well publicized but not well known. And what is not publicized, and what is not known at all, is that there is a great captive white population here too. No one has pointed out yet with any force that if I am not a man here, you are not a man here. You cannot lynch me and keep me in ghettos without becoming something monstrous yourselves. And furthermore, you give me a terrifying advantage.

You give me this advantage: that whereas you have never had to look at me, because you've sealed me away along with sin and hell and death and all the other things you didn't want to look at, including love, my life was in your hands, and I had to look at you. I know more about you, therefore, than you know about me. I've had to spend my life, after all—and all the other Negroes in the country have had to spend their lives—outwitting and watching white people. I had to know what you were doing before you did it. People talk about the new Negro, but he's been coming for three hundred years. The country thinks he's new because they've never had to look at him before. And they are looking at him now, not because there's been a change of heart, but only because they must.

It was never the intention of England or France or Portugal, or any of the colonial powers, to raise the colonial people to their level. No matter what they say now about highways and hospitals and penicillin, whatever was done in those colonies was not done for the natives. And the Belgians may not know this, but the natives do. What happened was very simple. You cannot walk into a country and stay there as long as the Europeans did and dig coal and iron and gold out of the earth and use it for yourself. Put all the natives in one place and have them working for you, and have a European sector where only Europeans live. By and by, it's inevitable that someone will make a connection between the machines you have and the power you have. And from there, it's just a matter of detail. Now the details can be bloody, or they can be less so; they will in any case be difficult.

We in this country now—and it really is one minute to twelve—can really turn the tide because we have an advantage that Europe does not have, and we have an advantage that Africa does not have, if we could face it. Black and white people have lived together here for generations, and now for centuries. Now, on whether or not we face these facts everything depends.

(1961)

Theater: The Negro In and Out

IT IS A SAD FACT that I have rarely seen a Negro actor really well used on the American stage or screen, or on television. I am not trying to start an artificial controversy when I say this, for in fact most American performers seem to find themselves trapped very soon in an "iron maiden" of mannerisms.

Somehow, the achieved record falls below the promise. Henry Fonda, for example, is one of the most accomplished actors around, but I find it very difficult to watch him because most of the roles he plays do not seem to me to be worth doing.

Moreover, it would seem to me that his *impulse* as an actor is very truthful; but the roles he plays are not. His physical attributes, and his quality of painful, halting honesty are usually at the mercy of some mediocre playwright's effort to justify the bankruptcy of the American male, e.g., the nebbish with whom he so gallantly struggles in *Two for the Seesaw*.

The point is that one can attend the Broadway theater, and most of the Off-Broadway theater all season long without ever being moved, or terrified, or engaged.

The spectacle on the stage does not attempt to re-create our experience—thus helping us to deal with it. The attempt is almost always in the opposite direction: to justify our fantasies, thus locking us within them.

Now, the figure of the Negro is at the very heart of the American confusion. Much of the American confusion, if not most of it, is a direct result of the American effort to avoid dealing with the Negro as a man. The theater cannot fail to reflect this confusion, with results which are unhealthy for the white actor, and disastrous for the Negro.

The character a white actor is called on to play is usually a wishful fantasy: the person, not as he is, but as he would like to see himself. It need scarcely be said, therefore, that the situations the playwright invents for this person have as their principal intention the support of this fantasy.

The Caine Mutiny Court Martial, A Majority of One, Tea and Sympathy, and *Tall Story* are all utterly untruthful plays. The entire purpose of the prodigies of engineering skill expanded on them is to make the false seem true. And this cannot fail, finally, to have a terrible effect on the actor's art, for the depths out of which true inspiration springs are precisely the depths he is forbidden to reach.

I am convinced that this is one of the reasons for the nerve-wracking *busyness* of our stage—"Keep moving, maybe nobody will notice that nothing's happening"—and the irritating, self-indulgent mannerisms of so many of our actors. In search of a truth which is not in the script, they are reduced to what seem to be psychotherapeutic exercises.

Listening to actors talk about the means they employ to "justify" this line, or that action, is enough to break the heart and set the teeth on edge. Sometimes the actor finds that no amount of skill will "justify" or cover up the hollowness or falsity of what he is called on to do. This is where the director comes in: it would seem that much of his skill involves keeping everything moving at such a clip, and to have so many things happening at once, that the audience will remain, in effect, safely protected from the play.

If this is true for the white actor, it is unimaginably worse for the Negro actor. The characters played by white actors, however untruthful they may essentially be, do depend on the accumulation of small, very carefully observed detail. Thus, Chester Morris, playing a thoroughly unreal father in *Blue Denim,* yet mimics the type so well that it is easy to be misled into believing that you once knew someone like him. But the characters played by Negro actors do not have even this advantage. White people do not know enough about Negro life to know which details to look for, or how to interpret such details as may have been forced on their attention.

To take one of the many possible examples: the scene in Reginald Rose's *Black Monday,* in which Juano Hernández is beaten to death. Hernández plays a janitor in the Deep South, you will remember, who is opposed to integration. He does not believe—so he informs a marvelously mocking and salty Hilda Simms—in pushing himself in "where he is not wanted." He is also telling this to his twelve-year-old grandson, who is beginning (somewhat improbably) to wonder if he is as good as white people.

Now, of course, we have all met such janitors and such Negroes. But their tone is very different and their tone betrays what they really feel. However servile they may appear to be, there is always a murderous rage, or a murderous fear, or both, not quite sleeping at the very bottom of their hearts and minds. The truth is that they do not have any real respect for white people: they despise them and they fear them. They certainly do not trust them. And when such a man confronts his nephew or his grandson, no matter what he says, there cannot fail to be brought alive in him envy and terror and love and hate. He has always hated his condition, even though he feared to change it, even though he may no longer be able to admit it.

If the playwright does not know this—as, on the evidence, I gather Mr. Rose did not—he cannot draw the character truthfully, and the actor who plays him is seriously handicapped.

This shows very painfully in the scene in which Hernández meets his death. His reaction to the effigy of a hanged Negro, in spite of all Mr. Hernández's skill, is false. This is not the first time he has seen such an effigy, and if he has been living in that town all his life, it is simply not possible for the white people there to surprise him—at least, they cannot surprise him by being wicked or by being afraid. They have always been that, and he knows that about them, if he knows nothing else. Any Negro facing, in such a town, three overheated white boys knows what he is in for.

He can try to outwit, flatter, cajole them, put them at their ease by humiliating himself—though at this point, the spectacle of his humiliation is probably not enough to set them at their ease; or if the chips are really, at last, thank heaven, down, he can resolve to take one of them with him. And even if all the foregoing guesswork is wrong, one thing remains indisputable: once attacked, he would certainly not be trying to get past his attackers in order to go to work. Not on that morning, not in that school, not with death staring at him out of the eyes of three young white men.

All of the training, therefore, all of the skill which Mr. Hernández has acquired, to say nothing of his talent—for it took a vast amount of talent to bring Lucas, in *Intruder in the Dust,* alive—is here not merely wasted, which would be bad enough; it is subverted, sabotaged, put at the mercy of a lie; for the wellspring on which the actor must draw, which is his own sense of life, and his own experience, is precisely, here, what Mr. Hernández cannot use. If he had, it would have torn the scene to pieces, and altered the course of the play. For the play's real intention, after all, is to say something about the integration struggle without saying anything about the root of it.

If you will examine the play carefully, you will find that the only really wicked people in the play are wicked because they are insane. They are covered, therefore, and the crimes of the Republic are hidden. If we get rid of all these mad people, the play seems to be saying, "We'll get together and everything will be all right." The realities of economics, sex, politics, and history are thus swept under the rug.

Now the Negro actor, after all, is also a person and was not born two seconds before he enters the casting office. By the time he gets to that office, he has probably been an elevator boy, a cab driver, a dishwasher, a porter, a longshoreman. His blood is already thick with humiliations, and if he has any sense at all, he knows how small are his chances of making it in the theater. He does a great deal of acting in the casting office—more, probably, than he will ever be allowed to do onstage. And, whatever his training, he is not there to get a role he really wants to play: he is there to get a role which will allow him to be seen.

It is all too likely that he has seen actors inferior to himself in training and talent rise far above him. And now here he is, once more, facing an essentially ignorant and uncaring white man or woman, who *may* allow him to play a butler or a maid in the show being cast. He dissembles his experience in the office, and he knows that he will probably be lying about it onstage. He also knows why; it is because nobody wants to know the story. It would upset them. To begin analyzing all of his probable reactions would take all of the space of this magazine, and then some. But resentment is compounded by the fact, as a Negro actress once observed to me, that not only does the white world impose the most intolerable conditions on Negro life, they also presume to dictate the mode, manner, terms, and style of one's reaction against these conditions.

Or, as a Negro playwright tells it, explaining how Ketti Frings came to adapt Richard Wright's *Long Dream* for the stage: "She was sitting by this swimming pool, see, and reading this book, and she thought, 'This would make a perfectly *darling* play.'"

"So she wrote the first few scenes and called out her Negro butler, chauffeur, and maid, and read it to them and asked, 'Now, isn't that the way you poor, downtrodden colored people feel about things?' 'Why, yes, Miss Frings,' they answered; and 'I thought so,' says the playwright."—And so we go on. And on and on.

The point of this introductory column—for the readers of the *Urbanite* will be hearing a great deal from me—is that the theater is perishing for the lack of vitality. Vitality, humanly and artistically speaking, has only one source, and that source is life. Now, the life actually being led on this continent is not the life which we pretend it is. White men are not what they take themselves to be, and Negroes are very different—to say the very least—from the popular image of them.

This image must be cracked, not only if we are to achieve a theater— for we do not really have a theater now, only a series of commercial speculations which result in mammoth musicals, and "daring" plays like *Compulsion* and *Inherit the Wind,* which are about as daring as a spayed tomcat— this image must be cracked if we intend to survive as a nation. The Negro-in-America is increasingly the central problem in American life, and not merely in social terms, in personal terms as well.

I intend, from time to time, in discussing the theater, to return to this point, for I think the time has come to begin a bloodless revolution. Only by a more truthful examination of what is really happening here can we realize the real aims of the theater, which are to instruct through terror and pity and delight and love. The only thing we can now do for the "tired businessman" is to scare the living daylights out of him.

Both the Albee plays at the York Theatre—*The Death of Bessie Smith* and *The American Dream*—left me rather waiting for the other shoe to fall. Both plays seemed to promise more than they delivered; but I am not at all certain that I know what it is that they promised. This is not, by the way, meant as a complaint or as a joke. I don't mind—in the theater, at any rate—having my cozy expectations swept out from under me; and I'm the type that enjoys being forced to ask myself just what the author had in mind. I was hardly ever moved "to the heart," as we say, by either of the Albee plays, but I *was* mystified, enraged, amused, and horrified. I don't know if you will like them or not, but I think you ought to see them.

To take the plays in the order in which they were presented: *The Death of Bessie Smith* takes place in the Deep South, much of it in a thoroughly demoralizing hospital. There is not a single attractive person in this play, unless one excepts the offstage Bessie Smith, and the good-natured but simple-minded type who takes her on the journey which ends in her death.

Neither Bessie nor this man have much to do with the main action of the play. There is a question in my mind as to whether they really do much to illuminate it, but we will discuss this in a moment. In the course of the play, Bessie Smith dies offstage and this is the extent, on the surface, anyway, of her connection with this drama.

The play's principal concern—I *think*—is with the character of a white Southern nurse. "Character" is perhaps not quite the word I want; rarely has less character been presented at greater or more unsympathetic length. I hesitate, possibly because I am a coward, to suppose this creature is intended, in any way, to represent the fair ladies of the South. And yet, she is clearly of no interest in herself, except clinically; and I must add that as I watched her, my own memories of Southern faces came flooding back, bringing with them the near-certainty that this horror, this emptiness, might very well be what the Southern face—and particularly the faces of the women—hide. I imagine that anyone who is old enough will not fail to be reminded of the faces and the personalities of the women who accused the Scottsboro boys of rape.

We first encounter this woman with her father—and they deserve each other—on the porch of their home. She is icily and methodically, and not for the first time—they certainly have nothing else to talk about—puncturing his delusions as to his person, his political ambitions, and his friendship with the mayor, who is a patient in the hospital where she works on the admissions desk.

The relationship between the father and daughter is absolutely unspeakable, as are almost all the other relationships in this play; but I was puzzled as to what, precisely, Mr. Albee wished me to make of it. It is a relationship which, like the character of the nurse, is really of no interest in itself, it being doomed, by the lack of resources in the people, to be static. They will have this conversation over and over, then they will die, or the curtain will fall: and what either we or they have learned in the meantime is a question.

It may be that Mr. Albee's intention was to reveal, as forcefully as possible, the depth of the Southern poverty and paranoia, and the extent of the sexual ruin. But if this is so, then I think he has miscalculated.

I sympathize with him in the dilemma to which his raw material, his personages, have drawn him. I am an American writer, too, and I know how it sets the teeth on edge to try to create, out of people clearly incapable of it—incapable of self-examination, of thought, or literally, of speech—

drama that will reveal them. But the solution is not, to my mind, to present these people as they see themselves or *as they are;* we must be enabled to see them as they have been or as they might become; otherwise, we merely judge them as specimens and feel nothing for them as human beings.

It has, perhaps, never been more difficult than it is now to illuminate the person beleaguered and bewildered by the irresponsibility and provincialism and worship of mediocrity which he, in his innocence, mistakes for democracy. On the other hand, it has possibly never been more important. So that I do not object to the deadly, hysterical stasis of the nurse, but to the fact that Mr. Albee never forces me to identify her inhumanity, her poverty, her terror, with my own.

For, in essence, the passionless brimstone exchanges which open the play *are* the play: the tone never changes, and we never learn very much more about the nurse, or the other people in the play, or about the community in which the action takes place. There is an arresting sequence between the nurse and a Negro orderly; but I must confess that the intention here was hopelessly muddled for me by the casting—I could not tell, at once, whether Harold Scott was playing a white man or a light Negro; and when it was clear that he was playing a Negro, I found myself distracted by the question of whether any Negro in the Deep South would so expose himself to this white witch. I did not know what to make of the intern, a dull type at best, it seemed to me; and whatever sympathy I might have been expected to feel for him was demolished by his incomprehensible passion to take the nurse to bed. (Whatever for?) This leaves, I believe, only the brief appearance of another, wonderfully distracted nurse, the offstage Bessie, and her last paramour.

And here, again, either I have totally misunderstood Mr. Albee's intention, or he has miscalculated. I expected, at some point in the play, some ruthless flash which would illuminate the contrast between the wonderfully reckless life and terrible death of Bessie Smith and the whited sepulchre in which the nurse is writhing. But this does not happen. Bessie Smith bleeds to death, the nurse is the only character who knows who she is— earlier, her father had protested her addiction to "nigger" music—and the nurse succumbs to hysteria. She announces that she, too, can sing and, horribly, tries.

I think I understand Mr. Albee's intention here, all right, but I think it fails of its effect: because there is no agony in it. People pay for the lives they lead and the crimes they commit and the blood-guiltiness from which they flee, whether they know they do or not. The effort not to know what one knows is the most corrupting effort one can make—which the nurse abundantly proves. But the anguish which comes when the buried knowledge begins to force itself to the light—which *must* be what is happening to the nurse upon the death of Bessie Smith—has driven countless thousands to madness or murder or grace, but certainly far beyond hysteria.

The American Dream turns out to be the gelded youth so admired here and now. It presents a much more bland and amusing surface, but can scarcely qualify, obviously, as a funny play. Its vision of the antiseptic passivity of American life, and the resulting death of the masculine sensibility, makes it more closely resemble a nightmare. I cannot synopsize this play, which offers even less in the way of story (and even more in the way of incident) than *Bessie Smith*. It begins at a marvelous clip, making its deadly observations with a salty, impertinent speed. ("I've got a right to all your money when you die," says Mommy to Daddy, "because I used to let you lie on top of me and bump your uglies." Daddy, needless to say, has long since given *that* up.) But it goes flat about halfway and finally surrenders much too quietly.

I came away with the feeling that it was a far better play than the author realized, and that he had given it up much too soon. Or that both plays were exercises, notes for work which Mr. Albee has yet to do. I imagine that he will find it necessary to do much more violence to theatrical forms than he has so far done if he is to get his story told.

It is possible that what I am really complaining about here is a certain coldness, intrinsic to Albee, which will always mar his work. But I doubt this. For one thing, the venom which has gone into the portraits of the nurse in *Bessie Smith,* and the parents in *American Dream* does not argue too great a detachment, but too indignant a distaste. And he has a strange way with language, a beat which is entirely his, which may be controlled by the head, but which seems to be dictated from the guts.

(1961)

Is *A Raisin in the Sun* a Lemon in the Dark?

This piece was written for *Tone* magazine as a rebuttal to a negative piece written by Chicago writer Nelson Algren (*The Man with the Golden Arm*, 1949).

Lorraine Hansberry (1930–1965), a native of Chicago, was an acclaimed African-American author and playwright. She is best known for her landmark play *A Raisin in the Sun* (1959), which was the first play on Broadway written by a black woman and the first directed by a black man (Lloyd Richards). The leading male role was played by Sidney Poitier, who revived it for the 1961 movie version. Hansberry and Baldwin became good friends.

Interestingly enough, Baldwin had a rather contentious relationship with Richard Wright (1908–1960), author of the award-winning, best-selling novel *Native Son* (1940), upon which the play of the same name was based, a dramatic collaboration between Wright and Pulitzer Prize–winning playwright Paul Green. Orson Welles directed the first incarnation back in 1941. Wright had been Baldwin's first big literary mentor—his hero, in fact—but Baldwin later would attack Wright's work in print, accusing it of being a prime example of "protest fiction," something Baldwin viewed as agitprop and inferior to high art. After Wright's death Baldwin would lament their lapsed friendship and claim that he had only been trying to impress Wright by being a "good student."

.   .   .

BOTH *Native Son* and *A Raisin in the Sun* are flawed pieces of work, though this is clearly not the point of Mr. Algren's argument. I do not place *Native Son* as highly as he does, and he claims too much for Richard Wright, who never found out many of the things Mr. Algren authoritatively speaks of him as "knowing." Neither do I think that *A Raisin in the Sun* is the meretricious creation he takes it to be. Furthermore, unlike Mr. Algren, I find a profound connection between the two works, and even certain rather obvious similarities.

This, naturally, has everything to do with the difference between my point of view and Algren's. Only politically, for example, does his rhetoric about being "rightful members of company of men" make any sense to me. Personally and artistically, it seems to me that this problem presents itself in ways which make the use of the word "rightful" rather questionable, if not rather terrifying.

In my own reading of *Native Son,* it seems to me that where the polemic is most strong, the novel is least true; and, conversely, that the real fury of the novel tends to complicate and compromise and finally, indeed, to invalidate the novelist's social and political attitudes.

A Raisin in the Sun is not nearly so massive and it would seem to be far less angry. But this last is not the case. It is a very angry play indeed, and to say that it is angry about real estate is like saying that *Native Son* is angry about airplanes. Bigger Thomas, you will remember, stands about on Chicago's street corners watching the airplanes flown by white men, wishing to rise into that sky. There are long exchanges between himself and his buddies, in which they pretend to be powerful, rich, white tycoons—"one of America's bald-headed men" is the way the sister in Miss Hansberry's play puts it, taunting her ambitious and conceited brother. The great flaw in *Native Son* is, it seems to me, involved with Wright's attempt to illuminate ruthlessly as unprecedented a creation as Bigger by means of the stock characters of Jan, the murdered girl's lover, and Max, the white lawyer. The force of Bigger's reality makes it impossible to believe in these two; though one can, of course, protect oneself against Bigger's reality by clinging to these shadowy and familiar figures; which is, indeed, in the event, what happened.

And the flaw in *Raisin* is not really very different. It involves the juxtaposition of the essentially stock—certainly familiar—figure of the mother with the intense (and unprecedented) figure of Walter Lee. Most Americans do not know that he exists. From the point of view of someone who knows that he exists and how bitter his life is, I could wish that the role of Lena Younger had been written with greater ambiguity. Part of the corrosive ambiguity of his mother's role in his life. This brings up the whole question of the role of the mother in Negro life, and the peculiar and horrible problems of the Negro woman. This theme is never overtly stated, but it runs throughout the play. Each of the women, the mother, the wife, and the daughter, are, on their own levels, grappling with the problem of how to create a haven of safety for Walter, so that he can be a man, play a man's role in the world, and yet not be destroyed. It is dangerous to be an American Negro male. America has never wanted its Negroes to be men, and does not, generally, treat them as men. It treats them as mascots, pets, or things. Every Negro woman knows what her man faces when he goes out to work, and what poison he will probably bring back. There is no guarantee that she will always be able to suck the poison out of him; the more particularly as the male's aspirations, and his failures, are so thoroughly bound up with herself. And if he is living where Walter lives, with a "dream" of buying a liquor store, flying an airplane, buying pearls for his wife, hitting the number—the entire family teeters on the edge of disaster. With every move he makes to bring the dream closer, disaster becomes more probable. On the other hand, should the dream fade, he fades with it; so do they, the women: and disaster has overcome them.

This is the reason that Walter's wife wearily tells him to eat his eggs. It is the reason his sister is so quick to turn on the brother she loves: she does not dare to trust his manhood, for it has no power in the world, and cannot protect her. And it is the reason, of course, that the mother plays so dominant a role in all their lives. *She* has been able to work when her husband could not find work. (All over the nation, at this moment, white matrons are extolling their maids and deploring their "no count" husbands). She has known what waited for Walter since his eyes opened on the world, and has tried to protect him from it. How can he fail, then, at the age of thirty-five, with his wife aging, and his son growing up, to flail about him like a man in a trap? For he *is* in a trap. And *why,* may I ask, and *how,* should his dreams be more noble than those of anyone else in this sad place? He is not presented, after all, as exceptional, merely as struggling—which is, perhaps, all things considered, quite exceptional enough.

I am not myself terribly worried about color TV and split-level houses, etc., since I consider my life to be already sufficiently compromised by the garbage of this century. My own rather melancholy feeling is that as long as people want these things, they will do everything in their power to get them; when they want something better, they will make it; all I can do in the meantime, it seems to me, is attempt to prove, by hard precept and harder example, that people can be better than they are. I see no point in railing against the American middle class as such. They are a pretty sorry lot, God knows, but they are suffering here in their tawdry splendor. What one has to do, I think, is undermine the standards by which they imagine themselves to live. As for the rise of the Negro into the middle class, I am not certain that what is happening in this country can be summed up quite so neatly. It doesn't look much like a rise to me; it looks more like an insane rout, with white people fleeing to the suburbs of cities, hotly pursued by Negroes. In any case, by the time anything we can comfortably speak of as a "rise" has occurred, this country will be, for better or worse, unrecognizable.

Well, I think I may be running out of space. But I do not know what Mr. Algren has in mind when he speaks of the right of the Negro to be himself. What, exactly, is this "self" of which Mr. Algren speaks so boldly? How does *Raisin in the Sun* deny the Negro this right? There are a great many Negroes in real estate, for example, and there are even a few in advertising. Are they or are they not claiming their right to be themselves? What are the wellsprings of Negro life?

No, I cannot agree that Miss Hansberry has written a play about real estate. Perhaps the real difference between her play and Wright's novel is that twenty-one years have passed and very little, for most of the Negroes in this country, has changed. Bigger died in his trap and Walter walks out of his, into the greater one. There is no other place for him to move. If he has left behind him something of value, it is up to those of us who know what value *is* to make certain that it is not entirely lost.

(1961)

As Much Truth As One Can Bear

Since World War II, certain names in recent American literature—Hemingway, Fitzgerald, Dos Passos, Faulkner—have acquired such weight and become so sacrosanct that they have been used as touchstones to reveal the understandable, but lamentable, inadequacy of the younger literary artists. We still hear complaints, for example, that World War II failed to produce a literary harvest comparable to that which we garnered from the first. We will discuss the idiocy of this complaint later.

Let one of us the younger attempt to create a restless, unhappy, free-wheeling heroine and we are immediately informed that Hemingway or Fitzgerald did the same thing better—infinitely better. Should we be rash enough to make any attempt to link the lives of some men with their time, we are sternly (or kindly) advised to reread *U.S.A.* It has all, it would seem, been done, by our betters and our masters. In much the same way, not so very long ago, it appeared that American poetry was destined to perish in the chill embrace of T. S. Eliot.

Neither I nor any of my confrères are willing to be defined or limited in this way. Not one of us suffers from an excess of modesty, and none of what follows is written in a complaining spirit. And it is certainly not my purpose here to denigrate the achievement of the four men I have named. On the contrary, I am certain that I and that handful of younger writers I have in mind have more genuine respect for this achievement than do most of their unbearably cacophonous worshippers.

I respect Faulkner enough, for example, to be saddened by his pronouncements on the race question, to be offended by the soupy rhetoric of his Nobel Prize speech, and to resent—for *his* sake—the critical obtuseness which accepted (from the man who wrote *Light in August*) such indefensibly muddy work as *Intruder in the Dust* or *Requiem for a Nun*.

It is useful, furthermore, to remember in the case of Hemingway that his reputation began to be unassailable at the very instant that his work began that decline from which it never recovered—at about the time of *For Whom the Bell Tolls*. Hindsight allows us to say that this boyish and romantic and inflated book marks Hemingway's abdication from the effort to understand the many-sided evil that is in the world. This is exactly the same thing as saying that he somehow gave up the effort to become a great novelist.

I myself believe that this is the effort every novelist must make, in spite of the fact that the odds are ludicrously against him, and that he can never, after all, *know*. In my mind, the effort to become a great novelist simply involves attempting to tell as much of the truth as one can bear, and then a little more. It is an effort which, by its very nature—remembering that men write the books, that time passes and energy flags, and safety beckons—is obviously doomed to failure. "Success" is an American word which cannot conceivably, unless it is defined in an extremely severe, ironical, and painful way, have any place in the vocabulary of any artist.

The example afforded by the later development, if one can call it that, of John Dos Passos is at least equally disturbing. And I suppose that there is no longer anything to say about Fitzgerald, at least not by me, and not now. Each of these men in his own way dramatizes for me the extraordinary hazards an American artist must run. Particularly, I must say, an American artist, whose tool is the common penny of language: who must try to deal with what words hide and what they reveal.

We live in a country in which words are mostly used to cover the sleeper, not to wake him up; and therefore, it seems to me, the adulation so cruelly proffered our elders has nothing to do with their achievement—which, I repeat, was mighty—but has to do with our impulse to look back on what we now imagine to have been a happier time. It is an adulation which has panic at the root.

I think that it is true, but I am willing to be corrected, that the previously mentioned giants have at least one thing in common: their simplicity. I do not refer to their styles (though, indeed, flying in the face of both critic and layman, I might be) but to their way of looking on the world. It is the American way of looking on the world, as a place to be corrected, and in which innocence is inexplicably lost. It is this almost inexpressible pain which lends such force to some of the early Hemingway stories—including "The Killers" and to the marvelous fishing sequence in *The Sun Also Rises;* and it is also the reason that Hemingway's heroines seem so peculiarly sexless and manufactured.

It is the sorrow of Gatsby, who searches for the green light, which continually recedes before him; and he never understands that the green light is there precisely in order to recede. Ben and Charley and Moorehouse and the entire cast of *U.S.A.* are tricked by life in just this way; nor is there any intimation in the book that we have, all, always, lived in a world in which dreams betray and are betrayed, where love dies or, more unbearably, fails to die, and where innocence *must* die, if we are ever to begin that journey toward the greater innocence called wisdom.

As for the work of Faulkner, which would seem, superficially, to escape these strictures, one has only to consider his vision, running throughout his work, of the gallant South. Even when he is most appalled by the crimes of his region—by which I do not so much mean the crimes committed against Negroes as the crimes his forebears and contemporaries have committed, and do commit, against themselves—he is testing it against the vision of a failed possibility.

One hears, it seems to me, in the work of all American novelists, even including the mighty Henry James, songs of the plains, the memory of a virgin continent, mysteriously despoiled, though all dreams were to have become possible here. This did not happen. And the panic, then, to which I have referred comes out of the fact that we are now confronting the awful question of whether or not all our dreams have failed. How have we managed to become what we have, in fact, become? And if we are, as indeed we seem to be, so empty and so desperate, what are we to do about it? How shall we put ourselves in touch with reality?

Writers are extremely important people in a country, whether or not the country knows it. The multiple truths about a people are revealed by that people's artists—that is what the artists are for. Whoever, for example, attempts to understand the French will be forced, sooner or later, to read

Balzac. And Balzac himself, in his own personality, illustrates all those vices, conundrums, delusions, ambitions, joys, all that recklessness, caution, patience, cunning, and revenge which activate his people. For, of course, he *is* those people; being French, like them, they operate as his mirror and he operates as theirs. And this is also entirely true of American writers, from James Fenimore Cooper to Henry James to William Faulkner.

Is it not possible to discern, in the features of Faulkner's Lucas, the lineaments of Fenimore Cooper's Uncas? And does not Lambert Strether of James's *The Ambassadors* come out of the loins of men who conquered a continent, destroying Uncas and enslaving Lucas, in order to build a factory which produces "unmentionable" articles—and which, in the absence of any stronger force, is now ruled by a strong-minded widow? What *is* the moral dilemma of Lambert Strether if not that, at the midnight hour, he realizes that he has, somehow, inexplicably, failed his manhood: that the "masculine sensibility," as James puts it, has failed in him? This "masculine sensibility" does not refer to erotic activity but to the responsibility that men must take upon themselves of facing and reordering reality.

Strether's triumph is that he is able to realize this, even though he knows it is too late for him to act on it. And it is James's perception of this peculiar impossibility which makes him, until today, the greatest of our novelists. For the question which he raised, ricocheting it, so to speak, off the backs of his heroines, is the question which so torments us now. The question is this: How is an American to become a man? And this is precisely the same thing as asking: How is America to become a nation? By contrast with him, the giants who came to the fore between the two world wars merely lamented the necessity.

These two strains in American fiction—nostalgia for the loss of innocence as opposed to an ironical apprehension of what such nostalgia means—have been described, not very helpfully, as the Redskin tradition as opposed to the Paleface. This has never made any sense to me. I have never read an American writer in whom the Redskin and the Paleface were not inextricably intertwined, usually, to be sure, in dreadful battle. Consider, for example, the tormented career of the author of *Tom Sawyer.* Or, for that matter, the beautiful ambiguity of the author of *Leaves of Grass.* And what was Hart Crane attempting to celebrate, in his indisputably Paleface fashion, in that magnificent failure which he called *The Bridge*?

It seems to me that the truth about us, as individual men and women and as a nation, has been and is being recorded, whether we wish to read it or not. Perhaps we cannot read it now, but the day is coming when we will

have nothing else to read. The younger writers, so relentlessly and unfa-
vorably compared to their elders, are nevertheless their descendants and
are under the obligation to go further than their elders went. It is the only
way to keep faith with them. The real difficulty is that those very same
questions, that same anguish, must now be expressed in a way that more
closely corresponds to our actual condition.

It is inane, for example, to compare the literary harvest of World War II
with that of World War I—not only because we do not, after all, fight wars
in order to produce literature, but also because the two wars had nothing
in common. We did not know, when we fought the first war, what we were
forced to discover—though we did not face it, and have not faced it yet—
when we fought the second. Between 1917 and 1941, the ocean, inconceiv-
ably, had shrunk to the size of a swimming pool.

In 1917, we had no enemies; 1941 marks our reluctant discovery—which,
again, we have not faced—that we had enemies everywhere. During World
War I, we were able to be angry at the atrocities committed in the name of
the Kaiser; but it was scarcely possible in World War II to be *angry* over the
systematic slaughter of six million Jews; nor did our performance at
Nuremberg do anything but muddy the moral and legal waters. In short,
by the time of World War II, evil had entered the American Eden, and it
had come to stay.

I am a preacher's son. I beg you to remember the proper name of that
troubling tree in Eden: it is "the tree of the knowledge of good and evil."
What is meant by the masculine sensibility is the ability to eat the fruit of
that tree, and live. What is meant by the "human condition" is that, indeed,
one has no choice: eat, or die. And we are slowly discovering that there are
many ways to die.

The younger American writers, then, to whom we shall, one day, be
most indebted—and I shall name no names, make no prophecies—are precisely those writers who are compelled to take it upon themselves to
describe us to ourselves as we now are. The loneliness of those cities
described in Dos Passos is greater now than it has ever been before; and
these cities are more dangerous now than they were before, and their citizens are yet more unloved. And those panaceas and formulas which have
so spectacularly failed Dos Passos have also failed this country, and the
world. The trouble is deeper than we wished to think: the trouble is in us.
And we will never remake those cities, or conquer our cruel and unbear-

able human isolation—we will never establish human communities—until we stare our ghastly failure in the face.

We will never understand what motivates Chinese or Cuban peasants until we ask ourselves who *we* are, and what we are doing in this lonely place. Faulkner's South, and grandfather's slaves, have vanished: the sun will never look on them again. The curtain has come down forever on Gatsby's career: there will be no more Gatsbys. And the green hills of Africa have come out of the past, and out of the imagination, into the present, the troubling world.

Societies are never able to examine, to overhaul themselves: this effort must be made by that yeast which every society cunningly and unfailingly secretes. This ferment, this disturbance, is the responsibility, and the necessity, of writers. It is, alas, the truth that to be an American writer today means mounting an unending attack on all that Americans believe themselves to hold sacred. It means fighting an astute and agile guerrilla warfare with that American complacency which so inadequately masks the American panic.

One must be willing—indeed, one must be anxious—to locate, precisely, that American morality of which we boast. And one must be willing to ask oneself what the Indian thinks of this morality, what the Cuban or the Chinese thinks of it, what the Negro thinks of it. Our own record must be read. And, finally, the air of this time and place is so heavy with rhetoric, so thick with soothing lies, that one must really do great violence to language, one must somehow disrupt the comforting beat, in order to be heard. Obviously, one must dismiss any hopes one may ever have had of winning a popularity contest. And one must take upon oneself the right to be entirely wrong—and accept penalties, for penalties there will certainly be, even here.

"We work in the dark," said Henry James, "we do what we can, our doubt is our passion and our passion is our task. The rest is the madness of art." This madness, thank heaven, is still at work among us here, and it will bring, inexorably, to the light at last the truth about our despairing young, our bewildered lovers, our defeated junkies, our demoralized young executives, our psychiatrists, and politicians, cities, towns, suburbs, and interracial housing projects. There is a thread which unites them all, and which unites every one of us. We have been both searching and evading the terms of this union for many generations.

.   .   .

We are the generation that must throw everything into the endeavor to remake America into what we say we want it to be. Without this endeavor, we will perish. However immoral or subversive this may sound to some, it is the writer who must always remember that morality, if it is to remain or become morality, must be perpetually examined, cracked, changed, made new. He must remember, however powerful the many who would rather forget, that life is the only touchstone and that life is dangerous, and that without the joyful acceptance of this danger, there can never be any safety for anyone, ever, anywhere.

What the writer is always trying to do is utilize the particular in order to reveal something much larger and heavier than any particular can be. Thus Dostoevsky, in *The Possessed,* used a small provincial town in order to dramatize the spiritual state of Russia. His particulars were not very attractive, but he did not invent them, he simply used what there was. Our particulars are not very attractive, either, but we must use them. They will not go away because we pretend that they are not there.

Not everything that is faced can be changed; but nothing can be changed until it is faced. The principal fact that we must now face, and that a handful of writers are trying to dramatize, is that the time has now come for us to turn our backs forever on the big two-hearted river.

(1962)

Geraldine Page: Bird of Light

I HAVE BORROWED Kazan's director's notes for *Sweet Bird of Youth*, from its first rehearsal to opening night. When I think back now to those five or six weeks of steadily mounting chaos, those desolate, work-lit stages, the makeshift props, the cardboard-tasting coffee, knocking steam pipes, the New York and, subsequently, the Philadelphia chill, I think of Gerry Page. In my mind's eye, she is standing perfectly still, upstage left, under the gloom and glare of the work light, intently watching Kazan mime a bit of business for the other actors. And she always seemed to me to be like that—terribly quiet and shy, but always watching.

The first days of rehearsal are always an utter shambles, at least in the memory; so, for that matter, are the last days; but, luckily for the theater, one's memory of intolerable nervous strain ends almost as soon as the strain does. I watched Kazan, who presumably knew what he was going to do with this improbable and disparate collection of actors. I certainly could tell nothing from the actors. They slouched or lurched or strode about, holding on to their books as though they were infants and looking as though they wondered what the hell they were doing here in this tiny, drafty theater, of all places. I was much too terrified of them all, of the mystic forces almost visibly clashing above their poor, doomed heads, to

do more than mutter the briefest of "good morning"s and "good night"s—
which, in those first days, was probably just as well. I was especially afraid
of Gerry because, to tell the truth, I was afraid *for* her. I simply could not
imagine her as the aging, desperately predatory, and somehow majestic
ex–movie queen that Tennessee Williams had created. And he had written
it, as always, somewhat larger and more livid than life. How was this open-
faced, quiet midwestern-type girl going to make herself believe in this creation? Or make *us* believe it? My sense of doom was strengthened when I
overheard someone whisper one day, "She's much too young for the part."
I thought so, too—and insufficiently elegant.

As we all now know, I could not possibly have been more wrong. But
now I find it nearly impossible to re-create my view of the steps which led
to this transformation. The most crucial steps, of course, did not take place
in my view at all, and I suppose that all I really saw were the results of a
process which had begun long before rehearsals started. She must have had
a very definite sense of the part and how to play it, for, as I now reconstruct
those first days, she seemed watchfully and patiently waiting to put her
conception to the test.

But her preternatural coolness, in this forest of knitted brows, left me
stupefied then. It was almost as though, with her wedding day upon her
and the bridegroom drawing nearer by the second, she yet lingered, in
some hideously compromising position, with another boy. "Oh," she said
to me one afternoon, "so-and-so is such a *worry* bird." So-and-so had vanished, as did nearly all the actors when they were not needed, gloomily, to
study his part. *Her* book was closed, in her lap. "Perhaps I *ought* to study,"
she said, with a smile—a smile meant, probably, to wipe the bewildered
and reproving look off my face—"but . . ." and her voice tinkled helplessly
into silence. I felt that she had put me down as another worry bird.

On the other hand, she was watching everything Kazan was doing up
there on the stage with the other actors. During the entire blocking-out
period, she impressed me tremendously with her speed and concentration,
but I got no hint of what she would do with the part; and whereas Kazan
gave me increasingly precise notes for the other actors, the clipboard is
strikingly sparse when it comes to instructions for Gerry Page. Moreover,
most of the notes for Gerry are extremely laconic. For instance, "Tell
Gerry she's inaudible" or "Tell Gerry I can't see her face." There is scarcely
ever on the clipboard any suggestion of what she should be thinking or
feeling on this or that movement, on this or that line; and the reason is that
her role was worked out in an extremely direct, knock-down-and-drag-out

way, and she never needed to be told anything twice. There was very little left for the clipboard by the time she and Kazan got through hammering away at a scene until it began to take the shape they wanted. Tiny little explosions occurred all along the way, illuminating, at first, not so much what Gerry was doing with the part as the treacherous difficulty of the part itself. It is difficult because this grotesque creature, the Princess, is always standing a little outside herself and commenting, with extreme distaste, on whatever she is doing. It is on this affliction that her precarious dignity depends. The first hint I caught of this was when Gerry, preparing, rather wearily, to listen to her beach-boy lover's* discourse, sits down at her wardrobe trunk, picks up her mirror, looks into it, and puts it down again. It was electrifying. It was terribly funny. It was terribly sad. And I also remember her achievement of that moment when the boy finishes his monologue and turns to her, saying, "Princess, will you help me?" And she holds out her arms, incurably predatory even as she is incurably lonely, but, also, at that moment, very beautiful and moving, because for that moment, if only in her own mind, she is both wife and mother and has again a human value for someone in the world.

Acting is (for me, anyway) one of the most mysterious of all the arts—mysterious because the instrument, the actor himself, without changing at all, undergoes such inexplicable transformations before one's eyes. I think that this sustained and steady tension between the real and the make-believe is healthy for the soul: it forces one to examine reality again. Seeing Gerry around the studio, or on television, had never caused me, really, to look at her, to wonder about her—and by "wonder" I don't mean the currently prevalent zoological sniffing which lacks even the primary virtue of curiosity—or, for that matter, to listen to her. I saw a girl who was enormously *sympathique*, not strikingly pretty, with a rather light, agreeable voice. That's all I saw. How in the world, then, did this girl manage to turn herself into a ruined and desperate harridan, with a voice that made one jump and with a face into which had somehow been burned the defeats, indignities, and agonies of a long and intolerable lifetime? I know that, technically and theatrically speaking, there are a great many answers to this question, although I also know that no one has ever really answered it. And when the same question confronts us, in life, in time, the answers are even more desperately makeshift. My point, anyway, is that all I saw of

*The role of her lover was played by Paul Newman.

Gerry is all that most of us, wandering in our grisly isolation through this world, ever see of any other person. Whoever forces this terrible truth once more on our attention has also helped us to bear it and to that extent, at least, has lessened it. It is a small light brought into a vast darkness—but a small light, considering, especially, what everyone is searching for, may be quite enough. As for the light which Gerry holds, may it burn long.

(1962)

From *What's the Reason Why?: A Symposium by Best-Selling Authors*: James Baldwin on *Another Country*

In the December 2, 1962, issue of *The New York Times,* the editors of the *Book Review* asked the year's best-selling authors, "what they believe there is about their book or the climate of the times that has made [it] so popular." *Another Country* had been on the best-seller list since June.

.   .   .

PEOPLE BOUGHT *Another Country* in considerably larger numbers than I imagined they would. I suppose this must have something to do with the fact that many more people than are willing to admit it lead lives not at all unlike the lives of the people in my book. I don't mean to compare myself to a couple of artists I unreservedly admire—Miles Davis and Ray Charles—but I would like to think that some of the people who liked my book responded to it in a way similar to the way they respond when Miles and Ray are blowing. These artists, in their very different ways, sing a kind of universal blues, they speak of something far beyond their charts, graphs, statistics, they are telling us something about what it is like to be alive. It is not self-pity which one hears in them, but compassion. And perhaps this is the place for me to say that I really do not, at the very bottom of my own mind, compare myself to other writers. I think I really helplessly model myself on jazz musicians and try to write the way they sound. I am not an intellectual, not in the dreary sense that word is used today, and do not want to be: I am aiming at what Henry James called "perception at the pitch of passion."

(1962)

The Artist's Struggle for Integrity

I REALLY DON'T LIKE WORDS like "artist" or "integrity" or "courage" or "nobility." I have a kind of distrust of all those words because I don't really know what they mean, any more than I really know what such words as "democracy" or "peace" or "peace-loving" or "warlike" or "integration" mean. And yet one is compelled to recognize that all these imprecise words are attempts made by us all to get to something which is real and which lives behind the words. Whether I like it or not, for example, and no matter what I call myself, I suppose the only word for me, when the chips are down, is that I am an artist. There is such a thing. There is such a thing as integrity. Some people are noble. There is such a thing as courage. The terrible thing is that the reality behind these words depends ultimately on what the human being (meaning every single one of us) believes to be real. The terrible thing is that the reality behind all these words depends on choices one has got to make, for ever and ever and ever, every day.

I am not interested really in talking to you as an artist. It seems to me that the artist's struggle for his integrity must be considered as a kind of metaphor for the struggle, which is universal and daily, of all human beings on the face of this globe to get to become human beings. It is not your fault, it is not my fault, that I write. And I never would come before you in the position of a complainant for doing something that I must do. What we might get at this evening, if we are lucky, is what the importance of this effort is. However arrogant this may sound, I want to suggest two propositions. The first one is that the poets (by which I mean all artists) are finally the only people who know the truth about us. Soldiers don't. Statesmen don't. Priests don't. Union leaders don't. Only poets. That's my first proposition. We know about the Oedipus complex not because of Freud but because of a poet who lived in Greece thousands of years ago. And what he said then about what it was like to be alive is still true, in spite of the fact that now we can get to Greece in something like five hours and then it would have taken I don't know how long a time.

The second proposition is really what I want to get at tonight. And it sounds mystical, I think, in a country like ours, and at a time like this when something awful is happening to a civilization, when it ceases to produce poets, and, what is even more crucial, when it ceases in any way whatever to believe in the report that only the poets can make. Conrad told us a long time ago (I think it was in *Victory*, but I might be wrong about that): "Woe to that man who does not put his trust in life." Henry James said, "Live, live all you can. It's a mistake not to." And Shakespeare said—and this is what I take to be the truth about everybody's life all of the time—"Out of this nettle, danger, we pluck this flower, safety." Art is here to prove, and to help one bear, the fact that all safety is an illusion. In this sense, all artists are divorced from and even necessarily opposed to any system whatever.

Let's trace it, just for kicks, for a minute. And I'll use myself. I won't say "me," but it's my story. The first thing an artist finds out when he is very, very young (when I say "young" I mean before he is fifteen, that is to say, before, properly speaking, he or she can walk or talk, before he or she has had enough experience to begin to assess his or her experience)—and what occurs at that point in this hypothetical artist's life is a kind of silence—the first thing he finds out is that for reasons he cannot explain to himself or to others, he does not belong anywhere. Maybe you're on the football team, maybe you're a runner, maybe you belong to a church, you certainly belong to a family; and abruptly, in other people's eyes—this is very important—you begin to discover that you are moving and you can't stop this movement to what looks like the edge of the world. Now what is crucial, and one begins to understand it much, much later, is that if you were this hypothetical artist, if you were in fact the dreamer that everybody says you are, if in fact you were wrong not to settle for the things that you cannot for some mysterious reason settle for, if this were so, the testimony in the eyes of other people would not exist. The crime of which you discover slowly you are guilty is not so much that you are aware, which is bad enough, but that other people see that you are and cannot bear to watch it, because it testifies to the fact that they are not. You're bearing witness helplessly to something which everybody knows and nobody wants to face, least of all the hypothetical misfit who has not learned how to walk or talk and doesn't know enough about experience to know what experience he has had.

Well, one survives that, no matter how. By and by your uncles and your parents and church stop praying for you. They realize it won't do a bit of good. They give you up, and you proceed a little further and your lovers put you down. They don't know what you're doing either, and you can't tell them 'cause you don't know. You survive this and in some terrible way, which I suppose no one can ever describe, you are compelled, you are corralled, you are bullwhipped into dealing with whatever it is that hurt you. And what is crucial here is that if it hurt you, that is not what's important. Everybody's hurt. What is important, what corrals you, what bullwhips you, what drives you, torments you, is that you must find some way of using this to connect you with everyone else alive. This is all you have to do it with. You must understand that your pain is trivial except insofar as you can use it to connect with other people's pain; and insofar as you can do that with your pain, you can be released from it, and then hopefully it works the other way around too; insofar as I can tell you what it is to suffer, perhaps I can help you to suffer less. Then, you make—oh, fifteen years later, several thousand drinks later, two or three divorces, God knows how many broken friendships and an exile of one kind or another—some kind of breakthrough, which is your first articulation of who you are: that is to say, your first articulation of who you suspect we all are.

Let me put it another way. When I was very young (and I am sure this is true of everybody here), I assumed that no one had ever been born who was only five feet six inches tall, or been born poor, or been born ugly, or masturbated, or done all those things which were my private property when I was fifteen. No one had ever suffered the way I suffered. Then you discover, and I discovered this through Dostoevsky, that it is common. *Everybody* did it. Not only did everybody do it, everybody's *doing* it. And all the time. It's a fantastic and terrifying liberation. The reason it is terrifying is because it makes you once and for all responsible to no one but yourself. Not to God the Father, not to Satan, not to anybody. Just you. If you think it's right, then you've got to do it. If you think it's wrong, then you mustn't do it. And not only do we all know how difficult it is, given what we are, to tell the difference between right and wrong, but the whole nature of life is so terrible that somebody's right is always somebody else's wrong. And these are the terrible choices one has always got to make.

All right, I said the cat survived all that, and—this is a very crucial thing—you know dirty socks can make you feel like nothing but a dirty sock. You walk into a room and somebody says, "What do you do?" And you say, "I write." And they say, "Yeah, but what do you *do*?" And you wonder, what *do* you do? And what's it for? Why don't you get a job? And somehow you can't, and finally you learn this in the most terrible way, because you try. You're in the position of someone on the edge of a field, and it's cold in the field, and there's a house over there, and there's fire in the house, and food and everything you need, everything you want, and you make all kinds of efforts to get into the house. And they would let you in; they would let you in. They're not being cruel. They recognize you as you come to the door, and they *can't* let you in. You get in, let us say, for five minutes and you can't stay. When I was much younger, people said to me—this is very serious and not just a confession, I'm not just being self-indulgent—"All right, you were working, now stop working. Forget it! Have a drink. Why are you so serious all the time? You can't write all the time, Jimmy. Relax." Have you ever had anyone tell you to relax?

All right, you get through all that and you make your first breakthrough, people have heard your name—and here comes the world again. The world you first encountered when you were fifteen. The world which has starved you, despised you. Here it comes again. This time it is bearing gifts. The phone didn't ring before—if you had a phone. Now it never stops ringing. Instead of people saying, "What do you do?" they say, "Won't you do this?" And you become, or you could become, a Very Important Person. And then—and this is a confession—you find yourself in the position of a woman I don't know who sings a certain song in a certain choir and the song begins: "I said I wasn't gonna tell nobody but I couldn't keep it to myself." You've come full circle. Here you are again, with it all to do all over again, and you must decide all over again whether you want to be famous or whether you want to write. And the two things, in spite of all the evidence, have nothing whatever in common.

Now what is it, at the point that the artist, since I must put it this way, begins to come of age, that he cannot keep to himself? This is the trickiest part of the whole argument. I was having lunch today with a very good friend of mine and a friend of his—and they're both artists. The friend of the friend is a man I admire very much but the other one is a cat I really dig. My friend is an actor and there's a role which we all know he ought to play. In fact, we all know—anyone who loves him—that he has no choice but to play it sooner or later and we all know that he's a little afraid to. And God knows he should be. But he knows he's got to do it. And his friend was saying to him—and I paraphrase it very awkwardly—you must remember that most people live in almost total darkness. It is true, said this friend, that we drink too much, we suffer from stage fright and you may get an ulcer or die of cancer, and it is true that it is all very, very hard and gets harder all the time. And yet people, millions of people whom you will never see, who don't know you, never will know you, people who may try to kill you in the morning, live in a darkness which—if you have that funny terrible thing which every artist can recognize and no artist can define— you are responsible to those people to lighten, and it does not matter what happens to you. You are being used in the way a crab is useful, the way sand certainly has some function. It is impersonal. This force which you didn't ask for, and this destiny which you must accept, is also your responsibility. And if you survive it, if you don't cheat, if you don't lie, it is not only, you know, your glory, your achievement, it is almost our only hope— because only an artist can tell, and only artists have told since we have heard of man, what it is like for anyone who gets to this planet to survive it. What it is like to die, or to have somebody die; what it is like to be glad. Hymns don't do this, churches really cannot do it. The trouble is that although the artist can do it, the price that he has to pay himself and that you, the audience, must also pay, is a willingness to give up everything, to realize that although you spent twenty-seven years acquiring this house, this furniture, this position, although you spent forty years raising this child, these children, nothing, none of it belongs to you. You can only have it by letting it go. You can only take if you are prepared to give, and giving is not an investment. It is not a day at the bargain counter. It is a total risk of everything, of you and who you think you are, who you think you'd like to be, where you think you'd like to go—everything, and this forever, forever.

Now I, if I may put it this way, and all my tribe, if I may put it that way, find this very hard to do, and it's very hard on my mother, on my sisters and my brothers and all my friends, and it's very hard on me, and I may fail in the next two seconds. But then one has got to understand—that is, I and all my tribe (I mean artists now)—that it is hard for me. If I spend weeks and months avoiding my typewriter—and I do, sharpening pencils, trying to avoid going where I know I've got to go—then one has got to use this to learn humility. After all, there is a kind of saving egotism too, a cruel and dangerous but also saving egotism, about the artist's condition, which is this: I know that if I survive it, when the tears have stopped flowing or when the blood has dried, when the storm has settled, I do have a type-writer which is my torment but is also my work. If I can survive it, I can always go back there, and if I've not turned into a total liar, then I can use it and prepare myself in this way for the next inevitable and possibly fatal disaster. But if I find that hard to do—and I have a weapon which most people don't have—then one must understand how hard it is for almost anybody else to do it at all.

And this is where the whole question in my own private, personal case of being an American artist, of being not yet sixty-five years old, and of being an American Negro artist in 1963 in this most peculiar of countries begins to be a very frightening assignment. One is dealing all the time with the most inarticulate people that I, in any case, have ever encountered, and I don't hesitate to say the most inarticulate group of people we are ever likely to encounter, I or anybody else, for a very long time, at least in this century. Inarticulate and illiterate and they're very particular and difficult to describe away, unlettered in the language, which may sound a little florid but there's no other way that I can think of to say it, totally unlet-tered in the language of the heart, totally distrustful of whatever cannot be touched, panic-stricken at the very first hint of pain. A people determined to believe that they can make suffering obsolete. Who don't understand yet a very physiological fact: that the pain which signals a toothache is a pain which saves your life. This is very frightening. It frightens me half to death, and I'm not talking now merely about race, and I'm certainly not talking merely about Southerners. I am talking really about two-thirds of my pub-lic and technical allies. People who believe that segregation is wrong. Peo-ple who march on picket lines who yet have overlooked something else and are still under the illusion, I think, that what they've overlooked has something to do with social questions and in my particular case anyway that it has something to do with Negroes. I would like to live long enough—don't misunderstand me, but I would like to live long enough—to see that word or the use to which it's put struck from the American vocabulary. In effect, there is no Negro problem. The problem is that one is still in a kindergarten, an emotional kindergarten, and the Negro in this country operates as some weird kind of gorilla who suddenly is breaking up all the blackboards. I am tired not only of being told to wait, but of people's saying, "What should I do?" They mean, "What should I do about the Negro problem; what should I do for you?" There is nothing you can do for me. There is nothing you can do for Negroes. It must be done for you. One is not attempting to save twenty-two million people. One is attempting to save an entire country, and that means an entire civilization, and the price for that is high. The price for that is to understand oneself. The price for that, for example, is to recognize that most of us, white and black, have arrived at a point where we do not know what to tell our children. Most of us have arrived at a point where we still believe and insist on and act on the principle, which is no longer valid, that this is such and such an optimum, that our choice is the lesser of two evils, and this is no longer true. Gonorrhea is not preferable to syphilis.

The time has come, it seems to me, to recognize that the framework in which we operate weighs on us too heavily to be borne and is about to kill us. It is time to ask very hard questions and to take very rude positions. And no matter at what price. It is time, for example, for one example, to recognize that the major effort of our country until today (and I am talking about Washington and all the way down to whoever heads the Women's Christian Temperance Union) is not to change a situation but to *seem* to have done it. It is spectacular for example, to have been forced ultimately to bring in the entire whatever-it-was—militia, U.S. marshals—to get James Meredith into school, and from a certain point of view, which I do not at all share, I can see that one could say that no other country would have done it. It's escaped everybody's notice that no other country would have had to. It is easy to admire the sit-in students in the South, and nothing is more delightful than to talk to Martin Luther King, whom I very much admire. But it is too easy to admire a Christian minister, especially if you take no responsibility for what's happening to him or to those people that he tries to represent. It is hard to begin to understand that the drift in American life towards chaos is masked by all these smiling faces and all these do-good efforts.

(1963)

We Can Change the Country

BEFORE I SAY ANYTHING ELSE, I have an announcement to make. I want all of you, and your wives and your children and your brothers-in-law and everyone you know, to resolve as of this moment that you will buy no presents for Christmas. And when I say no presents, I mean not a nail file, not a toothbrush, and I want you to tell your children, as of this moment and on Christmas Day, that the reason there is no Santa Claus this year is because we have lost the right—by the murder of our brothers and sisters—to be called a Christian nation. And until we regain that right, we cannot celebrate the birth of the Prince of Peace. And I am very serious about this for two reasons: (a) morally, I think this nation should be, for the foreseeable future, in mourning; (b) one must face the fact that this Christian nation may never have read any of the Gospels, but they do understand money.

We are not—we who are on the barricades in this unprecedented revolution—in the position of someone in the Congo or someone in Cuba. That is, we cannot take over the land. The terms of this revolution are precisely these: that we will learn to live together here or all of us will abruptly stop living. And I mean that. This is not, and never has been, a white nation. I am not a pupil or a ward of Senator Eastland.* I am an American.

*See footnote on page 11.

My forefathers bled and suffered and died to create this nation, and if my forefathers had not dammed all those rivers and picked all that cotton and laid all that track, there would not be an American economy today.

We are living, at the moment, through a terrifying crisis, and let me try to put it in the cruelest and most abrupt terms that I can. Let us say that a hundred years ago, when I was technically emancipated from the land and given over to the landlords and the bosses—let us say that I was happy in my place and that I loved doing all that singing and dancing down on the levee. Now I, and my father and my grandfather, to say nothing of my grandmother and her mother, never for a moment believed that we were singing and dancing down on the levee because we were so happy, and not for a moment does any black man that I've ever encountered believe that he really was what the country said he was. But what has happened is that the country (by "the country" I mean our government and most of our citizens) believes that I was happy in my place. They believe it so strongly that now they have the courage to ask, What does the Negro want? Well, I know what the Negro wants, and any man who is able to walk and talk knows what the Negro wants. If you know what *you* want, then you know what *I* want.

It is the American Republic—repeat, the American Republic—which created something which they call a "nigger." They created it out of necessities of their own. The nature of the crisis is that I am not a "nigger"—I never was. I am a man. The question with which the country is confronted is this: Why do you need a "nigger" in the first place, and what are you going to do about him now that he's moved out of his place? Because I am not what you said I was. And if my place, as it turns out, is not my place, then you are not what you said you were, and where's your place? There has never been in this country a Negro problem. I have never been upset by the fact that I have a broad nose, big lips, and kinky hair. *You* got upset. And now you must ask yourself why. I, for example, do not bring down property values when I move in. You bring them down when you move out.

Now there are several concrete and dangerous things that we must do to prevent the murder—and please remember there are several million ways to murder—of future children (by which I mean both black and white children). And one of them, and perhaps the most important, is to take a very hard look at our economic structure and our political institutions. For example, the North (for as long as I've been in the North, and I was born in the North) has prided itself on not being like the Southern racists. In the North they don't have signs up saying "white" and "colored." No one tells you where you can and cannot go. In the North, you have to find that out day by day, by what we call trial and error. But the moment you go anywhere near what The Man is really concerned about—I mean his pocketbook—what happened in Birmingham happens in New York.

New York is a segregated city. It is not segregated by accident; it is not an act of God that keeps the Negroes in Harlem. It is the real estate boards and the banks that do it. And when you attack that, that's where the power is. For example, I ask all of you to ask yourselves what would happen if Harlem refused to pay the rent for a month. We've got to bring the cat out of hiding. And where is he? He's hiding in the bank. We've got to flush him out. We have to begin a massive campaign of civil disobedience. I mean nationwide. And this is no stage joke. *Some laws should not be obeyed.*

Secondly, when I talk about our political institutions, there is no reason for any American to continue to be victimized by what we still refer to as the Republican and Democratic parties. Speaking for myself, I cannot imagine voting for any Republican, because the party contains Goldwater. I can't imagine voting for any Democrat, because that party contains East-land. It is important to bear in mind, or to recover the notion, that we are responsible for our government and the government is responsible to us. The government is supposed to represent *us.* It is time that the government knew that if the government does not represent us, if it insists on repre-senting a handful of nostalgic Southern colonels, the government will be replaced.

For a very long time, we have operated on the theory of the lesser of two evils. For example, I myself was so terrified of that salesman called Nixon that I allowed myself to be stampeded into the Kennedy camp. And I believe that was done, if you remember, by a phone call to Martin Luther King, when he was in jail. That swung the Negro vote. Well, the man has been in power for quite some time. If we care about this country—and not only the area of civil rights—it is time to serve notice on our representa-tives that they are under the obligation to represent us and that they cannot be said to represent us if they continually betray twenty million citizens. It is time to let the government know that we will no longer accept this pecu-liar, pathetic excuse: "We have no right to act." If they can invade Cuba, they can act. It is time to say, and unequivocally, that I—speaking now for myself, Jimmy Baldwin, and speaking for myself as though I were white even—I don't see any reason why I should invade Havana. I would much rather invade Miami.

The moral leaders of the Free World are in great trouble. This is not a free country, and if you doubt me, when you leave here, walk or ride up to

125th Street and walk through those streets and ask yourself what you'd feel like if you lived there, why you lived there if you did, and why it looks like a concentration camp. I mean the police walking two by two and three by three. Ask yourself what chances you would have, if you lived there, to get theft or fire or life insurance. Now, this, as I said, is not an act of God. It is an act of the nation, and it began not quite a hundred years ago when the North signed a bargain with the South: they would take me out of the cotton fields and lift me over to the factories, where I've been ever since. If you doubt me, check it out with your labor unions. Ask yourself why the Puerto Ricans and the Negroes are pushing carts in the Garment Center and nobody else.

Now we are here not only to mourn those children, who cannot really be mourned. We are here to begin to achieve the American Revolution. It is time that we the people took the government and the country into our own hands. It is perfectly possible to tap the energy of this country. There is a vast amount of energy here, and we can change and save ourselves. We don't have to be at the mercy forever of these sordid political machines. It is possible to create a third party, you know.

And finally, let me leave you with this: the government pretends it has no right to arrest Governor Wallace, but I know that governors have been impeached. The FBI has not been able to find a single bomber. In Alabama alone, fifty bombings and not one culprit—not yet. The FBI can't find them. Let me tell you why they can't find them. They can't afford to. They stay at the homes of the people who did the bombings. And when they come into town they investigate the students. We are the guilty party. When they come into Birmingham and Mississippi, they don't investigate the Ku Klux Klan or the White Citizens' Council or the mayor. They investigate the people in the streets . . .

If I had done one-tenth of what General Edwin Walker has done in Mississippi, if I had been inciting a mob to murder children, I would be in jail. When Robert Williams armed the Negroes in Monroe, North Carolina, the Justice Department hounded him out of this country on charges of kidnapping and called him—I've seen the posters in the post office myself—a psychopathic, dangerous, armed kidnapper. Well, General Edwin Walker is white and Robert Williams is black, and that is the reason one is in Cuba and the other is—probably working in the Justice Department. If we don't now move, literally move, sit down, stand, walk, don't go to work, don't pay the rent, if we don't now do everything in our power to change this country, this country will turn out to be in the position, let us say, of Spain, a country which is so tangled and so trapped and so immobilized by its interior dissension that it can't do anything else.

We have already paid a tremendous price for what we've done to Negro people. We have denied, and we are paying for the denial of the energy of twenty million people. No society can afford that. The future is going to be worse than the past if we do not let the people who represent us know that it is our country. A government and a nation are not synonymous. We can change the government, and we will.

(1963)

Why I Stopped Hating Shakespeare

EVERY WRITER in the English language, I should imagine, has at some point hated Shakespeare, has turned away from that monstrous achievement with a kind of sick envy. In my most anti-English days I condemned him as a chauvinist ("this England" indeed!) and because I felt it so bitterly anomalous that a black man should be forced to deal with the English language at all—should be forced to assault the English language in order to be able to speak—I condemned him as one of the authors and architects of my oppression.

Again, in the way that some Jews bitterly and mistakenly resent Shylock, I was dubious about Othello (what did he see in Desdemona?) and bitter about Caliban. His great vast gallery of people, whose reality was as contradictory as it was unanswerable, unspeakably oppressed me. I was resenting, of course, the assault on my simplicity; and, in another way, I was a victim of that loveless education which causes so many schoolboys to detest Shakespeare. But I feared him, too, feared him because, in his hands, the English language became the mightiest of instruments. No one would ever write that way again. No one would ever be able to match, much less surpass, him.

Well, I was young and missed the point entirely, was unable to go behind the words and, as it were, the diction, to what the poet was saying. I still remember my shock when I finally *heard* these lines from the murder scene in *Julius Caesar.* The assassins are washing their hands in Caesar's blood. Cassius says:

> Stoop then, and wash.—How many ages hence
> Shall this our lofty scene be acted over,
> In states unborn and accents yet unknown!

What I suddenly heard, for the first time, was manifold. It was the voice of lonely, dedicated, deluded Cassius, whose life had never been real for me before—I suddenly seemed to know what this moment meant to him. But beneath and beyond that voice I also heard a note yet more rigorous and impersonal—and contemporary: that "lofty scene," in all its blood and necessary folly, its blind and necessary pain, was thrown into a perspective which has never left my mind. Just so, indeed, is the heedless State overthrown by men, who, in order to overthrow it, have had to achieve a desperate single-mindedness. And this single-mindedness, which we think of (why?) as ennobling, also operates, and much more surely, to distort and diminish a man—to distort and diminish us all, even, or perhaps especially, those whose needs and whose energy made the overthrow of the State inevitable, necessary, and just.

And the terrible thing about this play, for me—it is not necessarily my favorite play, whatever that means, but it *is* the play which I first, so to speak, discovered—is the tension it relentlessly sustains between individual ambition, self-conscious, deluded, idealistic, or corrupt, and the blind, mindless passion which drives the individual no less than it drives the mob. "I am Cinna the poet, I am Cinna the poet . . . I am not Cinna the conspirator"—that cry rings in my ears. And the mob's response: "Tear him for his bad verses!" And yet—though one howled with Cinna and felt his terrible rise, at the hands of his countrymen, to death, it was impossible to hate the mob. Or, worse than impossible, useless; for here we were, at once howling and being torn to pieces, the only receptacles of evil and the only receptacles of nobility to be found in all the universe. But the play does not even suggest that we have the perception to know evil from good or that such a distinction can ever be clear: "The evil that men do lives after them; The good is oft interred with their bones . . ."

Once one has begun to suspect this much about the world—once one has begun to suspect, that is, that one is not, and never will be, innocent, for the reason that no one is—some of the self-protective veils between oneself and reality begin to fall away. It is probably of some significance, though we cannot pursue it here, that my first real apprehension of Shakespeare came when I was living in France, and thinking and speaking in French. The necessity of mastering a foreign language forced me into a new relationship to my own. (It was also in France, therefore, that I began to read the Bible again.)

My quarrel with the English language has been that the language reflected none of my experience. But now I began to see the matter in quite another way. If the language was not my own, it might be the fault of the language; but it might also be my fault. Perhaps the language was not my own because I had never attempted to use it, had only learned to imitate it. If this were so, then it might be made to bear the burden of my experience if I could find the stamina to challenge it, and me, to such a test.

In support of this possibility, I had two mighty witnesses: my black ancestors, who evolved the sorrow songs, the blues, and jazz, and created an entirely new idiom in an overwhelmingly hostile place; and Shakespeare, who was the last bawdy writer in the English language. What I began to see—especially since, as I say, I was living and speaking in French—is that it is experience which shapes a language; and it is language which controls an experience. The structure of the French language told me something of the French experience, and also something of the French expectations—which were certainly not the American expectations, since the French daily and hourly said things which the Americans could not say at all. (Not even in French.) Similarly, the language with which I had grown up had certainly not been the King's English. An immense experience had forged this language; it had been (and remains) one of the tools of a people's survival, and it revealed expectations which no white American could easily entertain. The authority of this language was in its candor, its irony, its density, and its beat: this was the authority of the language which produced me, and it was also the authority of Shakespeare.

Again, I was listening very hard to jazz and hoping, one day, to translate it into language, and Shakespeare's bawdiness became very important to me, since bawdiness was one of the elements of jazz and revealed a tremendous, loving, and realistic respect for the body, and that ineffable force which the body contains, which Americans have mostly lost, which I had experienced only among Negroes, and of which I had then been taught to be ashamed.

My relationship, then, to the language of Shakespeare revealed itself as nothing less than my relationship to myself and my past. Under this light, this revelation, both myself and my past began slowly to open, perhaps the way a flower opens at morning, but more probably the way an atrophied muscle begins to function, or frozen fingers to thaw.

The greatest poet in the English language found his poetry where poetry is found: in the lives of the people. He could have done this only through love—by knowing, which is not the same thing as understanding, that whatever was happening to anyone was happening to him. It is said that his time was easier than ours, but I doubt it—no time can be easy if one is living through it. I think it is simply that he walked his streets and saw them, and tried not to lie about what he saw: his public streets and his private streets, which are always so mysteriously and inexorably connected; but he trusted that connection. And, though I, and many of us, have bitterly bewailed (and will again) the lot of an American writer—to be part of a people who have ears to hear and hear not, who have eyes to see and see not—I am sure that Shakespeare did the same. Only, he saw, as I think we must, that the people who produce the poet are not responsible to him: he is responsible to them.

That is why he is called a poet. And his responsibility, which is also his joy and his strength and his life, is to defeat all labels and complicate all battles by insisting on the human riddle, to bear witness, as long as breath is in him, to that mighty, unnameable, transfiguring force which lives in the soul of man, and to aspire to do his work so well that when the breath has left him, the people—*all people!*—who search in the rubble for a sign or a witness will be able to find him there.

(1964)

The Uses of the Blues

THE TITLE "The Uses of the Blues" does not refer to music; I don't know anything about music. It does refer to the experience of life, or the state of being, out of which the blues come. Now, I am claiming a great deal for the blues; I'm using them as a metaphor—I might have titled this, for example, "The Uses of Anguish" or "The Uses of Pain." But I want to talk about the blues not only because they speak of this particular experience of life and this state of being, but because they contain the toughness that manages to make this experience articulate. I am engaged, then, in a discussion of craft or, to use a very dangerous word, art. And I want to suggest that the acceptance of this anguish one finds in the blues, and the expression of it, creates also, however odd this may sound, a kind of joy. Now joy is a true state, it is a reality; it has nothing to do with what most people have in mind when they talk of happiness, which is not a real state and does not really exist.

Consider some of the things the blues are about. They're about work, love, death, floods, lynchings; in fact, a series of disasters which can be summed up under the arbitrary heading "Facts of Life." Bessie Smith, who is dead now, came out of somewhere in the Deep South. I guess she was born around 1898, a great blues singer; died in Mississippi after a very long, hard—not *very* long, but very *hard*—life: pigs' feet and gin, many disastrous lovers, and a career that first went up, then went down; died on the road on the way from one hospital to another. She was in an automobile accident and one of her arms was wrenched out of its socket; and because the hospital attendants argued whether or not they could let her in because she was colored, she died. Not a story Horatio Alger would write. Well, Bessie saw a great many things, and among those things was a flood. And she talked about it and she said, "It rained five days and the skies turned dark as night" and she repeated it: "It rained five days and the skies turned dark as night." Then, "Trouble take place in the lowlands at night." And she went on:

> Then it thundered and lightnin'd and the wind began to blow
> Then it thundered and lightnin'd and the wind began to blow
> There's thousands of people ain't got no place to go

As the song makes clear, she was one of those people. But she ended in a fantastic way:

> Backwater blues done caused me to pack my things and go
> Because my house fell down
> And I can't live there no mo'.

Billie Holiday came along a little later and she had quite a story, too, a story which *Life* magazine would never print except as a tough, bittersweet sob story obituary—in which, however helplessly, the dominant note would be relief. She was a little girl from the South, and she had quite a time with gin, whiskey, and dope. She died in New York in a narcotics ward under the most terrifying and—in terms of crimes of the city and the country against her—disgraceful circumstances, and she had something she called "Billie's Blues": "My man wouldn't give me no dinner / Wouldn't give me no supper / Squawked about my supper and turned me outdoors / And had the nerve to lay a padlock on my clothes / I didn't have so many, but I had a long, long way to go."

And one more, one more—Bessie Smith had a song called "Gin House Blues." It's another kind of blues, and maybe I should explain this to you—a Negro has his difficult days, the days when everything has gone wrong and on top of it, he has a fight with the elevator man, or the taxi driver, or somebody he never saw before, who seems to decide to prove he's white and you're black. But this particular Tuesday it's more than you can take—

sometimes, you know, you can take it. But Bessie didn't this time, and she sat down in the gin house and sang: "Don't try me, nobody/'Cause you will never win/I'll fight the Army and the Navy/Just me and my gin."

Well, you know, that is all very accurate, all very concrete. I know, I watched, I was there. You've seen these black men and women, these boys and girls; you've seen them on the streets. But I know what happened to them at the factory, at work, at home, on the subway, what they go through in a day, and the way they sort of ride with it. And it's very, very tricky. It's kind of a fantastic tightrope. They may be very self-controlled, very civilized; I like to think of myself as being very civilized and self-controlled, but I know I'm not. And I know that some improbable Wednesday, for no reason whatever, the elevator man or the doorman, the policeman or the landlord, or some little boy from the Bronx will say something, and it will be the wrong day to say it, the wrong moment to have it said to me; and God knows what will happen. I have seen it all, I have seen that much. What the blues are describing comes out of all this.

"Gin House Blues" is a real gin house. "Backwater Flood" is a real flood. When Billie says, "My man don't love me," she is not making a fantasy out of it. This is what happened, this is where it is. This is what it is. Now, I'm trying to suggest that the triumph here—which is a very un-American triumph—is that the person to whom these things happened watched with eyes wide open, saw it happen. So that when Billie or Bessie or Leadbelly stood up and sang about it, they were commenting on it, a little bit outside it: they were accepting it. And there's something funny—there's always something a little funny in all our disasters, if one can face the disaster. So that it's this passionate detachment, this inwardness coupled with outwardness, this ability to know that, all right, it's a mess, and you can't do anything about it . . . so, well, you have to do something about it. You can't stay there, you can't drop dead, you can't give up, but all right, okay, as Bessie said, "picked up my bag, baby, and I tried it again." This made life, however horrible that life was, bearable for her. It's what makes life bearable for any person, because every person, everybody born, from the time he's found out about people until the whole thing is over, is certain of one thing: he is going to suffer. There is no way not to suffer.

Now, this brings us to two things. It brings us to the American Negro's experience of life, and it brings us to the American dream or sense of life. It would be hard to find any two things more absolutely opposed. I want to make it clear that when I talk about Negroes in this context I am not talking about race; I don't know what race means. I am talking about a social fact. When I say "Negro," it is a digression; it is important to remember that I am not talking about a people, but a person. I am talking about a man who, let's say, was once seventeen and who is now, let's say, forty, who has four children and can't feed them. I am talking about what happens to that man in this time and during this effort. I'm talking about what happens to you if, having barely escaped suicide, or death, or madness, or yourself, you watch your children growing up and no matter what you do, no matter *what* you do, you are powerless, you are really powerless, against the force of the world that is out to tell your child that he has no right to be alive. And no amount of liberal jargon, and no amount of talk about how well and how far we have progressed, does anything to soften or to point out any solution to this dilemma. In every generation, ever since Negroes have been here, every Negro mother and father has had to face that child and try to create in that child some way of surviving this particular world, some way to make the child who will be despised not despise himself. I don't know what "the Negro problem" means to white people, but this is what it means to Negroes. Now, it would seem to me, since this is so, that one of the reasons we talk about "the Negro problem" in the way we do is in order precisely to avoid any knowledge of this fact. Imagine Doris Day trying to sing:

> Papa may have, Mama may have,
> But God bless the child that's got his own.

People talk to me absolutely bathed in a bubble bath of self-congratulation. I mean, I walk into a room and everyone there is terribly proud of himself because I managed to get to the room. It proves to him that he is getting better. It's funny, but it's terribly sad. It's sad that one needs this kind of corroboration and it's terribly sad that one can be so self-deluded. The fact that Harry Belafonte makes as much money as, let's say, Frank Sinatra, doesn't really mean anything in this context. Frank can still get a house anywhere, and Harry can't. People go to see Harry and stand in long lines to watch him. They love him onstage, or at a cocktail party, but they don't want him to marry their daughters. This has nothing to do with Harry; this has everything to do with America. All right. Therefore, when we talk about what we call "the Negro problem" we are simply evolving means of avoiding the facts of this life. Because in order to face the facts of a life like Billie's or, for that matter, a life like mine, one has got to—the American white has got to—accept the fact that what he thinks he is, he is not. He has to give up, he has to surrender his image of himself, and apparently this is the last thing white Americans are prepared to do.

But anyway, it is not a question now of accusing the white American of crimes against the Negro. It is too late for that. Besides, it is irrelevant. Injustice, murder, the shedding of blood, unhappily, are commonplace. These things happen all the time and everywhere. There is always a reason for it. People will always give themselves reasons for it. What I'm much more concerned about is what white Americans have done to themselves; what has been done to me is irrelevant simply because there is nothing more you can do to me. But in doing it, you've done something to yourself. In evading my humanity, you have done something to your own humanity. We all do this all the time, of course. One labels people; one labels them "Jew," one labels them "fascist," one labels them "Communist," one labels them "Negro," one labels them "white man." But in the doing of this, you have not described anything—you have not described me when you call me a nigger or when you call me a Negro leader. You have only described yourself. What I think of you says more about me than it can possibly say about you. This is a very simple law, and every Negro who intends to survive has to learn it very soon. Therefore, the Republic, among other things, has managed to create a body of people who have very little to lose, and there is nothing more dangerous in any republic, any state, any country, any time, than men who have nothing to lose.

Because you have thus given him his freedom, the American Negro can do whatever he wills; you can no longer do anything to him. He doesn't want anything you've got; he doesn't believe anything you say. I don't know why and I don't know how America arrived at this peculiar point of view. If one examines American history, there is no apparent reason for it. It's a bloody history, as bloody as everybody else's history, as deluded, as fanatical. One has only to look at it from the time we all got here. Look at the Pilgrims, the Puritans—the people who presumably fled oppression in Europe only to set up a more oppressed society here—people who wanted freedom, who killed off the Indians. Look at all the people moving into a new era, and enslaving all the blacks. These are the facts of American history as opposed to the legend. We came from Europe, we came from Africa, we came from all over the world. We brought whatever was in us from China or from France. We *all* brought it with us. We were not transformed when we crossed the ocean. Something else happened. Something much more serious. We no longer had any way of finding out, of knowing who we were.

Many people have said in various tones of voice, meaning various things, that the most unlucky thing that happened in America was the presence of the Negro. Freud said, in a kind of rage, that the black race was the folly of America and that it served America right. Well, of course, I don't quite know what Freud had in mind. But I can see that, in one way, it may have been the most unlucky thing that happened to America, since America, unlike any other Western power, had its slaves on the mainland. They were here. We had our slaves at a time, unluckily for us, when slavery was going out of fashion. And after the Bill of Rights. Therefore, it would seem to me that the presence of this black mass here as opposed to all the things we said we believed in and also at a time when the whole doctrine of white supremacy had never even been questioned is one of the most crucial facts of our history. It would be nightmarish now to read the handbooks of colonialists a hundred years ago; even ten years ago, for that matter. But in those days, it was not even a question of black people being inferior to white people. The American found himself in a very peculiar position because he knew that black people were people. Frenchmen could avoid knowing it—they never met a black man. Englishmen could avoid knowing it. But Americans could not avoid knowing it because, after all, here he was, and he was, no matter how it was denied, a man, just like everybody else. And the attempt to avoid this, to avoid this fact, I consider one of the keys to what we can call loosely the American psychology. For one thing, it created in Americans a kind of perpetual, hidden, festering, and entirely unadmitted guilt. Guilt is a very peculiar emotion. As long as you are guilty about something, no matter what it is, you are not compelled to change it. Guilt is like a warm bath or, to be rude, it is like masturbation: you can get used to it, you can prefer it, you may get to a place where you cannot live without it, because in order to live without it, in order to get past this guilt, you must act. And in order to act, you must be conscious and take great chances and be responsible for the consequences. Therefore, liberals, and people who are not even liberals, much prefer to discuss "the Negro problem" than to try to deal with what this figure of the Negro really means personally to them. They still prefer to read statistics, charts, Gallup polls, rather than deal with the reality. They still tell me, to console me, how many Negroes bought Cadillacs, Cutty Sark, Coca-Cola, Schweppes last year; how many more will buy Cadillacs, Cutty Sark, Coca-Cola, and Schweppes next year. To prove to me that things are getting better. Now, of course, I think it is a very sad matter if you suppose that you or I have bled and suffered and died in this country in order to achieve Cadillacs, Cutty

Sark, Schweppes, and Coca-Cola. It seems to me if one accepts this speculation about the luxury of guilt that the second reason must be related to
the first. That has to do with the ways in which we manage to project onto
the Negro face, because it is so visible, all of our guilts and aggressions and
desires. And if you doubt this, think of the legends that surround the
Negro to this day. Think, when you think of these legends, that they were
not invented by Negroes, but they were invented by the white Republic.
Ask yourself if Aunt Jemima or Uncle Tom ever existed anywhere and why
it was necessary to invent them. Ask yourself why Negroes until today are,
in the popular imagination, at once the most depraved people under
heaven and the most saintly. Ask yourself what William Faulkner really
was trying to say in *Requiem for a Nun,* which is about a nigger, whore, dope
addict, saint. Faulkner wrote it. I never met Nancy, the nun he was writing
about. He never met her either, but the question is, why was it necessary
for him and for us to hold on to this image? We needn't go so far afield. Ask
yourself why liberals are so delighted with the movie *The Defiant Ones.* It
ends, if you remember, when Sidney Poitier, the black man, having been
chained interminably to Tony Curtis, the white man, finally breaks the
chain, is on the train, is getting away, but no, he doesn't go, doesn't leave
poor Tony Curtis down there on the chain gang. Not at all. He jumps off
the train and they go buddy-buddy back together to the same old Jim Crow
chain gang. Now this is a fable. Why? Who is trying to prove what to
whom? I'll tell you something. I saw that movie twice. I saw it downtown
with all my liberal friends, who were delighted when Sidney jumped off
the train. I saw it uptown with my less liberal friends, who were furious.
When Sidney jumped off that train they called him all kinds of unmentionable things. Well, their reaction was at least more honest and more
direct. Why is it necessary at this late date, one screams at the world, to
prove that the Negro doesn't really hate you, he's forgiven and forgotten all
of it? Maybe he has. That's not the problem. *You* haven't. And that *is* the
problem:

> I love you, baby,
> But can't stand your dirty ways.

There's one more thing I ought to add to this. The final turn of the
screw that created this peculiar purgatory which we call America is that
aspect of our history that is most triumphant. We really did conquer a continent; we have made a lot of money; we're better off materially than any-

body else in the world. How easy it is as a person or as a nation to suppose that one's well-being is proof of one's virtue; in fact, a great many people are saying just that right now—you know, "We're the best nation in the world because we're the richest nation in the world." The American way of life has proven itself, according to these curious people, and that's why we're so rich. This is called "Yankee virtue" and it comes from Calvin, but my point is that I think this has again something to do with the American failure to face reality. Since we have all these things, we can't be so bad, and since we have all these things, we are robbed, in a way, of the incentive to walk away from the TV set, the Cadillac, and go into the chaos out of which and only out of which we can create ourselves into human beings.

To talk about these things in this country today is extremely difficult. Even the words mean nothing anymore. I think, for example, what we call "the religious revival" in America means that more and more people periodically get more and more frightened and go to church in order to make sure they don't lose their investments. This is the only reason that I can find for the popularity of men who have nothing to do with religion at all, like Norman Vincent Peale, for example—only for example; there're lots of others just like him. I think this is very sad. I think it's very frightening. But Ray Charles, who is a great tragic artist, makes of a genuinely religious confession something triumphant and liberating. He tells us that he cried so loud he gave the blues to his neighbor next door.

How can I put it? Let us talk about a person who is no longer very young, who somehow managed to get to, let us say, the age of forty, and a great many of us do, without ever having been touched, broken, disturbed, frightened—forty-year-old virgin, male or female. There is a sense of the grotesque about a person who has spent his or her life in a kind of cotton batting. There is something monstrous about never having been hurt, never having been made to bleed, never having lost anything, never having gained anything because life is beautiful, and in order to keep it beautiful you're going to stay just the way you are and you're not going to test your theory against all the possibilities outside. America is something like that. The failure on our part to accept the reality of pain, of anguish, of ambiguity, of death has turned us into a very peculiar and sometimes monstrous people. It means, for one thing, and it's very serious, that people who have had no experience have no compassion. People who have had no experience suppose that if a man is a thief, he is a thief; but, in fact, that isn't the most important thing about him. The most important thing about him is that he is a man and, furthermore, that if he's a thief or a murderer or whatever he is, *you* could also be and you would know this, anyone would know this who had really dared to live. Miles Davis once gave poor Billie Holiday one hundred dollars and somebody said, "Man, don't you know she's going to go out and spend it on dope?" and Miles said, "Baby, have you ever been sick?"

Now, you don't know that by reading, by looking. You don't know what the river is like or what the ocean is like by standing on the shore. You can't know anything about life and suppose you can get through it clean. The most monstrous people are those who think they are going to. I think this shows in everything we see and do, in everything we read about these peculiar private lives, so peculiar that it is almost impossible to write about them, because what a man *says* he's doing has nothing to do with what he's *really* doing. If you read such popular novelists as John O'Hara, you can't imagine what country he's talking about. If you read *Life* magazine, it's like reading about the moon. Nobody lives in that country. That country does not exist and, what is worse, everybody knows it. But everyone pretends that it does. Now, this is panic. And this is terribly dangerous, because it means that when the trouble comes, and trouble always comes, you won't survive it. It means that if your son dies, you may go to pieces or find the nearest psychiatrist or the nearest church, but you won't survive it on your own. If you don't survive your trouble out of your own resources, you have not really survived it; you have merely closed yourself against it. The blues are rooted in the slave songs; the slaves discovered something genuinely terrible, terrible because it sums up the universal challenge, the universal hope, the universal fear:

> The very time I thought I was lost
> My dungeon shook and my chains fell off.

Well, that is almost all I am trying to say. I say it out of great concern. And out of a certain kind of hope. If you can live in the full knowledge that you are going to die, that you are not going to live forever, that if you live with the reality of death, you can live. This is not mystical talk; it is a fact. It is a principal fact of life. If you can't do it, if you spend your entire life in flight from death, you are also in flight from life. For example, right now you find the most unexpected people building bomb shelters, which is very close to being a crime. It is a private panic which creates a public delusion that some of us will be saved by bomb shelters. If we had, as human beings, on a personal and private level, our personal authority, we would know better; but because we are so uncertain of all these things, some of us, apparently, are willing to spend the rest of our lives underground in concrete. Perhaps, if we had a more working relationship with ourselves and with one another, we might be able to turn the tide and eliminate the propaganda for building bomb shelters. People who in some sense know who they are can't change the world always, but they can do something to make it a little more, to make life a little more human. Human in the best sense. Human in terms of joy, freedom which is always private, respect, respect for one another, even such things as manners. All these things are very important, all these old-fashioned things. People who don't know who they are privately, accept as we have accepted for nearly fifteen years, the fantastic disaster which we call American politics and which we call American foreign policy, and the incoherence of the one is an exact reflection of the incoherence of the other. Now, the only way to change all this is to begin to ask ourselves very difficult questions.

I will stop now. But I want to quote two things. A very great American writer, Henry James, writing to a friend of his who had just lost her husband, said, "Sorrow wears and uses us but we wear and use it too, and it is blind. Whereas we, after a manner, see." And Bessie said:

> Good mornin', blues.
> Blues, how do you do?
> I'm doin' all right.
> Good mornin'.
> How are you?

(1964)

What Price Freedom?

PART OF THE PRICE that Americans have paid for delusion, part of what we have done to ourselves, was given to us in Dallas, Texas. This happened in a civilized nation, the country which is the moral leader of the Free World, when some lunatic blew off the President's head. Now, I want to suggest something, and I don't want to sound rude, but we all know that it has been many generations and it hasn't stopped yet that black men's heads have been blown off—and nobody cared. Because, as I said before, it wasn't happening to a person, it was happening to a "nigger."

We all know that this country prides itself in something it calls "upward mobility." "Upward mobility" means, among other things, other sinister things, that if you were born a poor boy—say, you are born in the ghetto, or in the backwoods someplace, or in Sicily, and you can't speak English very well yet—it means that if you work hard and save your pennies and be a good boy (or know how to be a bad boy) you can get to be a junior executive by the time you are thirty. That is what "upward mobility" means and that is *all* it means. It does not apply, of course, to one-tenth of the population. A black boy born in the backwoods and a black boy born in the ghetto knows he is not going to get out of the ghetto by saving his pennies and being a nice boy. Now, if I am imprisoned in the ghetto, somebody is keeping me there. I can't walk out because of the warden. There are two people you always find in prison: the man in the prison and the man who is keeping him there. I, as the prisoner, have a terrible advantage since I have to understand by the time I am twelve the nature of the prison and *your* nature, since you are my warden, and then I have to figure out how to outwit you and how to lick you and I do, and I manage, very often anyway, to survive all your prisons, but you, the wardens, have not. If we in this country had a stronger grasp of reality—and when I say "reality" I mean the reality of another human being—another human being!—if we had not lost that, then the assassination of Medgar Evers would have aroused the country *then.*

He was a father; he had a wife; he had children; he was an American! He was also killed, we are told, by a lunatic. I am suspicious of these "lunatics" who crop up in the most inconvenient or convenient times and places. In any case, I don't care what hand pulled the trigger; he was put to death by the same oligarchy who still intend, with the country's help, to keep the Negro in his place. That is why he died and that is why nobody cared.

Six kids were murdered in Birmingham on a Sunday and in Sunday school in a Christian nation, and nobody cared. And because nobody cared *then,* we are in this trouble *now;* because the forces which we have allowed to take over in this country also killed poor President Kennedy, and not because—let us tell the truth—not because he had turned into John Brown and not because he was a great civil rights leader. Let's not be so pious as to make a myth out of what we *know.* He died for a very simple and also very complex reason, and when one examines the reason we are seeing something that all of our communications systems deny. What he did was break the bargain the country had struck around the turn of the century, when we agreed in the North that we would do what we wanted to with "our niggers" and in the South you would do what you wanted with "your niggers." That is what created the "Solid South," and he broke the bargain, poor man. When James Forman talks about "one man, one vote," if we really should achieve one man, one vote, that is the end of the Southern oligarchy and that really is also the end of the Democratic Party as we now know it.

That fact suggests to me some of the dimensions of the crisis which we now face. How can I put this? I was trying to suggest before that what the country has done to one-tenth of its citizens has had a disastrous effect on the country. It is obvious—or maybe it is not so obvious, as it seems to be a controversial point, but it seems to me obvious—that if you are intending to establish, to live in, to create a democracy, then you have a responsibility to all of your citizens. It would seem obvious to me that any son, any native son or daughter, has all the rights that any other native son or daughter has.

It's bad enough for this not to be so; that's bad enough. But what is really much worse is the system of lies, evasions, and naked oppression designed to pretend this isn't so. It is one thing to trample a kid half to death or to death—that is bad enough—but it is quite another thing to then be told by the agents of that oppression, "Be patient; we will do better tomorrow." The question will cross your mind just for a moment: "You will do *what* better tomorrow?" No, no, the militancy and the vitality that I heard in the music here today come from the kind of energy which allows you, which in fact forces you, to examine everything, taking nothing for granted. To say that it has been this way for the last two hundred years, but that it will *not* be this way for the next five minutes; that if, for example, you don't think you can work in the Democratic Party, you don't have to— there are other things. It is a vitality, in short, which allows you to believe, to act on the belief, that it is *your* country, and your responsibility to your country is to *free it*, and to free it you have to *change* it.

Americans are the youngest country, the largest country, and the strongest country, we like to say, and yet the very notion of change, *real* change, throws Americans into a panic and they look for any label to get rid of any dissenter. A country which is supposed to be built on dissent, built on the value of the individual, now distrusts dissent at least as much as any totalitarian government can and debases the individual in many ways because it places security and money above the individual; and when these things are cultivated and honored in the country, no matter what else it may have, it is in danger of perishing, because no country can survive, it *cannot* survive, without a patient, active responsibility for all its citizens. This country now, in terms of its politicians, always seems to feel "it is out of our hands"; "we can't do anything." A country which has no objective need to do so is always talking about the lesser of two evils. I hope you see what I am trying to suggest. I am trying to suggest that in order for me as a black citizen of this country to begin to be a free man here, in order for that to happen, a great many other things have to happen. I cannot be, even if I wanted to be, fitted into the social structure as it now stands; there is no possibility of opening it up to let me in. In the very same way, in the Deep South, Christian churches do not have many Christians in their congregations, and when I move into the congregation, and when the church itself embraces all Christians, the church will have had to change.

In order for us to survive and transcend the terrible days ahead of us, the country will have to turn and take me in its arms. Now, this may sound mystical, but at bottom that is what has got to happen, because it is not a matter of *giving me* this or that; it is not yours to give me. Let us be clear about that. It is not a question of whether they are going to give me any freedom. I am going to take my freedom. That problem is resolved. The real problem is the price. Not the price I will pay, but the price the country will pay. The price a white woman, man, boy, and girl will have to pay in themselves before they look on me as another human being. This metamorphosis is what we are driving toward, because without that we will perish—indeed, we are almost perishing now.

Internal dissension in this country has had a terrifying effect all over the world, because we are locked in civil war. Now, some of the changes which begin to achieve the liberation of a country have to be awkward and disturbing; and just think about one single aspect of this problem—jobs and freedom. The economy cannot employ all of its white people. And in my view one of the reasons for this—and I am deliberately not talking about the fantastic nuclear situation which is costing so much money—one of the reasons for this is that a great deal of the energy of this economy goes into creating things that nobody needs and nobody wants and everybody buys. Nobody needs a new car every year, and it doesn't really matter what kind of toothpaste you use, you know; these things are not important. And in order for me to get a job, we have to have ways of getting everybody a job, and we are not going to do it the way we are doing it now. That's a fact! And as for freedom, I will tell you what I know about freedom, and you will think I don't have any political sense. I know that James Forman, for example, and many of the students he leads, are much, much freer than most of the white people I know in this country. For that matter, I am too. The reason is, I think, the reason is that in order to be free—let's look some facts of your life in the face—you have to look into yourself and know *who you are,* at least know who you are, and decide what you want or at least what you will *not* have, and will *not* be, and take it from there. People are as free as they wish to become. If one thinks of Americans in this way, "freedom" is used here as a synonym for "comfort." People think they are free because they don't have a military machine oppressing them; but one of the simplest ways to lose freedom is to stop fighting for it and stop respecting it. And when it goes that way, something much worse happens, I think: when freedom goes that way, it completely vanishes, and nobody cares. Chaos takes its place, rather like what we watched in Germany—and again, this is going to be a horrible example. I still believe when a country has lost all human feeling, you can do anything to anybody and justify it, and we do know that in this country we have done just that. The nature of our crisis then, it seems to me, is that those of us who will not live unless we can be free make this known. The events, the terrible events of the last days, have done nothing to alter this determination. In fact, if one had been undecided or uncertain before about what it meant to try to liberate oneself in this country, one is undecided no longer, because now we have seen with our own eyes the danger we are in. We have seen with our own eyes what happens to a society when it allows itself to be ruled by the least able and the most abject among us. We have seen what happens when the word "democracy" is taken to be a synonym for mediocrity; is not taken to mean to raise all of its members to the highest possible level, but on the contrary to reduce such members as aspire to excellence down to the lowest common denominator.

We have begun to see what happens to a country when it is run according to the rules of a popularity contest; we have begun to see that we ourselves are far more dangerous for ourselves than Khrushchev or Castro. What we do not know about our black citizens is what we do not know about ourselves; and what we do not know about ourselves is what we do not know about the world—and the world knows it. Nothing can save us—not all our money, nor all our bombs, nor all our guns—if we cannot achieve that long-, long-, long-delayed maturity.

(1964)

The White Problem

I SHOULD SAY TWO THINGS before I begin. One: I beg you to hold somewhere in the center of your mind the fact that this is a centennial year, that we are celebrating, this year, one hundred years of Negro freedom. Two: we are speaking in the context of the Birmingham crisis. And in this attempt to speak to you, I am going to have to play entirely, as they say, by ear. I want you to reconsider, or really to listen to, for the first time, the last two lines of an extremely celebrated song, as though you were an actor, and you were on the stage, under the necessity to deliver Hamlet's soliloquy "To be or not to be," etc., as though these lines had never been heard before. These two lines could be considered extremely corny, but I ask you to take them seriously. They are a question. The two lines I want you to pretend you are delivering on some stage, somewhere in the world, as though these lines had never been heard before, are these:

> Oh, say, does that star-spangled banner still wave
> O'er the land of the free and the home of the brave?

And now please try to make a certain leap with me. I have one more quotation I want to give you, which comes from Nietzsche—it has been on my mind all week long. At some point, the man says:

I stand before my highest mountain, and before my longest journey, and, therefore, must I descend deeper than I have ever before descended.

There are several thousand things one must attempt to suggest, due to the context in which we are speaking. In the life of a woman, in the life of a man, in anybody's life, there are always many elements at work. The crucial element I wish to consider here is that element of a life which we consider to be an identity; the way in which one puts oneself together, what one imagines oneself to be; for one example, the invented reality standing before you now, who is arbitrarily known as Jimmy Baldwin. This invented reality contains a great number of elements, all of them extremely difficult, if not impossible, to name. The invented reality has struck a certain kind of bargain with the world: he has a name, we know what he does, and we think, therefore, that we know who he is. But it is not that simple. The truth, forever, for everybody, is that one is a stranger to oneself, and that one must deal with this stranger day in and day out—that one, in fact, is forced to create, as distinct from invent, oneself. Life demands of everyone a certain kind of humility, the humility to be able to make the descent that Nietzsche is talking about.

Life does not offer one as many choices as one would like to believe. In my life—and in your life, too, I am sure—when young, one supposes that there is some way to avoid disaster. Let me try to spell that out a little. When I was a little boy, for example, I used to tell my mother, "I'm going to do this, I'm going to do that, I'm going to go here and I'm going to go there, I'm going to be a writer—I'm going to *do, do, do, be* this." Mama would look at me and say, "It's more than a notion."

It took me a long time, a very long time, to begin to realize that she was right, and begin to realize what she meant. I, like all of us, thought I knew what I wanted, and I thought I knew who I was, and—like all of us—I thought that whatever it was I wanted and wherever I wanted to go, I could achieve without paying my dues. For one of the things that one cannot imagine, especially when one is young, is how to pay your dues. You don't even know that there are dues to be paid. Later on, one begins to discover, with great pain, and very much against one's will, that whatever it is you want, what you want, at bottom, must be to *become yourself*: there is nothing else to want. Whatever one's journey is, one's got to accept the fact that disaster is one of the conditions under which you will make it. (The journey, I mean, not "make it" in the American sense.) And you will learn a certain humility, because the terms that you have invented, which you think describe and define you, inevitably collide with the facts of life. When this collision occurs—and, make no mistake, this is an absolutely inevitable collision—when this collision occurs, like two trains meeting head-on in a tunnel, life offers you the choice, and it's a very narrow choice, of holding on to your definition of yourself or saying, as the old folks used to say, and as everybody who wants to live has to say: *Yes, Lord.*

Which is to say yes to life. Until you can do that, you've not become a man or a woman. Now, in this country this inability to say yes to life is part of our dilemma, which could become a tragic one; it is part of the dilemma of being what is known as an American. The collective effort until this moment, and the collective delusion until this moment, has been precisely my delusion when I was a little boy: that you could get what you wanted, and become what you said you were going to be, painlessly. Furthermore, if one examines for a second, or if one tries to define, the proper noun "American," one will discover that the noun equates with a catalogue of virtues, and with something called, plaintively enough, "I Am an American" Day. To be an American means, I gather—check me out, you think about it—that, though Greeks, Armenians, Turks, Frenchmen, Englishmen, Scots, Italians, may be corrupt, sexual, unpredictable, lazy, evil, a little lower than the angels, Americans are not—quite overlooking the fact that the country was settled by Englishmen, Scots, Germans, Turks, Armenians, etc. Every nation under heaven is here, and not, after all, for a very long time.

I think that it might be useful, in order to survive our present crisis, to do what any individual does, is forced to do, to survive his crisis, which is to look back on his beginnings. The beginnings of this country (it seems to me a banality to say it, but, alas, it has to be said) have nothing whatever to do with the myth we have created about it. The country did not come about because a handful of people in various parts of Europe said, "I want to be free," and promptly built a boat or a raft and crossed the Atlantic Ocean. Not at all, not at all. In passing, let me remark that the words "liberty" and "freedom" are terribly misused words. Liberty is a genuine political possibility, in spite of the fact that the word is so often used as a slogan; and freedom—which, as I understand it, is beyond politics, though affecting politics and affected by it—may be the very last thing that people want. The very last thing. Anyway, the people who settled the country, the people who came here, came here for one reason, no matter how disguised. They came here because they thought it would be better here than wherever they were. That's why they came. And that's the only reason that they came. Anybody who was making it in England did not get on the

Mayflower. It is important that one begin to recognize this because part of the dilemma of this country is that it has managed to believe the myth it has created about its past, which is another way of saying that it has entirely denied its past. And we all know, I think, what happens to a person who is born where I was born, say, in Harlem, and goes into the world pretending that he was born in Sutton Place. And what happens to a person, however odd this may sound, also happens to a nation, a nation being, when it finally comes into existence, the achievement of the people who make it up; and the quality of the nation being absolutely at the mercy of, defined and dictated by, the nature and the quality of its people.

Let me point, if I may, to another thing, which is really the same thing. The Italian immigrant arriving from Italy, for example, or the son of parents who were born in Sicily, makes a great point of not speaking Italian, because he's going to become an American. And he can't bear his parents, because they are backward. This may seem a trivial matter. But it is of the utmost importance when a father is despised by his son, and this is one of the facts of American life, and is what we are really referring to, in oblique and terrible fashion, when we talk about upward mobility.

In this extraordinary endeavor to create the country called America, a great many crimes were committed. And I want to make it absolutely clear, or as clear as I can, that I understand perfectly well that crime is universal, and as old as mankind, and I trust, therefore, that no one will assume that I am indicting or accusing. I'm not any longer interested in the crime. People treat each other very badly and always have and very probably always will. I'm not talking about the crime; I'm talking about denying what one does. This is a much more sinister matter. We did several things in order to conquer the country. There existed, at the time we reached these shores, a group of people who had never heard of machines, or, as far as I know, of money—which we *had* heard about. We promptly eliminated them; we killed them. I'm talking about the Indians, in case you don't know what I'm talking about. Well, people have done that for centuries, but I'm willing to bet anything you like that not many American children being taught American history have any real sense of what that collision was like, or what we really did, how we really achieved the extermination of the Indians, or what that meant. And it is interesting to consider that very few social critics, very few, have begun even to analyze the hidden reasons for the tremendous popularity of the cowboy–Indian legend in American life, a legend so powerful that it still, in 1963, dominates the American television screen. I suspect that all those cowboy–Indian stories are designed to reassure us that no crime was committed. We've made a legend out of a massacre. In which connection, if I may digress for a moment, there used to be an old joke going around among Negroes. If you remember the Lone Ranger, he was white, of course, and he had a sidekick called Tonto, an Indian. There's always a good Indian. He rode around with the Lone Ranger, and according to my memory of the story, Tonto and the Lone Ranger ran into this ambush of nothing but Indians. And the Lone Ranger said, "What are we going to do, Tonto?" And Tonto said, "What do you mean, 'we'?"

Well, I tell that joke in order to point out something else. It's a Negro joke. One of the other things we did in order to conquer the country, physically speaking, was to enslave the Africans. Now slavery, like murder, is one of the oldest human institutions. So we cannot quarrel about the facts of slavery. That is to say, we could, but that's another story. We enslaved them because, in order to conquer the country, we had to have cheap labor. And the man who is now known as the American Negro, who is one of the oldest Americans, and the *only* one who never wanted to come here, did the dirty work, hoed the cotton—in fact, it is not too much to say that without his presence, without that strong back, the American economy, the American nation, would have had a vast amount of trouble creating that capital of which we are now so proud, and to which we claim Negroes have never contributed anything. If the Negro had not done all that totin' of barges and liftin' of bales, America would be a very different country, and it would certainly be a much poorer country.

The people who settled the country had a fatal flaw. They could recognize a man when they saw one. They knew he wasn't—I mean *you can tell,* they knew he wasn't—anything *else* but a man; but since they were Christian, and since they had already decided that they came here to establish a free country, the only way to justify the role this chattel was playing in one's life was to say that he *was not* a man. For if he wasn't a man, then no crime had been committed. That lie is the basis of our present trouble. It is an extremely complex lie. If, on the one hand, one man cannot avoid recognizing another man, it is also true then, obviously, that the black man in captivity, and treated like an animal, and told that he was, *knew* that *he* was, a man being oppressed by other men who did not even have the courage to admit what they were doing. When the African, in Africa, enslaved other men, he did not pretend that he was merely breaking in oxen.

Let me tell you a small anecdote. I was in Dakar about a year ago, in Senegal, and just off Dakar there is a very small island, which was once the property of the Portuguese. It is simply a rock with a fortress; from Africa, it is the nearest point to America. My sister and I went to this island to visit something called the Slave House. The house was not terribly large. It looks a little like houses you see in New Orleans. That's the truth. It's got two stories and a courtyard and a staircase on each side, sweeping stone staircases. I assume that the captains and the slavers lived upstairs; downstairs were the slave quarters. You walked through a kind of archway, very dark, very low, made of stone, and on either side of you were a series of cells, with stone floors and rusted bits of iron still embedded in the walls. This may be my imagination, but it seemed to me that the odor was still there, that I could still smell it. What it must have smelled like, with all those human beings chained together, in such a place. I remember that they couldn't speak to each other, because they didn't come from the same tribe. In this corridor, as I say, there are the cells on either side of you, but straight ahead, as you enter the archway, or corridor, is a very much smaller doorway, cut out of the stone, which opens on the sea. You go to the edge of the door, and look down, and at your feet are some black stones and the foam of the Atlantic Ocean, bubbling up against you. The day that we were there, I tried, but it was impossible—the ocean is simply as vast as the horizon—I tried to imagine what it must have felt like to find yourself chained and speechless, speechless in the most total sense of that word, on your way *where*?

There were some French tourists around and I confess that for a moment I almost hit one of them on the head. They wouldn't have known why.

Anyway, it was the black man's necessity, once he got here, to accept the cross; he had to survive, to manage somehow to outwit his Christian master; what he was really facing when he got here was the Bible and the gun. But I'm not complaining about that now, either. What is most terrible is that American white men are not prepared to believe my version of the story, to believe that it happened. In order to avoid believing that, they have set up in themselves a fantastic system of evasions, denials, and justifications, which system is about to destroy their grasp of reality, which is another way of saying their moral sense.

What I am trying to say is that the crime is not the most important thing here. What makes our situation serious is that we have spent so many generations pretending that it did not happen. Ask yourself on what assumptions rest those extraordinary questions which white men ask, no matter how politely. On what assumption rests the question "Would you let your sister marry one?" It's based on some preoccupation in the minds of white men. God knows I'm not interested in marrying your sister. I mean that. On what assumption, again, rests the extraordinary question "What does the Negro want?" The question betrays a flight from reality which is absolutely unimaginable: if we weren't dealing with what, in the public mind, is a *Negro,* the question could never be asked; we'd know damn well what he wanted. We know very well that *we* would not like to live the way we compel Negroes to live. Anyone who asks "What does the Negro want?" is saying, in another way, that he does not wish to be told, is saying that he is afraid to change, is afraid to pay his dues.

Let's go back, for a minute, to where I started. Let's go back to Nietzsche: "I stand before my highest mountain, and before my longest journey, and, therefore, must I descend deeper than I have ever before descended." And we spoke a little earlier about the necessity, when the collision between your terms and life's terms occurs, of saying yes to life. That's the descent. The difference between a boy and a man is that a boy imagines there is some way to get through life safely, and a man knows he's got to pay his dues. In this country, the entire nation has always assumed that I would pay their dues for them. What it means to be a Negro in this country is that you represent, you are the receptacle of and the vehicle of, all the pain, disaster, sorrow which white Americans think they can escape. This is what is really meant by keeping the Negro in his place. It is why white people, until today, are still astounded and offended if, by some miscalculation, they are forced to suspect that you are not happy where they have placed you. This is true; and I'm not talking about the Deep South. People finally say to you, in an attempt to dismiss the social reality, "But you're so bitter!" Well, I may or may not be bitter, but if I were, I would have good reasons for it: chief among them that American blindness, or cowardice, which allows us to pretend that life presents no reasons, to say nothing of opportunities, for being bitter.

In this country, for a dangerously long time, there have been two levels of experience. One—to put it cruelly, but, I think, quite truthfully—can be summed up in the images of Doris Day and Gary Cooper: two of the most grotesque appeals to innocence the world has ever seen. And the other, subterranean, indispensable, and denied, can be summed up, let us say, in the tone and in the face of Ray Charles. And there has never been in this country any genuine confrontation between these two levels of experience. Let me force you, or try to force you, to observe a paradox. Though almost all white Americans come from Europe, Europe understands the

American Negro better than they understand the white American. White Americans find it extremely difficult to establish any dialogue between themselves and Europeans for the very good reason, no doubt, that they have yet to break into communion with themselves; but black Americans and Europeans know what it is to suffer, and are far beyond any hope of innocence. A bill for the American endeavor to get from the cradle to the grave looking like Eisenhower has now come in.

White people are astounded by Birmingham. Black people aren't. White people are endlessly demanding to be reassured that Birmingham is really on Mars. They don't want to believe, still less to act on the belief, that what is happening in Birmingham (and I mean this, and I'm not exaggerating; there are several thousand ways to kill or castrate a man) is happening all over the country, and has been for countless generations; they don't want to realize that there is not one step, one inch, no distance, morally or actually, between Birmingham and Los Angeles.

Now, it is entirely possible that we may all go under. But until that happens, I prefer to believe that since a society is created by men, it can be remade by men. The price for this transformation is high. White people will have to ask themselves precisely why they found it necessary to invent the nigger; for the nigger is a white invention, and white people invented him out of terrible necessities of their own. And every white citizen of this country will have to accept the fact that he is not innocent, because those dogs and those hoses are being turned on American children, on American soil, with the tacit consent of the American Republic; those crimes are being committed in your name. Black people will have to do something very hard, too, which is to allow the white citizen his first awkward steps toward maturity. We have, indeed, functioned in this country in precisely that way for a very long time—we were the first psychiatrists here. If we can hang on just a little bit longer, all of us, we may make it. We've got to try. But I've tried to outline what I take to be some of the conditions for our survival.

(1964)

Black Power

Stokely Carmichael (1941–1998), later known as Kwame Toure, was a Trinidadian-born activist. Beginning with the Student Nonviolent Coordinating Committee, and often protesting alongside Martin Luther King Jr. and other luminaries of the civil rights movement, he would go on to become "Honorary Prime Minister" of the Black Panther Party—thus making a move from nonviolence to advocating violent rebellion.

During the late 1960s and early 1970s Baldwin had a love-hate relationship with the party. Though he tried to support it, many of its members found him to be too close to the establishment and not enough of a radical and were critical of his sexuality. Nonetheless, Baldwin came to the Panthers' defense time and time again, even helping them out financially. Carmichael would later distance himself from the Panthers. He was replaced as party chairman by H. Rap Brown.

This essay was written in response to Carmichael's book *Black Power* (1967), which, among other things, condemned the Vietnam War, praised Marxist rebels like Che Guevara, and encouraged the overthrow of the current United States government.

.   .   .

I FIRST MET STOKELY CARMICHAEL in the Deep South when he was just another nonviolent kid, marching and talking and getting his head whipped. This time now seems as far behind us as the Flood, and if those suffering, gallant, betrayed boys and girls who were then using their bodies in an attempt to save a heedless nation have since concluded that the nation is not worth saving, no American alive has the right to be surprised—to put the matter as mildly as it can possibly be put. Actually, Americans are not at all surprised; they exhibit all the vindictiveness of the guilty; what happened to those boys and girls, and what happened to the civil rights movement, is an indictment of America and Americans, and an enduring monument, which we will not outlive, to the breathtaking cowardice of this sovereign people.

Naturally, the current in which we all were struggling threw Stokely and me together from time to time—it threw many people together, including, finally, Martin Luther King and Malcolm X. America sometimes resembles, at least from the point of view of the black man, an exceedingly monotonous minstrel show; the same dances, same music, same jokes. One has done (or been) the show so long that one can do it in one's sleep. So it was not in the least surprising for me to encounter (one more time) the American surprise when Stokely—as Americans allow themselves the luxury of supposing—coined the phrase "black power." He didn't coin it. He simply dug it up again from where it's been lying since the first slaves hit the gangplank.

I have never known a Negro in all my life who was not obsessed with black power. Those representatives of white power who are not too hopelessly brainwashed or eviscerated will understand that the only way for a black man in America not to be obsessed with the problem of how to control his destiny and protect his house, his women, and his children is for that black man to become in his own mind the something-less-than-a-man which this Republic, alas, has always considered him to be. And when a black man, whose destiny and identity have always been controlled by others, decides and states that he will control his own destiny and rejects the identity given to him by others, he is talking revolution.

In point of sober fact, he cannot possibly be talking anything else, and nothing is more revelatory of the American hypocrisy than their swift perception of this fact. The "white backlash" is meaningless twentieth-century jargon designed at once to hide and to justify the fact that most white Americans are still unable to believe that the black man is a man—in the same way that we speak of a "credibility gap" because we are too cowardly to face the fact that our leaders have been lying to us for years. Perhaps we suspect that we deserve the contempt with which we allow ourselves to be treated.

In any case, I had been hoping to see Stokely again, in Paris. But I now learn that he has arrived in New York and that his passport has been lifted. He is being punished by a righteous government, in the name of a justly wrathful people, and there appears to be a very strong feeling that this punishment is insufficient. If only, I gather, we had had the foresight to declare ourselves at war, we would now be able to shoot Mr. Carmichael for treason. On the other hand, even if the government's honorable hands are tied, the mob has got the message. I remember standing on a street corner in Selma during a voting registration drive. The blacks lined up before the courthouse, under the American flag; the sheriff and his men, with their helmets and guns and clubs and cattle prods; a mob of idle white men standing on the corner. The sheriff raised his club and he and his deputies beat two black boys to the ground. Never will I forget the surge in the mob; authority had given them their signal. The sheriff had given them the right—indeed, had very nearly imposed on them the duty—to bomb and murder; and no one has ever accused that sheriff of inciting to riot, much less of sedition.

No one has ever accused ex-Governor Wallace of Alabama—"ex" in name only—of insurrection, although he had the Confederate flag flying from the dome of the capitol the day we marched on Montgomery. The government would like to be able to indict Stokely, and many others like him, of incitement to riot; but I accuse the government of this crime. It is, briefly, an insult to my intelligence, and to the intelligence of any black person, to ask me to believe that the most powerful nation in the world is unable to do anything to make the lives of its black citizens less appalling.

It is not unable to do it; it is only unwilling to do it. Americans are deluded if they suppose Stokely to be the first black man to say, "The United States is going to fall. I only hope I live to see the day." Every black man in the howling North American wilderness has said it, and is saying it, in many, many ways, over and over again. One's only got to listen, again, to all those happy songs. Or walk to Harlem and talk to any junkie, or anybody else—if, of course, they will talk to you. It was a nonviolent black student who told Bobby Kennedy a few years ago that he didn't know how much longer he could remain nonviolent; didn't know how much longer he could take the beatings, the bombings, the terror. He said that he would never take up arms in defense of America—never, never, never. If he ever picked up a gun, it would be for very different reasons; trembling, he shook his finger in Bobby Kennedy's face and said, with terrible tears in his voice, "When I pull the trigger, kiss it goodbye!"

That boy has grown up, as have so many like him—we will not mention those irreparably ruined, or dead; and I really wonder what white Americans expected to happen. Did they really suppose that fifteen-year-old black boys remain fifteen forever? Did they really suppose that the tremendous energy and the incredible courage which went into those sit-ins, wade-ins, swim-ins, picket lines, marches was incapable of transforming itself into an overt attack on the status quo? I remember that same day in Selma watching the line of black would-be voters walk away from the courthouse which they had not been allowed to enter. And, I thought, the day is coming when they will not line up anymore.

That day may very well be here—I fear it is here; certainly Stokely is here, and he is not alone. It helps our situation not at all to attempt to punish the man for telling the truth. I repeat: we have seen this show before. This victimization has occurred over and over again, from Frederick Douglass to Paul Robeson to Cassius Clay to Malcolm X. And I contest the government's right to lift the passports of those people who hold views of which the government—and especially *this* government—disapproves. The government has the duty to warn me of the dangers I may encounter if I travel to hostile territory—though they never said anything about the probable results of my leaving Harlem to go downtown and never said anything about my travels to Alabama—but it does not have the right to use my passport as a political weapon against me, as a means of bringing me to heel. These are terror tactics.

Furthermore, *all* black Americans are born into a society which is determined—repeat, determined—that they shall never learn the truth about themselves or their society, which is determined that black men shall use as their only frame of reference what white Americans convey to them of their own potentialities, and of the shape, size, dimensions, and possibilities of the world. And I do not hesitate for an instant to condemn this as a crime. To persuade black boys and girls, as we have for so many generations, that their lives are worth less than other lives, and that they can live only on terms dictated to them by other people, by people who despise them, is worse than a crime; it is the sin against the Holy Ghost.

Now, I may not always agree with Stokely's views, or the ways in which he expresses them. My agreement, or disagreement, is absolutely irrelevant. I get his message. Stokely Carmichael, a black man under thirty, is saying to me, a black man over forty, that he will not live the life I've lived, or be corralled into some of the awful choices I have been forced to make: *and he is perfectly right.* The government and the people who have made his life, and mine, and the lives of all our forefathers, and the lives of all our brothers and sisters and women and children an indescribable hell has no right, now, to penalize the black man, this so-despised stranger here for so long, for attempting to discover if the world is as small as the Americans have told him it is. And the political implications involve nothing more and nothing less than what the Western world takes to be its material self-interest.

I need scarcely state to what extent the Western self-interest and the black self-interest find themselves at war, but it is precisely this message which the Western nations, and this one above all, will have to accept if they expect to survive. Nothing is more unlikely than that the Western nations, and this one above all, will be able to welcome so vital a metamorphosis. We have constructed a history which is a total lie, and have persuaded ourselves that it is true. I seriously doubt that anything worse can happen to any people.

One doesn't need a Stokely gloating in Havana about the hoped-for fall of the United States, and to attempt to punish him for saying what so many millions of people feel is simply to bring closer, and make yet more deadly, the terrible day. One should listen to what's being said, and reflect on it; for many, many millions of people long for our downfall, and it is not because they are Communists. It is because ignorance is in the saddle here, and we ride mankind. Let us attempt to face the fact that we *are* a racist society, racist to the very marrow, and we are fighting a racist war. No black man in chains in his own country, and watching the many deaths occurring around him every day, believes for a moment that America cares anything at all about the freedom of Asia. My own condition, as a black man in

America, tells me what Americans really feel and really want, and tells me who they really are. And, therefore, every bombed village is my hometown.

That, in a way, is what Stokely is saying, and that's why this youth can so terrify a nation. He's saying the bill is in, the party's over, are we going to live here like men or not? Bombs won't pay this bill, and bombs won't wipe it out. And Stokely did not begin his career with dreams of terror but with dreams of love. Now he's saying—and he's not alone, and he's not the first—if I can't live here, well then, neither will you. You couldn't have built it without me; this land is also mine; we'll share it or we'll perish, *and I don't care.*

I *do* care—about Stokely's life, my country's life. One's seen too much already of gratuitous destruction, one hopes, always, that something will happen in the human heart which will change our common history. But if it doesn't happen, this something, if this country cannot hear and cannot change, then we, the blacks, the most despised children of the great Western house, are simply forced, with both pride and despair, to remember that we come from a long line of runaway slaves who managed to survive without passports.

(1968)

The Price May Be Too High

As so often happens in this time and place, a real question, with important repercussions, is rendered nearly trivial by the terms in which the question is expressed. Beneath the terms, of course, lie the deadly assumptions on which black and white relations in this country have rested for so long. These assumptions are suggested in a famous song: "If you white, all right / If you brown, hang around / But if you black, step back!"

The question is not whether black and white artists can work together—artists need each other, despite all those middlebrow rumors to the contrary. The question is whether or not black and white *citizens* can work together. Black artists remember how much white artists have stolen from them, and this certainly creates a certain tension; but the rejection by many black artists of white artistic endeavor contains far more than meets the public eye. What black artists are rejecting, when the rejection occurs, is not the possibility of working with white artists. What they are rejecting is that American system which makes pawns of white men and victims of black men and which really, at bottom, considers all artistic effort to be either irrelevant or threatening.

It is very strange to be a black artist in this country—strange and dangerous. He must attempt to reach something of the truth, and to tell it—to use his instrument as truthfully as he knows how. But consider what Sambo's truth means to the governors of states, the mayors of cities, the chiefs of police departments, the heads of boards of education! The country pretends not to know the reasons for Sambo's discontent; but Sambo must deal not only with his public discontent and daily danger but also with the dimensions of his private disaster. How, given the conditions of his life here, is he to distinguish between the two? (There may not *be* a distinction and that may be the moral of the tale, and not only for poor Sambo.) Assuming he survives the first dues-paying time and becomes more or less articulate, to whom is he to address himself? Artists are produced by people who need them, *because* they need them. The black artist has been produced, historically speaking, anyway, by people who are both black and white, by people whose lifestyles differ so crucially that he is in perpetual danger of lapsing into schizophrenia and can certainly be considered the issue of a divorce. Or a rape.

I will state flatly that the bulk of this country's white population impresses me, and has so impressed me for a very long time, as being beyond any conceivable hope of moral rehabilitation. They have been white, if I may so put it, too long; they have been married to the lie of white supremacy too long; the effect on their personalities, their lives, their grasp of reality, has been as devastating as the lava which so memorably immobilized the citizens of Pompeii. They are unable to conceive that their version of reality, which they want me to accept, is an insult to my history and a parody of theirs and an intolerable violation of myself.

Well, then, for the sake of one's sanity, one simply ceases trying to make them hear. If they think that things are more important than people—and they do—well, let them think so. Let them be destroyed by their things. If they think that I was happy being a slave and am now redeemed by having become—and on their terms, as they think—the equal of my overseers, well, let them think so. If they think that I am flattered by their generosity in allowing me to become a sharecropper in a system which I know to be criminal—and which is placed squarely on the backs of nonwhite people all over the world—well, let them think so. Let the dead bury their dead. And it is not only the black artist who arrives at this exasperated and merciless turning point. For that matter, it is not even an attitude recently arrived at. If one's ancestors were slaves here, it is an attitude which can be called historical.

The ground on which black and white artists may be able to work together, to learn from each other, is simply not provided by the system under which artists in this country work. The system is the profit system, and the artists and their work are "properties." No single word more aptly sums up the nature of this particular beast. In such a system, it makes perfect sense that Hollywood would turn out so "liberal" an abomination as *If He Hollers, Let Him Go!* while leaving absolutely unnoticed and untouched such a really fine and truthful study of the black-white madness as, for example, Ernest J. Gaines's *Of Love and Dust*. For that matter, it makes perfect sense that Hollywood lifted the title *If He Hollers, Let Him Go!* from a fine novel by Chester Himes, published about twenty years ago, and has yet to announce any plans to film it, which, all things considered, is probably just as well. What it comes to is that the system under which black and white artists in this country work is geared to the needs of a people who, so far from being able to abandon the doctrine of white supremacy, seem prepared to blow up the globe to maintain it.

And *if* white people are prepared to blow up the globe in order to maintain that faith of their fathers which placed Sambo in chains, then they are certainly willing to allow him his turn on television, stage, and screen. It is a small price for white people to pay for the continuance of their domination. But the price of appearing may prove to be too high for black people to pay. The price a black actor pays for playing, in effect, a white role—for being "integrated," say, in some soupy soap opera—is, at best, to minimize and, at worst, to lie about everything that produced him, about everything he knows. White people don't want to hear what he knows, and the system can't afford it. What *is* being attempted is a way of involving, or incorporating, the black face into the national fantasy in such a way that the fantasy will be left unchanged and the social structure left untouched. I doubt that even American "know-how" can achieve anything so absurd and so disastrous; but anyway, I think that we may one day owe a great debt to those who have refused to play this particular ball game. What they are rejecting is not a people, but a doctrine, and their seeming separation may prove to be one of the few hopes of genuine union that we have ever had in this so dangerously divided house.

(1969)

The Nigger We Invent

On March 18, 1969, Baldwin appeared, along with Betty Shabazz, the widow of Malcolm X (El-Hajj Malik El-Shabazz), before a House Select Subcommittee gathered that day in New York City and chaired by Representative James H. Scheuer of New York. They spoke in support of a House bill to establish a national commission on "Negro History and Culture."

· · ·

MR. BALDWIN. I would like to make a suggestion before I begin. I brought with me Mrs. Betty Shabazz, who is Malcolm X's widow.

MR. SCHEUER. Would you like to invite her to testify with you?

MR. BALDWIN. Yes.

I am much in favor of the proposed legislation. I have to be honest with you and say that it occurs to me that the principal problem one faces in teaching Negroes their culture is that we will find that impossible to do without teaching American history, in a sense, then, for the first time. The

burden under which the Negro child operates in this country, as your
previous witnesses have indicated, is that he has no sense of identity.

It occurs to me that this involves a great national waste on the part of
the morale of the child who is black. It appears to me that it is a great
national waste not only for a Negro child but for any child growing up in
this country. Anyone who is black is taught, as my generation was taught,
that Negroes are not a civilization or culture, and that we came out of the
jungle and were saved by the missionary.

Not only is this something awful to me, which eventually puts me on
the street corner, but it's awful to everyone. You cannot educate a child if
you first destroy his morale. That is why they leave school. You cannot
educate him if he sees what is happening to his fathers, if he sees Ph.D.'s
toting garbage.

If he sees in fact on the one hand no past and really no present and
certainly no future, then you have created what the American public likes to
think of, in the younger generation, as the nigger we invent and the nigger
they invent. What has happened is that you destroy the child from the cradle.

MR. SCHEUER. It is the institutionalization of the prophecy.

MR. BALDWIN. If the cat cannot join a union no matter how many pennies
he saves, he will still be at the bottom of the barrel. There is really nothing
you can do with him. By and by, he will not listen to you and he will not
listen to me. I am not a witness nor a hope. I am proof of what the country
does to you if you are black. That is true even if I am Jackie Robinson.

MR. SCHEUER. Do you think that this legislation in a minor way—none of us
suggest that it is a great panacea—might bring together the talent that would
produce a program to open up the doors of our education system, of our
textbooks, of our media, to portray the role of the Negro in American life,
and in world affairs, so that the Negro would have an enhanced self-image
and so that the white child would have a true sense of Negro contributions?

MR. BALDWIN. That is the hope of the proposed bill. But we would be
deluding ourselves if we did not understand that the particular history of my
forefathers in this country can change the climate in this country. That
climate is not one of flattery.

MR. SCHEUER. I think the Anti-Riot Commission Report says that as it is, as
you have been doing for many years.

MR. BALDWIN. You have to face the fact that in the textbook industry—the
key word there is "industry"—McGraw-Hill is not yet about to destroy all its

present textbooks and create new ones, because they will not be bought by the colleges and by the schools, at least not yet in St. Louis, or in Maryland, or New Orleans, or for that matter in New York. It is, after all, a profit-motive industry.

One cannot expect a business to put itself out of business under altruistic motives. One has got to find some way, then, it would seem to me, to indicate to the textbook industry, which is a great stumbling block here, that would indicate to them that it is in their self-interest.

For example, the terrifying thing in the minds of the public was Malcolm X. One of the reasons you got Malcolm X was because when he was quite young and wanted to become a lawyer, his teacher advised him to do something that a colored person could do, like become a carpenter.

Only the child, or the brother or sister or the mother of that child, knows what happens to that child's morale at that time. This is ingrained in the American mythology. It will not be tomorrow that it is uprooted. We have to begin.

We are beginning late, I must say, but any beginning is better than none. But I don't think we should pretend that it is going to be easy.

MR. SCHEUER. Can you give us any recommendations of yours as to how this proposal of ours can be improved and how it can be refined and how it can be given a clearer direction? Can you give us any insights as to how we can do the job better?

MR. BALDWIN. If I were you and sitting where you are sitting, there are some people I would get in touch with. I would get in touch with Sterling Brown out of the University of Washington; I would talk to John [Hope] Franklin. I am not in agreement with Mr. [Roy] Innis entirely about this being an all-black commission. I would also talk to William Styron, but I would talk to people like Sterling Brown.

MR. SCHEUER. Did you say you were not in agreement that it should be all Negro?

MR. BALDWIN. I think it would be self-defeating. As I read it, it would be an attempt to teach American history. I am a little bit hard-bitten about white liberals.

MR. SCHEUER. Is that a pejorative phrase when you use it?

MR. BALDWIN. It can be. I don't trust people who think of themselves as liberals. I do trust some white people, like Bill [Styron], he is not a Negro. He is a Deep Southern cat who has paid his dues and he has been through the fire and he knows what it is about. I trust him more than Max Lesher. What I am saying is that I don't trust missionaries.

I don't want anybody working with me because they are doing something for me. What I want them to do is to work in their own communities. I want you to tell your brothers and your sisters and your wife and your children what it is all about. Don't tell me, because I know already. You see what I mean?

You have the power. But to answer you and go back to your question, I think one of the stumbling blocks is that the nature of the black experience in this country does indicate something about the total American history which frightens Americans. It brings up all those things you have talked about and want to talk about.

It brings up the real history of the country—the history of our relationships with Mexicans and slaves. All these points contradict the myth of American history. It attacks the American identity in a sense.

Shirley Temple would be a different person if she were black.

MR. SCHEUER. She probably would be a member of Congress.

MR. BALDWIN. We can't prove that by the members of Congress. You see what I mean. Someone like Sterling Brown is an old poet and an old blues singer. He knows more than, say, a man my age. He can tell you things which I cannot, about you and me. It is a level of experience about which Ray Charles sings and of which all Americans are still terrified.

If we are going to build a multiracial society, which is our only hope, then one has got to accept that I have learned a lot from you, and a lot of it is bitter, but you have a lot to learn from me, and a lot of that will be bitter. That bitterness is our only hope. That is the only way we get past it. Am I making sense to you?

MR. SCHEUER. Absolutely.
Congressman Gus Hawkins of California.

MR. HAWKINS. I must apologize for being called out of the room, Mr. Baldwin.

I certainly think that you have offered some very wonderful suggestions and some good comments. I particularly enjoyed what I considered to be the point that you made that the objective of such a commission would be to teach American history, making it plain and clear that the history of the black man in America is that part of American history. There is not reason to separate it.

You feel that competent persons, both black and white, should be engaged in doing this?

MR. BALDWIN. It is our common history. My history is also yours.

MR. HAWKINS. I certainly agree with you, Mr. Baldwin. I certainly appreciate this opportunity that you have afforded us.

MR. SCHEUER. Congressman [William] Hathaway of Maine.

MR. HATHAWAY. Mr. Baldwin, I would take it that you would agree that perhaps we should expand the scope of the bill to cover not only the history of the culture but also the contemporary heroes.

MR. BALDWIN. Yes, but you must understand that, speaking as black Americans, my heroes have always been [seen] from the point of view of white Americans as bad niggers. Cassius Clay is one of my heroes but not one of yours.

I on the other hand am not suggesting that this commission should establish a hall of fame for great Negroes at all. What I am trying to suggest is that you recognize the role that my heroes—as distinguished from yours— have played in American life and the reasons why all my heroes came to such bloody ends.

From my point of view, Muhammad Ali Clay, without discussing his affiliations or what I may think of him, has been hanged by the public as a bad nigger. He is going to be an example to every other Negro man. Those are my heroes. Those are not the heroes of the American public. You will find yourself up against that fact before many days have passed.

Do you see what I mean? As long as my heroes are not yours, then the bitterness in the ghetto increases hour by hour and grows more and more dangerous and does not only blow up the ghetto but blows up the cities.

When I came back from New York a few weeks ago, I came back during the garbage strike, when all New York looked just like Harlem.

MR. SCHEUER. It looked just like South Bronx, the district I represent, and I was happy to see the rest of the city have what the residents of Harlem and Bedford-Stuyvesant put up with 365 days of the year. It was a salutary experience.

MR. BALDWIN. When you unleash a plague, it covers the entire city and nation. What has been happening to me all of these years is now beginning to happen to all of you, and this was inevitable. What we are involved with here is an attempt to have ourselves, and we need each other for that.

My history, though, contains the truth about America. It is going to be hard to teach it.

MR. HATHAWAY. Perhaps we should tell more of the truth about our heroes, such as George Washington and Abraham Lincoln, who are built up in history books almost as myths. We know that they had frailties. We know that they made a lot of mistakes. Those mistakes are never built up, so that the white man has the impression immediately that his heroes are almost gods.

MR. BALDWIN. I don't think that any kid believes any of those legends about George Washington and his cherry tree—"I cannot tell a lie" and all that nonsense.

MR. HATHAWAY. I think at certain stages they do. After a while they get to believe that it is not true.

MR. BALDWIN. I never did.

This is fine. I think it does a disservice to a child to tell him things which are not true. Children cannot really be fooled. For example, and I will be very brief, you remember that several years ago the Birmingham church school was bombed and there were four girls killed in there. They were not killed by some madman, but by a mad society, which is not only located in Birmingham. At that time some of us threw together an ad hoc committee to prevent celebrations on Christmas Day. We had lost the right as a Christian nation to celebrate the birth of Christ. I discovered during this that Santa Claus is not needed by children, but by grown-ups. People say we couldn't do that because the children would be so upset. The fact is that it wasn't true; what they really meant was that *they* would be upset.

We give them those legends and they try to survive them, but no kid has ever believed anything written about George Washington. Anyway, even if they did, by the time they are seventeen they have got to revise their whole estimate of reality around the fact of human beings, not legends.

I think the sooner one learns the truth, the better. Do I make myself clear?

MR. HATHAWAY. I am just wondering whether I agree with you. Perhaps we just need a more realistic appraisal of what our heroes should be.

MR. BALDWIN. Anyway, leaving aside the hypothetical matters, the black kid in the ghetto doesn't believe in these heroes for a moment. You begin the process of the breakdown of communication virtually from the cradle.

I really didn't believe at the time I was seven the Pledge of Allegiance, and no black boy I knew did, either. For very good reasons, too. I didn't believe it, in effect, because the country didn't believe it. I didn't believe it because *you* didn't believe it. If you had believed it, I would have been in a different place. My father would have been a very different man. You didn't believe it, so I didn't. You can't fool a kid. You still don't believe it, and so they don't, and they won't believe it until you do. You have to prove that you do.

MR. HATHAWAY. By action?

MR. BALDWIN. Yes. Let me get a job, allow me the right to protect my women, my house, my children. That is all the Negro wants: his autonomy. Nobody hates you. The time is far gone for that. I simply want to live my life.

I suggest, too, that the kids all up and down this country in the streets of all our cities are coming to ruin and are going on the needle. They are coming to nothing. This is a waste no country can afford.

I am the flesh of your flesh and bone of your bone; I have been here as long as you have been here—longer—I paid for it as much as you have. It is my country, too. Do recognize that that is the whole question. My history and culture has got to be taught. It is yours.

MR. HATHAWAY. Do you think that there is some hope that if the culture is brought back to white America that the black America has a better chance?

MR. BALDWIN. Yes. This would involve a change in your institutions. It is not just a matter of passing a bill. The Christian church in this country is a very popular institution. But this has always been a racist institution, and we take this as immoral.

Once I become a part of that church, that institution is a different institution. It is not a matter of letting me into it; it has to change. This is true for all American institutions—including schools and the textbook industry.

You are to accept the fact that I am the darker brother, and the key word there is "brother." Whereas you from Europe came here voluntarily, I was kidnapped, and my history was destroyed here. For your purposes, this has to be faced. I am not trying to be bitter or anything. This is the way it is.

MR. SCHEUER. I would like to emphasize that we are in entire accord with you in that we want the institutions to change. We want the textbook industry to change; we want the teaching industry to change. We want the radio and television and press industry to change, and we hope that this commission could start to do the hard intellectual work and play the leadership role to induce change.

This commission, if it is anything, will be a change effort. We would like to have your views on how it can best be achieved to perfect the design of this commission so that it will open up doors.

MR. BALDWIN. I am not gifted in this area. Let me offer a suggestion. You can do whatever you like with it. We are talking about mass media. One is up against this: There is a very successful movie going around which I saw a few days ago in Hollywood. It is called *Guess Who's Coming to Dinner.* This movie is about an interracial marriage, I suppose. Sidney Poitier plays a very beautiful and modest role. That is all he ever plays. This is the mass media for you.

Now, if one is going to deal with the mass media, you have to be aware that you are reaching two publics: the white people in this country and abroad; I talked to some people in London who adored it and think it is true. But, of course, when I watch it, some cat in the ghetto is watching it; it may do great things for your morale, but it does terrible things to him. He recognizes that the movie is a cop-out. Mr. Poitier is not an ordinary citizen. It obviously would be a different movie if he were able to play a real man.

I am not overstating my case; the movie does say that in order for me to marry this particular white chick, I have to be what he is in the movie. Well, that is not so of any white person, he can marry whomever he wants to marry. I am trying to say that the structure of the mass media is such that I think you ought to be aware that there would be a tremendous resistance.

You will hear what I have heard for years. "It is great and powerful, but it is not for our readers." Or—"It is a risky picture and we can't do it." The mass media is mainly a form of escape, and someone said many, many years ago that no white person is going to make his escape personality black, especially in this country. I don't think we should be deluded about that.

MR. SCHEUER. Here exactly is that kind of a challenge that we hope the commission will face squarely.

MR. BALDWIN. We are terribly penalized in this country, every single one of us, famous and obscure. It is like being what America still considers one of your niggers. This commission has to begin to break down that terrifying heritage, which, after all, destroys the white child, too.

MR. SCHEUER. That was the point I was trying to make with Mr. Innis before you came. The 90-percent white majority has as much or more of an interest in this purification process, because they are deprived by not knowing of Negro history and culture.

MR. BALDWIN. They are frightened. I don't hate white people; I don't have to. I am not afraid of you. You face a Southern deputy, and he *does* hate you—because he is scared to death of you. He is the one who is in trouble, and that is the man you have to liberate.

MR. SCHEUER. We can't thank you enough for coming to see us. You certainly deserve the door prize for having come the longest distance. We are grateful, and we benefited enormously by your views.

MRS. SHABAZZ. I am in complete accord with this bill and in teaching black history in the schools. Some of the things I have heard I have disagreed with, and some I have agreed with. I think primarily the problem is one of getting black history in the schools. If it is wanted by blacks and whites, I think this would solve some of the problems, if cooperation is wanted.

This is needed to curb the things that are going on and some terrible things that will continue to go on. I think a lot of the hysteria has been created primarily by whites, who basically have not understood blacks, who have not treated them as human beings.

Everyone has basic emotions of hate, fear, and love, and I think the whites in this country have used the machinery of propaganda very skillfully. You find blacks who want to know something about their history and you find whites who don't understand or who are fearful. They will publicize this sort of thing as a hate gathering and a hate meeting, when actually it could possibly be a historical meeting that whites and blacks could learn from.

(1969)

Speech from the Soledad Rally

The Soledad Brothers was the name given to three black inmates who were charged with the January 1970 beating death of John V. Mills at Soledad State Prison in California. George Jackson (twenty-nine), John Clutchette (twenty-eight), and Fleeta Drumgo (twenty-six) were accused of killing the white prison guard in retaliation for the earlier shooting deaths of three black inmates at San Quentin by another guard, whose case had been dismissed by a grand jury as "justifiable homicide."

At the age of nineteen Jackson had been given a peculiar sentence: from one year to life, after being convicted for stealing $70.20 from a gas station. The year of the prison killing he published a book—*Soledad Brother: The Prison Letters of George Jackson (1964-1970)*. The noted French ex-convict, playwright, and novelist Jean Genet wrote the introduction. The reviewer for the *New York Times* called it "the most important single volume from a black since *The Autobiography of Malcolm X*." The book earned significant awards and praise and international support.

On April 20, 1971, a rally was held at the Central Hall in Westminster, England. The rally drew over three thousand people and raised over two thousand pounds. This is the speech Baldwin delivered that day. According to his biographer, Baldwin was so taken with Jackson's writing and story that he wanted to make a film based on Jackson's life.

Later that same year, on August 22, George Jackson was shot and killed in an attempt to escape from San Quentin Prison during an uprising he caused. Five other men lost their lives that day.

The head of his defense committee and the organizer for the 1971 rally, Professor Angela Y. Davis, had already been involved in another dramatic escape attempt in 1970, which resulted in four deaths. She was free on bail at this time, awaiting trial in California. (See "An Open Letter to My Sister Angela Y. Davis," p. 206.)

.   .   .

I CAN'T KEEP YOU very long, because the hall's going to close very soon, and I must tell you this: that I was very honored and very excited to be here, because of what I've heard and because of the feeling in the hall. I haven't got time to go into all that, either, so let me tell you, let me simply say two things: we've heard a lot in my country lately, and you've heard a lot in your country too, about law and order. And people ask me from time to time if "Mr. Baldwin, does that mean that you're advocating violence?" And by and by you hear the question so long and so often that you begin to understand that in the question there is a threat, and what the question really means is: "If you have the effrontery to seem to be advocating violence, you must bear in mind that we have the police forces, we have the tanks, we have the helicopters, we have the guns, we have the mace, we have the chemicals, we got the jury, we got the judge, and we got *you*! It means: if you don't like where you are, we can keep you where you *is*!"

Now, there are people in England and there are people in France, and there are sounds—no matter how quiet it is kept—from people in America who are aware of what is happening to them and what criminal action has been taken against their lives. I don't merely mean black lives: that's merely the greatest metaphor, the most visible symptom of the rottenness of a certain state, of the end of a certain history. Because, let us face this fact—it's a brutal fact and everyone here and many more people than that, whether or not they want to, will be forced to deal with the central fact of this century, and it is a very simple fact, so simple that no one wants to face it—that this civilization, including this hall, including that extraordinary god the Europeans found in the desert, and dragged all the way to England—that invention and this hall and this economy and the bank of the Holy Ghost which stands in Rome were built on a principle which is politely called cheap labor. If we translate that from the high English into where I was born, it means that every dark child born—and this was the intention of a civilization—was born to be used for the profit of white people. And this hall in which we stand is yet more important than the guns, the fleets, the bombs, because this hall represents the ways in which black people were taught to despise themselves.

Now, something very serious happens in a civilization because the reason we're here tonight is not merely because of the performance of my unhappy country; it is not merely because of the fate of Angela Davis and the Soledad Brothers or the Third World all over the world; it isn't even merely because of the bloody slaughter in Vietnam. It is because every Western government is implicated and is guilty of and responsible for the shoddy performance of my country. Mr. Nixon, who sits in Washington, is also *your* President.

Now, what is important here, what is happening in this century is for the first time within the history of anyone living anywhere, a certain group of people who have always been despised, who were born to be shoeshine boys, who were born to be political prisoners, in fact were born to be used, have discovered, as it happens in time, what happened to them. And they have begun to understand that if they are going to liberate themselves, they have to begin it first of all within themselves. No one is going to do it for them.

Alas, it is called power. And alas, people who have power very rarely have morals: the power corrodes the morals. Someone said earlier this evening that it is not the judge's court, it is *our* court. It is not Mr. Reagan's Sacramento—my blood is in that soil! Senator Eastland, if he is still alive—and it's difficult to tell—never had any legal rights to his job. Governor Wallace holds his job illegally, because *I* did not vote for him. And if that is so, that means the machinery which put into power Mr. Nixon, Mr. Agnew, Mr. Mitchell and his charming wife, and is afraid to get rid of King Lear—otherwise known as Hoover—also hold its job illegally. I did not vote for that machine. I don't have a swimming pool unpaid for in California. I am not worried about whom my children may or may not play with. I'm not worried about . . . There's something obscene about a people who are willing to send their sons off to be slaughtered by the *thousands* in a foreign jungle and are afraid to have them make love to the boy or girl next door.

History, in short, has achieved its own bankruptcy. That puts on our shoulders an enormous responsibility. We have no way. When Martin was alive, we marched and we petitioned; many people died, many people went mad, many people have been forgotten. That was a heroic endeavor, but it will never come again. Now, what is beginning to happen, and in spite of all the things that have happened to all our brains for all these generations, to divide black people from black people, to divide Indians from West Indians, to divide me from you, to divide whites from whites, it is absolutely true, *absolutely true,* that if George Jackson and Angela Davis and my child have no life, have no future, no one in this room has any future.

We cannot afford, to put it briefly, all those prisoners in South Africa. We cannot afford all those European-trained leaders in what we call Africa. We cannot afford, for the sake of our lives and our children's lives, to suppose that any country or any civilization has a right to murder half the world and menace all the rest in the name of profits. It is perfectly possible, in short . . . now I'll have to leave you.

[*Interruption: "What is 'civilization'?"*]

"Civilization" is a word used by those who think of themselves as civilized because they describe you as uncivilized!

I want to leave you with one thing, one thing only. We are the victims and we are the result of a doctrine called white supremacy, which came into the world God knows how many years ago, it doesn't matter now. Now, it is over. We cannot fall into the same trap. Now, I must tell you that white people are, in the generality, terrified of being identified with black people, because, of course, they don't want to be treated like a nigger. What white people have to understand, in spite of their sad history, is that they invented the nigger—I didn't! And if they invented the nigger, then they are guilty of what they've always accused me of, which is acting like one!

Black people will have to understand, though it won't be easy, that history creates strange children, and our responsibility is to the children we will produce and to the world which we will create. The world which we have to create has to evolve itself in such a way that never again will a man like Ronald Reagan or a man like Governor Wallace or a man like Richard Nixon *or* (I don't want to speak about your country, I'm a guest here!) Enoch Powell!—hold public office again. *These* are the men who should be kept away from all children, should never be allowed to drive cars! But the fact that these men are in power proves the bankruptcy of the civilization which has put them there. That is all I mean.

[*Interruption from black woman protesting about black children in Britain being put into "subnormal" schools.*]

Let me say one thing: that woman's voice, that woman's voice is what you have to hear. We're responsible to that, and if the people who rule us don't hear that voice, then something terrible will happen to us.

(1971)

A Challenge to Bicentennial Candidates

ONE GROWS UP EARLY on my street, and so I started looking for you around the time that I—and later my brothers—began selling shopping bags, shining shoes, scavenging for wood and coal, scavenging, period. I was about seven, certainly no more than that, and as my brothers approached this august and independent age, they joined me in the streets.

My father, before me, also looked for you, for a long while. He gave up, finally, and died in an asylum. Perhaps I use the word "asylum" with some bitterness. My father was a big, strong, handsome, healthy black man, who liked to use his muscles, who was accustomed to hard labor. He went mad and died in Bedlam because, being black, he was always "the last to be hired and the first to be fired."

He—we—therefore, spent much of our lives on welfare, and my father's pride could not endure it. He resented, and eventually came to hate, the people who had placed him in this condition and who did not even have the grace or courage to admit it.

My father wasn't stupid and, God knows, he wasn't lazy. But his condition, against which I watched him struggle with all the energy that he had, was blamed on his laziness; and his wife (who knew better) and his children (who didn't) were assured, merely by the presence of the welfare worker, of his unworthiness. No wonder he died in an American asylum—and at the expense, needless to say, of the so-victimized American taxpayer. (My father was also an American taxpayer, and he paid at an astronomical rate.)

I gather, from the speeches I read and hear, and I see, in the sullen bewilderment in the faces of all the American streets, that the principal gift the Bicentennial candidate can offer the American people is freedom from the poor—a stunning gift indeed for so original a people, a people whose originality resides entirely and precisely in the poverty which drove them to these shores. It is like offering the American people, on their birthday, freedom from the past and freedom from any responsibility for the present: for the poor are always with us; and they can also be against us.

The Bicentennial candidate is to offer for our birthday freedom from the discontented, freedom from the criminals who roam our streets; he is to offer, out of such a dangerous history, at so dangerous a time, nothing less than freedom from danger. America's birthday present, on its two hundredth birthday, is to be the final banishment of the beast in the American playground.

The niceties of rhetoric, the pretense of democracy, and the explosive global situation prevent the candidate from identifying this beast too precisely, but real Americans know that the American taxpayer is being ruined by the worthless and undeserving poor. You can vote with your feet in this country (so someone said to my father, somewhere between the Reconstruction and the First World War): "If you don't like it in this state, move." And so my father did, dear candidate, possibly looking for you. All the way from the Southern cotton fields to the ghettoes, factories, prisons, and riots of the North, real Americans know that the American taxpayer is being ruined by the Indian/Chicano/Mexican/Puerto Rican/black. These dominate the welfare rolls, and the prison populations, and roam, and make unlivable, the streets of the American cities.

I am saddened indeed to be forced to recognize that my father's anguish—to say nothing of my brothers'—has cost the Republic so dearly. I should have thought it cheaper, on the whole, for the American taxpayer to have found a way of allowing my father—and my brothers—to walk on earth, rather than scraping together all those pennies to send a man to walk on the moon. Man cannot live by nuclear warheads alone; so I would have thought. I would have thought that the ceaseless proliferation, the buying and selling and stockpiling, of weapons was a far more futile and expensive endeavor than the rehabilitation of our cities. Cities, after all, are meant to be lived in, and weapons are meant to kill.

I may be somewhat bewildered by the passion with which so many labor for death against life. I could have hoped that pride in America's birthday might have invested the citizens of the great Republic with such pride in their children that they would resolve—at last, and, God knows, not a moment too soon—to educate these children, and build schools and create teachers for that purpose.

The coalition of special interests which rule the American cities, and the collusion between these interests and the boards of education, are responsible for the disaster in the schools. Or, in other words, schools are located in "neighborhoods," and neighborhoods are created—or, more precisely, in human terms, destroyed—by those who own the land and who are determined to preserve, out of a cowardice called nostalgia, the status quo.

Perhaps it is not too much to ask of the ex-governor of New York [Nelson A. Rockefeller], he of the merry wink, and the casual billions, exactly why the reclamation of the land, in Harlem, began with the destruction of the black nationalist bookstore on 125th Street and Seventh Avenue, and, catty-corner from it, on 125th Street and Seventh Avenue, the destruction of the Hotel Theresa. These two institutions were, in Harlem, what in Africa is called the "palaver tree," the place where we discussed and attempted to reclaim our lives. For my father, of course, the "palaver tree" would have been another place, the Lafayette Theatre, long before it was destroyed. For my younger brothers and sisters, and my nieces and my nephews, it was the balcony from which Fidel Castro spoke: spoke, dear candidate, to *them*, from the balcony of a Harlem hotel. The listening crowd knew nothing of Cuba, and couldn't have cared less about communism; but they knew that someone was speaking to them.

It would seem to me that the American social disaster is a tremendous burden on the American taxpayer. It is an investment on which his only return is chaos.

Of course, the candidate will answer, his unhappy priorities are dictated by the responsibility of protecting the "free world."

If the candidate really believes this, and is not merely wondering on what unhappy market he can dump our excess Coca-Cola, I challenge him to take a look at what he thinks he is protecting. I dare the candidate to take to the "chitterling" or the "fried chicken" or the Muslim or the Baptist or the Holy Roller circuit: to walk, not ride, through the black streets of Washington, D.C., and Watts and Detroit and Chicago and San Francisco and Boston and Philadelphia and Pittsburgh and Baltimore, and, yes, Atlanta, and Cleveland, and Gary, and Jackson, and New York. I dare him to teach to, speak to, not merely bow before, any class in any school in any ghetto.

I challenge the candidate to visit Harlem Hospital, and then stand in the streets and explain to the Harlem populace how Harlem Hospital comes about. I challenge the candidate to justify the methadone program. I challenge him to visit the prisons of this country, from hamlet to hamlet and coast to coast, even daring to go so far as to question Senator Eastland's plantation: and not to wait, as in the case of the late and much lamented J. Edgar, until he is safely dead.

I challenge the candidate to love the country which he claims to love to the entire extent of love: to face it, this present chaos, and help the country to face itself, and, for the sake of all our children, to change it.

(1976)

The News from All the Northern Cities Is, to Understate It, Grim; the State of the Union Is Catastrophic

I CAN SCARCELY BELIEVE that I first met Martin Luther King Jr. twenty-one years ago, in Atlanta. I find it nearly impossible to believe that my stocky younger brother, which is the way I thought of him, has been dead for ten years. Ten years!

The mind and the heart refuse and resist the knowledge. (So does the body, perhaps: this note has been delayed for twenty-four hours because the moment I began to write it, I fell ill.) Searching for a kind of lucidity, one picks up the sorrowful chronology and holds on to it. Yes, for example, it was 1957 when we first met. Martin was stealing a few days from Montgomery to work on his book. The blacks in Montgomery were still marching. Yes, I last saw him alive in 1968 in New York, and, yes, I was in Hollywood, in 1968, when he was murdered in Memphis.

And this *is* 1978. Ten years ago, I was working on the screen version of *The Autobiography of Malcolm X,* and was sitting beside a California swimming pool, with Billy Dee Williams, when the phone rang and a friend's voice told us that Martin had been shot. And I really feel, as I write this now, the same unbelieving wonder, the same shock and helpless rage.

I have a dream.

One looks around this country now, remembering those words, and that passion. A vast amount of love and faith and passion, and blood, have gone into the attempt to transform and liberate this nation.

To look around the United States today is enough to make prophets and angels weep, and, certainly, the children's teeth are set on edge. This is not the land of the free; it is only very unwillingly and sporadically the home of the brave, and all that can be said for the bulk of our politicians is that, if they are no worse than they were, they are certainly no better.

I have a dream.

I was in Boston last year, twenty years after meeting Martin, twenty-three years after the Supreme Court decision outlawing segregation in the schools. Just before I got there, young, white patriots attempted to bayonet a black American citizen with the American flag. Someone apparently prevailed on the young patriots to apologize—it was never intended that the flag should be used for such a purpose—and that would appear, for the moment, to be the extent of change in Boston.

I was in Atlanta, which is visibly desegregated in all the downtown hotels. "But don't let it fool you," a black matron said to me. "This is just about the only level on which we ever meet. It's window dressing."

Now, as was the case twenty years ago, whatever amenities are being arranged in Atlanta, they can have no effect on the state of Georgia. In North Carolina, the frame-up of the "Wilmington Ten" has now been justified by the governor of the state. The news from all the Northern cities is, to understate it, grim; the state of the Union is catastrophic. And when this is true for white Americans, the situation of blacks is all but indescribable.

Yes, I have a dream: for Martin really knew something about this country and had discovered a lot about the world. At the point, precisely, that he could mix the American domestic morality with America's role in the world, he became dangerous enough to be shot.

Americans refuse to perceive that theirs is not a white country; they can scarcely avoid suspecting that this is not a white world. It is no accident, for me, therefore, that the role which Andrew Young now plays on the troubled stage of the world is a role for which he was prepared, whether consciously or not, by his work with Martin. For, what Martin saw on the mountaintop was a future beyond these shores, and an identity beyond this struggle.

(1978)

Lorraine Hansberry at the Summit

The famous meeting Baldwin recounts here with then Attorney General Robert F. Kennedy took place in New York City in May of 1963 at the 24 Central Park South Kennedy family residence.

.   .   .

I MUST, NOW, FOR VARIOUS REASONS—some of which, I hope, will presently become apparent—do something which I have very deliberately never done before: sketch the famous Bobby Kennedy meeting. I have talked about it or around it, and a day is coming when I will be compelled to deliver my entire testimony. But, for the moment, I want merely to suggest something of Lorraine Hansberry's beauty and power on that day; and what the incomprehension that day's encounter was to cause the nation and, presently, and until this hour, the world.

Let us say that we all live through more than we can say or see. A life, in retrospect, can seem like the torrent of water opening or closing over one's head and, in retrospect, is blurred, swift, kaleidoscopic like that. One does not wish to remember—one is perhaps not *able* to remember—the holding of one's breath under water, the miracle of rising up far enough to breathe, and then, the going under again; or the tremendous difference between the light beneath the water and the light when one comes up to the sky.

Lorraine would not be very much younger than I am now if she were alive. She would be forty-nine, and I am fifty-five. But she was very much younger than I when we met—she being twenty-nine then, and I being thirty-four. At the time of the Bobby Kennedy meeting, she was thirty-three. That was one of the very last times I saw her on her feet, and she died at the age of thirty-four. The fact that I would not now be much older than she if she were alive is one of the reasons I miss her so much—we could have such times together now!

People forget how young everybody was. Bobby Kennedy, for another, quite different, example, was thirty-eight. His father had been ambassador at the Court of St. James's—among other quite stunning distinctions—and it goes without saying (nor was it his fault) that he had not the remotest concept of poverty. I doubt that poverty can be imagined, and the attitudes of the American middle class, or the middle class anywhere, are proof that the memory obliterates poverty with great speed and efficiency.

In a sense, therefore, the meeting took place in that panic-stricken vacuum in which black and white, for the most part, meet in this country. I am not now speaking of conscious attitudes, but of history. White people do not wish to be reminded whence they came by the poverty which is, they hope, behind them. Neither do they wish, for the most part, to enter into black suffering—it was Bobby Kennedy, after all, who, referring to the Irish past, said that a Negro could become President in forty years. He really did not know why black people were so offended by this attempt at reassurance. But a black woman pointed out that she resented and rejected such encouragement from the son of an Irish immigrant, who had arrived on these shores long after she had been auctioned here.

It is to be remembered that, at the time of the meeting, Medgar Evers had but lately been blown away at the age of thirty-seven. Malcolm and Martin (both to be murdered at the age of thirty-nine) are still with us. Birmingham, Alabama, has already had its effect on, among others, Julian Bond, a youngster, and Jerome Smith, not much older, and Angela Davis. Angela had known the children blown away in that Birmingham Sunday school. This event invested her with a resolution which was eventually to land her on the FBI's Most Wanted List.

Telescoping, severely now, the details, I had just come off the Southern road, and principally from Birmingham, when Bobby Kennedy asked me to throw this meeting together. I had met Bobby Kennedy once at a White

House function and had told him, with some vehemence, that I wanted to talk to him about the role of the FBI in the Deep South. He had looked at me as though he was thinking that it might not be a bad idea to hand me over to the FBI but was very cordial. I suppose. Anyway, this encounter had something to do with his reason for calling me. I called, among others, Miss Lena Horne, who said that she "never" flew. She nevertheless arrived the next day. I found her wearing a beige suit, sitting in Bobby Kennedy's lobby and complaining that she had a "hole" in her shoe from guiding this plane across the continent. She had just driven in from Idlewild—soon to be renamed Kennedy.

The meeting had been called so swiftly that I had not been able to find Lorraine or Jerome [Smith]. I think that it was my brother David who managed to find them both; but anyway, here they were: Lorraine, Jerome, and David.

And here came Burke Marshall and Bobby Kennedy, and we went on up to the suite.

There were many more people than I can name here. Let us say that I simply called black or white people whom I trusted, who would not feel themselves compelled to be spokesmen for any organization or responsible for espousing any specific point of view. I called the people who had, I knew, paid some dues and who knew it. Rip Torn, for example, a white Southerner, though that does not describe him, was here; and the black sociologist Kenneth Clark; and Harry Belafonte, a very good man on the Southern road and a very good man indeed; and Ed[win "Bill"] Berry of the Chicago Urban League; others. But I am trying to talk about Lorraine.

The meeting began quietly enough until Lorraine responded to Bobby's failure to understand or reply to Jerome's passionate query as to the real role of the U.S. government in, for example, Birmingham. Bobby—and here I am not telescoping but exercising restraint—had turned away from Jerome, as though to say, "I'll talk to all of *you*, who are civilized. But who is *he?*"

Lorraine said (in memory, she is standing, but I know she was sitting—she towered, that child, from a sitting position), "You have a great many very accomplished people in this room, Mr. Attorney General, but the only man you should be listening to is that man over there. That is the voice," she added, after a moment during which Bobby sat absolutely still staring at her, "of twenty-two million people."

As Mr. Kennedy did not appear to understand this, Miss Horne eventually—and as the afternoon wore on, perpetually—attempted to clarify it, saying, for example, "If you are so proud of your record, Mr. Attorney General, *you* go up to Harlem into those churches and barber shops and pool halls, and *you* tell the people. *We* ain't going to do it, because *we* don't want to get shot."

I think I was watching everything. But I know I was watching Lorraine's face. She wanted him to *hear*. Her face changed and changed, the way Sojourner Truth's face must have changed and changed or, to tell the truth, the way I have watched my mother's face change when speaking to someone who could not hear—who yet, and you know it, will be compelled to hear one day.

We wanted him to tell his brother the President to personally escort to school, on the following day or the day after, a small black girl already scheduled to enter a Deep South school.

"That way," we said, "it will be clear that whoever spits on that child will be spitting on the nation."

He did not understand this, either. "It would be," he said, "a meaningless moral gesture."

"We would like," said Lorraine, "from you, a moral commitment."

He did not turn from her as he had turned away from Jerome. He looked insulted—seemed to feel that he had been wasting his time.

But he reacted very strongly to Jerome's answer to his question "Would you take up arms to defend this country?" The answer was, "Never! Never! Never!"

Bobby Kennedy was surprised that any American could feel that way. But something got through to him when this same answer was reiterated later—by a black voice shouting, "When I pull the trigger, kiss it goodbye!"

Well, Lorraine sat still, watching all the while and listening with a face as still, as beautiful, and as terrifying as her face must have been at that moment when she told us, "My Lord calls me. He calls me by the thunder. I ain't got long to stay here." She put that on her tape recorder in her own voice at the moment she realized that she was about to die.*

The meeting ended with Lorraine standing up. She said, in response to Jerome's statement concerning the perpetual demolition faced every hour of every day by black men, who pay a price literally unspeakable for attempting to protect their women, their children, their homes, or their lives, "That is all true, but I am not worried about black men—who have done splendidly, it seems to me, all things considered."

---

*The quoted words are heard in the documentary short film *Lorraine Hansberry: The Black Experience in the Creation of Drama*, 1975, directed by Ralph J. Tangney.

Then, she paused and looked at Bobby Kennedy, who, perhaps for the first time, looked at her.

"But I am very worried," she said, "about the state of the civilization which produced that photograph of the white cop standing on that Negro woman's neck in Birmingham."

Then, she smiled. And I am glad that she was not smiling at me. She extended her hand.

"Goodbye, Mr. Attorney General," she said, and turned and walked out of the room.

We followed her. Perhaps I can dare to say that we were all, in our various ways, devastated, but I will have to leave it at that.

I had forgotten that I was scheduled to be interviewed by Dr. Kenneth Clark, and we were late. We were hurried into the car. We passed Lorraine, who did not see us. She was walking toward Fifth Avenue—her face twisted, her hands clasped before her belly, eyes darker than any eyes I had ever seen before—walking in an absolutely private place.

I knew I could not call her.

Our car drove on; we passed her.

And then, we heard the thunder.

(1979)

On Language, Race, and the Black Writer

WRITERS ARE OBLIGED, at some point, to realize that they are involved in a language which they must change. And for a black writer in this country to be born into the English language is to realize that the assumptions on which the language operates are his enemy. For example, when Othello accuses Desdemona, he says that he "threw a pearl away richer than all his tribe." I was very young when I read that and I wondered, "Richer than *his* tribe?" I was forced to reconsider similes: "as black as sin," "as black as night," "blackhearted."

In order to deal with that reality at a certain time in my life, I left the United States and went to France, where I was unable to speak to anybody because I spoke no French. I dropped into a silence in which I heard, for the first time, the beat of the language of the people who had produced me. For the first time, I was able to hear that music.

When I was in elementary school there were no black writers or white writers whom I could regard as models. I did not agree at all with the moral predicament of Huckleberry Finn concerning Nigger Jim. It was not, after all, a question about whether I should be sold back into slavery.

I am a witness to and a survivor of the latest slave rebellion, or what American newspapers erroneously term the civil rights movement. I put it that way because Malcolm X and I met many years ago when Malcolm was debating a very young sit-in student on a radio station which had asked me to moderate the discussion. Malcolm asked the student a question which I now present to you: "If you are a citizen, why do you have to fight for your civil rights? If you are fighting for your civil rights, then that means you are not a citizen." Indeed, the "legalisms" of this country have never had anything to do with its former slaves. We are still governed by the slave codes.

When I say a "slave rebellion," I mean that what is called the civil rights movement was really insurrection. It was co-opted. It is a fact that the latest slave rebellion was brutally put down. We all know what happened to Medgar Evers. We all know what happened to Malcolm X. We all know what happened to Martin Luther King. We know what happened to Fred Hampton and Mark Clark, and so many more. The list is long. That is the result of slave rebellion.

A very brutal thing must be said: The intentions of this melancholic country as concerns black people—and anyone who doubts me can ask any Indian—have always been genocidal. They needed us for labor and for sport. Now they can't get rid of us. We cannot be exiled and we cannot be accommodated. Something's got to give. The machinery of this country operates day in and day out, hour by hour, to keep the nigger in his place.

When I was young, I used to run an elevator—murderously, but I ran it. I am not needed to run that elevator anymore. Black people are no longer needed to do a whole lot of things we used to do. On the other hand, we are here. This coming summer is going to be a difficult one. In every city in this nation now, black fathers are standing in the streets watching black sons; they're watching each other. Neither fathers nor sons have any place to go, and it is not their fault. It has nothing to do with their value, their merit, their capabilities.

There may be nothing worse under heaven, there may be no greater crime, than to attack a man's integrity, to attempt to destroy that man. For I know that in spite of the American Constitution, in spite of all the born-again Christians, my father was not a mule and not a thing, that my sister was not born to be the plaything of idle white sheriffs.

Black people find themselves between a rock and a hard place. Our presence in this country terrifies every white man walking. This nation is not now, never has been, and now never will be a white country. There is not a white person in this country, including our President and all his friends, who can *prove* he's white.

The people who settled this country came from many places. It was not so elsewhere in the world. In France, they were French; in England, they were English; in Italy, they were Italian; in Greece, they were Greek; in

Russia, they were Russian. From this I want to point out a paradox: blacks, Indians, Chicanos, Asians, and that beleaguered handful of white people who understand their history are the only people who know who they are.

When the Europeans arrived in America, there was a moment in their lives when they had to learn to speak English, when they became guys named Joe. Guys named Joe couldn't speak to their fathers because their fathers couldn't speak English. That meant a rupture, a profound rupture, with their own history, so that they could become guys named Joe. And in doing so, Joe never found out anything else about himself.

Black people in this country come out of a history which was never written down. The links between father and son, between mother and daughter, until this hour and despite all the dangers and trials to which we have been subjected, remain strong and alive. And if we could do that— and we have done that—then we can deal with what now lies before us.

Every white person in this country—and I do not care what he or she says—knows one thing. They may not know, as they put it, "what I want," but they know *they would not like to be black here.* If they know that, then they know everything they need to know, and whatever else they say is a lie.

The American idea of racial progress is measured by how fast I become white. It is a trick bag, because they know perfectly well that I can never become white. I've drunk my share of dry martinis. I have proved myself civilized in every way I can. But there is an irreducible difficulty. Something doesn't work. Well, I decided that I might as well act like a nigger.

The black people of this country stand in a very strange place, as do the white people of this country—and almost for the very same reason, though we approach it from different points of view. I suggest that what the rulers of this country don't know about the world which surrounds them is the price they pay for not knowing me. If they couldn't deal with my father, how are they going to deal with the people in the streets of Tehran? I could have told them, if they had asked.

There is a reason that no one wants our children educated. When we attempt to do it ourselves, we find ourselves up against a vast machinery of racism which infects the country's entire system of education. I know the machinery is vast, ruthless, cunning, and thinks of nothing, in fact, but itself, which means us, because we are a threat to the machinery. We have already lived through a slave rebellion. We cannot pick up guns, because they've got the guns. We cannot hit those streets again, because they're waiting for us. We have to do something else.

Before each slave rebellion there occurred something which I now call "noncooperation" by the slaves. How to execute this in detail today is something each one of us has to figure out. But we could begin with the schools—by taking our children out of those schools, taking them off those buses. Everybody knows, who thinks about it, that you can't change a school without changing a neighborhood, and you can't change a neighborhood without changing the city, and there ain't nobody prepared to change the city, because they want the city to be white. America's cities are going to crumble when the white people move out to get away from the niggers. Every crisis in every city is caused by that. How can we expect people who cannot educate their *own* children to educate anybody else? This will be, well, contested.

But black people hold the trump. When you try to slaughter people, you create a people with nothing to lose. And if I have nothing to lose, what are you going to do to me? In truth, we have one thing to lose—our children. Yet we have never lost them, and there is no reason for us to do it now.

We hold the trump. I say it: patience, and shuffle the cards.

(1979)

Of the Sorrow Songs: The Cross of Redemption

Though Baldwin originally wrote this piece as a review for James Lincoln Collier's *The Making of Jazz* (1979), the essay turns into a meditation and manifesto about race and music.

.   .   .

JULY 29, 1979

I WILL LET THE DATE STAND: but it is a false date. My typewriter has been silent since July 6th, and the piece of paper I placed in the typewriter on that day has been blank until this hour.

July 29th was—is—my baby sister's birthday. She is now thirty-six years old, is married to a beautiful cat, and they have a small son, my nephew, one of my many nephews. My baby sister was born on the day our father died: and I could not but wonder what she, or our father, or her son, my nephew, could possibly make of this compelling investigation of our lives.

It is compelling indeed, like the nightmare called history: and compelling because the author is as precise as he is deluded.

Allow me, for example, to paraphrase, and parody, one of his statements, and I am not trying to be unkind:

There have been two authentic geniuses in jazz. One of them, of course, was Louis Armstrong, the much loved entertainer, striving for acceptance. The other was a sociopath named Charlie Parker, who managed . . . to destroy his career—and finally himself.

Well, then: *There have been two authentic geniuses in art. One of them, of course, was Michelangelo, the much beloved court jester, striving to please the Pope. The other was a misfit named Rembrandt, who managed . . . to destroy his career—and finally himself.*

If one can believe the first statement, there is absolutely no reason to doubt the second. Which may be why no one appears to learn anything from history—I am beginning to suspect that no one *can* learn anything from the nightmare called history. These are my reasons, anyway, for attempting to report on this report from such a dangerous point of view.

I have learned a great deal from traversing, struggling with, this book. It is my life, my history, which is being examined—defined: therefore, it is my obligation to attempt to clarify the record. I do not want my nephew—or, for that matter, my Swiss godson, or my Italian godson—to believe this "comprehensive" history.

People cannot be studied from a distance. It is perfectly possible that we cannot be studied at all: God's anguish, perhaps, upon being confronted with His creation. People certainly cannot be studied from a safe distance, or from the distance which we call safety. No one is, or can be, the other: there is nothing in the other, from the depths to the heights, which is not to be found in me. Of course, it can be said that, "objectively" speaking, I do not have the temperament of an Idi Amin, or Somoza, or Hitler, or Bokassa. Our careers do not resemble each others', and for that I do thank God. Yet, I am aware that, at some point in time and space, our aspirations may have been very similar, or had we met, at some point in time and space—at school, say, or looking for work, or at the corner bar—we might have had every reason to think so. They are men, after all, like me; mortal, like me; and all men reflect, are mirrors for, each other. It is the most fatal of all delusions, I think, not to know this: and the root of cowardice.

For neither I nor anyone else could have known from the beginning what roads we would travel, what choices we would make, nor what the result of these choices would be: in ourselves, in time and space, and in that nightmare we call history. Where, then, is placed the "objective" speaker, who can speak only after, and never before, the fact? Who may or may not have perceived (or received) the truth, whatever the *truth* may be? What does it mean to be "objective"? What is meant by "temperament"? And how does temperament relate to experience? For I do not know, will never know, and neither will you, whether it is my experience which is responsible for my temperament, or my temperament which must be taken to task for my experience.

I am attacking, of course, the basis of the language—or, perhaps, the *intention* of the language—in which history is written; am speaking as the son of the Preacher Man. This is exactly how the music called *jazz* began, and out of the same necessity: not only to redeem a history unwritten and despised, but to checkmate the European notion of the world. For until this hour, when we speak of history, we are speaking only of how Europe saw—and sees—the world.

But there is a very great deal in the world which Europe does not, or cannot, see: in the very same way that the European musical scale cannot transcribe—cannot write down, does not understand—the notes, or the price, of this music.

Now, the author's research is meticulous. Collier has had to "hang" in many places—has "been there," as someone predating "jazz" might put it: but he has not, as one of my more relentless sisters might put it, "been there and back."

My more relentless sister is merely, in actuality, paraphrasing, or bearing witness to, Bessie Smith: "picked up my bag, baby, and I tried it again." And so is Billie Holiday, proclaiming—not complaining—that "my man wouldn't want me no breakfast/Wouldn't give me no dinner/Squawked about my supper/And threw me out doors/Had the nerve to lay/A matchbox on my clothes."

"I didn't," Billie tells us, "have so many. But I had a long, long ways to go."

Thus, Aretha Franklin demands "Respect," having "stolen" the song from Otis Redding (as Otis Redding tells it, sounding strangely delighted to declare himself the victim of this sociopathological act). Aretha dared to "steal" the song from Otis because not many men, of any color, are able to make the enormous confession, the tremendous recognition, contained in "try a little tenderness."

And if you can't get no satisfaction, you may find yourself boiling a bitch's brew while waiting for someone to bring me my gin! or start walking toward the weeping willow tree or ramble where you find strange fruit—black, beige, and brown—hanging just across the tracks where it's tight like that and you do not let the sun catch you crying. It is always "Farewell to Storyville."

For this celebrated number has only the most passing, and, in truth, impertinent, reference to the red-light district of New Orleans, or to the politician for whom it was named: a certain Joseph Story. What a curious way to enter, briefly, history, only to be utterly obliterated by it: which is exactly what is happening to Henry Kissinger. If you think I am leaping, you are entirely right. Go back to Miles, Max, Dizzy, Yardbird, Billie, Coltrane: who were not, as the striking—not to say quaint—European phrase would have it, "improvising": who can afford to improvise, at those prices?

By the time of "Farewell to Storyville," and long before that time, the demolition of black quarters—for that is what they were, and are, considered—was an irreducible truth of black life. This is what Bessie Smith is telling us, in "Back Water Blues." This song has as much to do with a flood as "Didn't It Rain" has to do with Noah, or as "If I Had My Way" has to do with Samson and Delilah, and poor Samson's excess of hair. Or, if I may leap again, there is a song being born, somewhere, as I write, concerning the present "boat people," which will inform us, in tremendous detail, how ships are built. There is a dreadful music connecting the building of ovens with the activity of contractors, the reality of businessmen (to say nothing of business) and the reality of bankers and flags, and the European middle class, and its global progeny, and Gypsies, Jews, and soap: and profit.

The music called "jazz" came into existence as an exceedingly laconic description of black circumstances, and as a way, by describing these circumstances, of overcoming them. It was necessary that the description be laconic: the iron necessity being that the description not be overheard. Or, as the indescribably grim remnants of the European notion of the "nation-state" would today put it, it was absolutely necessary that the description not be "decoded." It has not been "decoded," by the way, any more than the talking drum has been decoded. I will try to tell you why.

I have said that people cannot be described from a distance. I will now contradict myself and say that people *can* be described from a distance: the distance that they themselves have established between themselves and what we must, helplessly, here, call life. Life comes out of music, and music comes out of life: without trusting the first, it is impossible to create the second. The rock against which the European notion of the nation-state has crashed is nothing more—and absolutely nothing less—than the question of identity: *Who am I? And what am I doing here?*

This question is the very heart, and root, of the music we are discussing: and contains (if it is possible to make this distinction) not so much a moral judgment as a precise one.

The Irish, for example, as it now, astoundingly, turns out, never had the remotest desire to become English; neither do the people of Scotland, or Wales; and one can suppose that the people of Canada, trapped as they are between Alaska and Mexico, with only the heirs of the doctrine of Manifest Destiny between themselves and these two definitely unknown ports of call, distract themselves with the question of whether they are French or English only because their history has now allowed them the breathing space to find out what in God's name(!) it means to be Canadian. The Basques do not wish to be French *or* Spanish; Kurds and Berbers do not wish to be Iranian *or* Turkish.

If one travels from Naples, to Rome, to Torino, it can by no means be taken for granted that the "nation"—hammered into a "nation," after all, quite recently—ever agreed, among themselves, to be that. The same is true of an equally arbitrary invention, Germany: Bavaria is not Berlin. For that matter, to be in Haifa is not at all like being in Jerusalem, and neither place resembles Nazareth. Examples abound: but at this moment, the only nations being discussed are those which have become utilitarian but otherwise useless—Sweden, for example, or Switzerland, which is not a nation, but a bank. There are those territories which are considered to be "restive" (Iran, Greece) or those which are "crucial," or "unstable"—or, incomprehensibly, both: Japan, for example, is "crucial" *and* "unstable." Peru, for the moment, is merely "unstable," though one keeps on it a nervous eye: and though we know that there's a whole lot of coffee in Brazil, we don't know who's going to drink it. Brazil threatens to become, as we quite remarkably put it, one of the "emerging" nations, like Nigeria, because those decisions, in those places, involve not merely continents, but the globe. Leaving aside the "crafty East"—China and Russia—there are only embarrassments, like the British colonial outpost named for a merciless, piratical *murderer/colonizer* named Cecil Rhodes.

What, indeed, you may well ask, has all this to do with *The Making of Jazz*—a book concerned, innocently and earnestly enough, with the creation of black American music?

That music is produced by, and bears witness to, one of the most obscene adventures in the history of mankind. It is a music which creates, as what we call History cannot sum up the courage to do, the response to that absolutely universal question: *Who am I? What am I doing here?*

How did King Oliver, Ma Rainey, Bessie, Armstrong—a roll call more vivid than what is called History—Bird, Dolphy, Powell, Pettiford, Coltrane, Jelly Roll Morton, the Duke—or the living, again, too long a roll call: Miss Nina Simone, Mme Mary Lou Williams, Carmen McRae, the Count, Ray, Miles, Max—forgive me, children, for all the names I cannot call. How did they, and how *do* they, confront that question—and make of that captivity a song?

For the music began in captivity, and is still, absolutely, created in captivity. So much for the European vanity, which imagines that with the single word "history" it controls the "past," defines the "present"; and therefore cannot but suppose that the "future" will prove to be as willing to be brought into captivity as the slaves they imagine themselves to have discovered, as the "nigger" they had no choice but to invent.

Be careful of inventions: the invention describes you, and will certainly betray you. Speaking as the son of the Preacher Man, I know that it was never intended, in any way whatever, that either the Father or the Son should be heard. Take that any way you will: I am trying to be precise.

If you know—as a black American *must* know, discovers at his mother's breast, and then in the eyes of his father—that the world which calls itself "white" and which has the further, unspeakable cowardice of calling itself "free"—if you will dare imagine that I, speaking now as a black witness to the white condition, see you in a way that you cannot afford to see me, if you can see that the invention of the black condition creates the trap of the white identity, you will see that what a black man *knows* about a white man stems, inexorably, from the white man's description of who, and what, he takes to be the other—in this case, the black cat: me.

You watch this innocent criminal destroying your father, day by day, hour by hour—your *father!*—despising your mother, your brothers, and your sisters; and this innocent criminal will cut you down without any mercy if any one of you dares to say a word about it.

And not only is he trying to kill you. He would also like you to be his accomplice—discreet and noiseless accomplice—in this friendly, democratic, and, alas, absolutely indispensable action. "I didn't," he will tell you, "make the world."

You think, but you don't say, to your friendly murderer, who, sincerely, means you no harm: "Well, baby, somebody better. And, in a great big hurry."

Thus, you begin to see; so, you begin to sing and dance; for those responsible for your captivity require of you a song. You begin the unimaginable horror of contempt and hatred; then, the horror of self-contempt and self-hatred. "What did I do? to be so black, and blue?" If you survive—as, for example, the "sociopath" Yardbird did not, as the "junkie" Billie Holiday did not—you are released onto the tightrope tension of bearing in mind, every hour, every second, drunk, or sober, in sickness or in health, those whom you must not even begin to depend on for the truth, and those to whom you must not lie.

It is hard to be black, and therefore officially, and lethally, despised. It is harder than that to despise so many of the people who think of themselves as white, before whose blindness you present the obligatory historical grin.

And it is harder than that, out of this devastation—Ezekiel's valley: "Oh, Lord, can these bones live?"—to trust life, and to live a life, to love, and be loved.

It is out of this, and much more than this, that black American music springs. This music begins on the auction block.

Now, whoever is unable to face this—the auction block; whoever cannot see that that auction block is the demolition, by Europe, of all human standards: a demolition accomplished, furthermore, at that hour of the world's history, in the name of "civilization"; whoever pretends that the slave mother does not weep, until this hour, for her slaughtered son, that the son does not weep for his slaughtered father; or whoever pretends that the white father did not, literally, and knowing what he was doing, hang, and burn, and castrate, his black son—whoever cannot face this can never pay the price for the "beat" which is the key to music, and the key to life.

Music is our witness, and our ally. The "beat" is the confession which recognizes, changes, and conquers time.

Then, history becomes a garment we can wear, and share, and not a cloak in which to hide; and time becomes a friend.

(1979)

Black English: A Dishonest Argument

Baldwin gave this speech at Wayne State University, an urban school located in Detroit, Michigan, in 1980.

.　　.　　.

I SHALL BEGIN BY SAYING a very difficult thing. Sometimes it happens that you walk into a response which almost makes your presence and your response a little, not exactly redundant, but close to that. We all know why we are here. So all I can do is comment on the reasons for our presence here tonight and on the fact, as I put it in London, where they believe in history, that this is a historical event. We are speaking inevitably in the shadow of, and we'll get around to this in a moment, the question of black English, a question which has only come up in this country, as of this date.

I want to suggest that history is not the past. It is the present. We carry our history with us. We *are* our history. If we pretend otherwise, to put it very brutally, we literally are criminals. We just saw our history, just heard it, not five minutes ago [referring to the Tennessee Baptist Choir's rendition of black history in song]. I have been to a place which the Western world pretends has not happened. I'm talking about the auction block. We are also talking about the automobile assembly line. I want to make this clear, sitting in your town, talking in your town. One of the architects of this peculiar town is a man named Henry Ford, who is probably responsible for building it—paying workers, black and white; clubbing down workers, black and white—who was a friend of Hitler's; who was no friend of the Jews. (He hadn't yet heard about us.) I challenge anyone alive to challenge me on that.

Now, in this peculiar place, in this peculiar time, in this peculiar country, we have had an argument which presents itself as being concerned with the validity of what is called "black English." No one has yet demanded of Thomas Jefferson or his heirs in exactly what language they wrote the Declaration of Independence. Once one has reminded this country of the fact that, in perfect English, it was written, and not a thousand years ago, in an official document, that black men had no rights which white men were bound to respect. It was not a thousand years ago, the Dred Scott decision. It was not a thousand years ago that a black man was declared three-fifths of a man. I am almost old enough to remember it. I missed it by a very short time.

Actually, we all know something very important that has brought me here. Let me try to spell it out for you, again. And let me suggest that the argument concerning black English is one of the most dishonest arguments in the history of a spectacularly dishonest nation. I kid you not. I grew up in Harlem. I was a shoeshine boy. I scrubbed toilets. And I can still cook. I was dealing with cops before I was seven years old and sleeping in basements before I was ten, watching my mother and my father, my brothers and my sisters, in the land of the free and the home of the brave, living as though every day was going to be our last. Now, how exactly do you expect me to explain that, to describe that to Greer Garson when she comes to teach me English? There is an irreducible gap between my teacher and my experience, between my teacher and my education. I would not have said it when I was ten, could not have said it when I was thirteen, but I can say it now: I don't want anyone I love, including my nieces, my nephews, my great-nieces, my great-nephews, to grow up to be like Jimmy Carter, Ronald Reagan, and all those people.

I tell you something else, a *very* important matter. The language forged by black people in this country, on this continent, as the choir just told you, got us from one place to another. *We* described the auction block. We described what it meant to be there. We survived what it meant to be torn from your mother, your father, your brother, your sister. We described it. We survived being described as mules, as having been put on earth only for the convenience of white people. We survived having *nothing* belonging to us, not your mother, not your father, not your daughter, not your son. And *we* created the only language in this country.

We are the only people in this country, in this part of the North American wilderness, who have never denied their ancestors. A very important matter, for the price of the American ticket—from Russia, from Italy, from Spain, from England—was to pretend you didn't know where you came from; and, furthermore, that you would not pay dues for where you came from. It's called "upward mobility." No one with a job in England got on the *Mayflower.* I'm the only American who knows he didn't want to come here. I know what is happening in Boston is that all those descendants of the Irish potato famine came here. The price of the ticket was to cease being Irish, cease being Greek, cease being Russian, cease being whatever you had been before, and to become "white." And *that* is why this country says it's a white country and really believes it is.

I beg you to bear in mind when I use the word "white" that I am *not* talking as the other side of the Ku Klux Klan. There is no one, there is not a living soul in this country, who can prove he is white. Not one! They can't prove that they're white because I've been here too long, and that's the truth, no matter how they cut it. My problems are not *only* black; my problems are also *white.* They know it. They lynched me, they burned me, they castrated me—*knowing* what they were doing—and they're doing it until this hour. *That* is what these arguments are about.

A child comes to school—better say *my* child—five or six years old, and meets Greer Garson. He just does what everybody else does, especially children: he describes his environment. You describe your environment in order to control it, in order to find out what it is, in order to find out who and where you are. That is what a child does—this is wood, this is paper, this is fire. You got to find out the reality which surrounds you. You got to be able to describe it. You got to be able to describe your mother and your father and your uncles and your junkie cousin. If you aren't able to describe it, you will not be able to survive it.

Now, I described to Greer Garson what happened to my father last night, who just came out of jail. Why doesn't he get a job? Why doesn't he get a *job?* The only people in the world who will not be fooled are children. A child knows if you despise him. And if you despise that child, he will not learn anything from you.

Now, one hears from a long time ago that "white is merely a state of mind." I add to that, white is a moral choice. It's up to you to be as white as you want to be and pay the price of that ticket. You cannot tell a black man by the color of skin, either. But this is a democracy.

A child knows that the teacher despises his attempts to describe what happened to his father, to describe his living room—by that time he's already too old to describe the roaches and the rats. He is too young to describe the landlord and too frightened to describe the streets—and yet he is trying to control his environment. That is what and why he's trying to articulate. And yet, the teacher—and in this case the teacher is America—despises him and his descriptions. They manage to create, deliberately, in every generation, the nigger they want to see.

That is how it happens, and it is not an act of God. Do you understand what I'm saying? The most famous American opera, the greatest American opera, the *only* American opera, as far as I know, is called *Porgy and Bess.* Tell me what language that was written in and by whom. "Summertime"— what about the other lines? In short, Mr. Heyward, whom I have nothing against at all, could describe us, or the man who wrote *Show Boat.* We, the blacks, can be described by others, but we are forbidden to describe ourselves.

Not a thousand years ago, it was illegal to teach a slave to read. Not a thousand years ago, the Supreme Court decided that separate could not be equal. And today, as we sit here, no one is learning anything in this country. You see a nation which is the leader of the rest of the world, that had to pay the price of *that* ticket, and the price of *that* ticket is we're sitting in the most illiterate nation in the world. THE MOST ILLITERATE NATION IN THE WORLD. A monument to illiteracy. And if you doubt me, all you have to do is spend a day in Washington. I am serious as a heart attack.

I'm trying to say something, and I want you to hear it. We *have* no models. The black American *has* no antecedent. *We,* in this country, *on* this continent, in the most despairing terms, created an identity which had never been seen before in the history of the world. We created that music. Nobody else did, and the world lives from it, though it doesn't pay us for it. In the storm which has got to overtake the Western world, we are the only bridge between their history which is the past and their history which is the present. We are the only black Westerners. We are the only people under heaven, the black Americans, who have paid so much for their father's father's father's father's father and mother.

We are the only people in the world—in the world!—who know anything about this country. Nobody else does. Nobody. Nobody else knows white Americans except black Americans. No one else cares about the white American. He can fool the world, but he can't fool me. He can't fool us. We are the only hope this country has.

I attest to this: the world is not white; it never was white, cannot be white. White is a metaphor for power, and that is simply a way of describing Chase Manhattan Bank. That is all it means, and the people who tried to rob us of identity have lost their own. And when you lose that, when a people lose *that,* they've lost everything on which they depended, which is the bottom of their moral authority, and their moral authority is the power to persuade me that I should be like them. But I have decided that I would rather be me than be like Maggie Thatcher or Ronald Reagan or Teddy Kennedy. I have realized there ain't enough raisins in this fuckin' pie to feed *nobody.* White people don't *give* nothin' to each other, so I know they ain't gon' *give* to me. They had children dragging carts through mines before they got to me.

Furthermore, you ain't got no pie to share with me. I know that what you call the "energy crisis" means that I am no longer forced to sell what I produce, to you, at your prices. That's what it means. Before the Cuban Revolution, people were forced to grow sugar, called sugar cane; cut it for us—I mean, for the American government—at our prices; sell it to us, at our prices; then buy it back from us, a year later, in canes, at our prices. It was then called "cane sugar."

Everybody knows that one of the things hiding behind what you call the "energy crisis" is the profit motive. If you don't know that, it's a bullshit tip. We call ourselves a sovereign people; we say we are governed with the consent of the governed. It's a nation that I care the most about—I wouldn't be here otherwise. But it's the most super nation I know since Germany, where the Jews presumably walked into the gas rooms and turned themselves into soap, and it was done with the consent of the world, and nobody stopped it.

Finally, what I am saying is this. I am saying that the Western world has lost whatever authority it had. The moral authority in the Western world is gone. And it is gone forever. It is gone, not because of the criminal record—everybody's record is criminal. It is gone because you cannot do one thing and pretend you're doing another! None of us, who are sitting around in some of the true limbo out-of-space, which we call "now," waiting to be saved, civilized, or discovered, have the moral authority to say anything. And this is called America, where Columbus got lost and thought he had found India. That is why the people—the Reds, the Native Americans—have been called Indian; they had to say *something* to Queen Isabella. All geography now is doubtful, and where we are now, on the medieval map there was a place where the world ended. On the map it said, "Here are dragons." But we are men.

(1980)

This Far and No Further

IT IS HARD TO BE CLEAR in these matters: yet, I hazard that Society—with a capital S—is a direct result of the actual and moral options offered by the State. And yet, on the other hand, the State as we know it is very largely, if not entirely, the result of the actual and moral exhaustion of society, with a small s. The actual, baffling, continuing, and wounding relations which obtain among human beings cause us to long for Authority as deeply as we long for water: and the personal authority surrenders to a larger one, which, if it cannot save us from death, can protect us from chaos. (To be Catholic, with a large C, for example, is not at all the same thing as being catholic.)

Hence, we need victims: object lessons. And this need, which never fails to announce itself as Moral, has nothing whatever to do with morality or any moral hope. This need becomes the quicksand in which all hope of the moral life expires.

Yet, there lives, always and with unpredictable results, within the human being who *is* society something which that Society which controls him—and which he has created—can never know, or reach. It is this inchoate, largely incoherent, and irrepressible energy which has demolished empires. Every State, without exception, co-opts, corrupts, or destroys all those within its proclaimed jurisdiction—and sometimes, as in the present century, beyond it—capable of saying, "No." But no State has been able to foresee or prevent the day when their most ruined and abject accomplice— or most expensively dressed prostitute—will growl, "This far and no further."

Or what their children have been watching, or how they will act on what they have seen; and what they see.

Now, the State creates the Criminal, of every conceivable type and stripe, because the State cannot operate without the Criminal. The nature of their operation demands fraud, coercion, secrecy, and the power to intimidate: in no way whatever, for example, do the tactics of the financier or the successful racketeer differ from those of the FBI or the CIA—or, for that matter, the cop on the corner. Your intimidated neighbor may be, at this very moment, telling the FBI everything he thinks he knows about you. And your neighbor is not betraying you. He knows that where there's smoke, there must be fire: he has been enlisted in the service of Authority, which knows more than he—about you. And, of course, the good Lord alone has any idea of what they may know about *him*. Hanging over his head is the choice of becoming a Criminal accomplice or a Prisoner.

Anyone old enough to remember the McCarthy era and the shameful case—among others—of the Rosenbergs knows what I am talking about.

If the State creates the Criminal, and uses him, until—for reasons of State—it becomes necessary that he be, with extreme prejudice, terminated, it simply throws the Prisoner into Society's lap. This has the effect of reassuring Society that Society is being protected while, at the same time, causing him to hate the Prisoner (far more than he hates the Criminal) because the Prisoner—so he is told, every hour on the hour—is costing him an awful lot of money. Without pursuing the fascinating economics of a system which permits the State to profit from the Criminal while forcing Society to pay for the Prisoner, it is interesting that Society numbly shakes the collective head when told—not asked—about the latest expensive bash at the Pentagon. Now, of course, the prisons are full of Criminals. This is not, however, what distinguishes a prison or a penitentiary from the streets we walk or a bank or a church or an advertising agency. The Criminal, that is, may or may not be a Prisoner, and the Prisoner may or may not be a Criminal. All that we can really claim to *know* about the Prisoner is that he or she is a human being, like ourselves, who has been *caught*, who has been *incarcerated*. He/she went mad with an axe or a razor or a knife or a gun or raped someone or killed someone to get his/her fix or got caught with dope or stole forty or seventy or a hundred dollars. But rarely is the Prisoner someone who has managed to embezzle, say, two or three million dollars. Rarely is it someone who has managed to bankrupt the public trust: rare and spectacular it is that the Prisoner has been dragged from the seats of power. A very great Criminal, Franco, for but one example, was never hauled before the moral Western tribunal on any charge; created a multitude of prisoners, to say nothing of corpses; and died, allegedly senile and infantile but otherwise quite peacefully, in bed. In his *own* bed. However many men he may have caused to be tortured to death, however many men he caused to live and die with the prison stink of multitudes of men in their nostrils, Franco, the Criminal, never had to undergo the perpetual indignity of the Prisoner.

I once flew quite a long way to see a friend of mine in prison. I was coming as a journalist, and had so informed the Warden by telephone, the day before: for the case was, essentially, political, and I was to do an interview. I was on assignment from a black paper, a weekly. But no, said the Warden, only reporters from daily papers were allowed. I had never heard of this limitation before; but, then, there was no reason that I should have—though I *did* realize, suddenly, that there were no black daily newspapers in America, and my friend is black. Well, I got another assignment, from a daily, and presented myself at the prison. I sat alone in the Warden's office for quite some time—fighting paranoia, one may say, but I yet had to face the fact that Authority was not overjoyed by my arrival. And I was resigning myself to the probable necessity of having to leave and come back another day—for visiting hours were almost over—when I was allowed in, with a distinctly chilling assignment.

My friend had refused—as I knew—to work in the prison factory at prison prices. He wanted a Union wage. The Warden was sure that I understood how disruptive this was for the prison routine and how unrealistic and inconsiderate my friend was being. I think that I assured him that I did, may have offered him my heartfelt sympathy: I was capable, at that moment, of saying anything. The Warden wanted me—if I was really the friend I claimed to be—to persuade his Prisoner to be cooperative: it would help when the time came for him to appear before the Parole Board.

What a terrifying apprehension of crime and punishment! I had flown nearly ten thousand miles to see a brother I loved in order to deliver a far from veiled threat: *Cooperate, or . . . ?*

I suppose that all that a man can learn in prison is *why he is there:* an unimaginably lonely and private assessment, which nevertheless, at the very least, releases him from the Society's presumption as to why he is there. I do not pretend, in any way whatever, to be able to assess the price the person who is the Prisoner pays: but I know that prisons do not rehabilitate, because it is not their purpose and it is not in their power. One is not rehabilitated by learning to cooperate with the structure designed to debase the person into the Prisoner. Nor do men repent in "penitentiaries": the word itself reveals the mercilessly self-righteous Puritan delusion. Repentance is a private matter, and no more than forgiveness can it be coerced. Society, responsive to the will and the needs of the State, slams the door on the Prisoner with the vindictive vehemence of the blow meant to shatter a mirror.

I visited Death Row prisoners not long ago, and so I am compelled to point out that the Prisoner is likely, on the whole, to be inescapably visible: Death Row, like the ghetto, is dark with dark faces. The incarceration of the Prisoner reveals nothing about the Prisoner, but reveals volumes concerning those who hold the keys. And finally, then, since I am an American discussing American Prisoners, we are also discussing one more aspect of the compulsive American dream of genocide.

On different levels, the Artist and the Prisoner must fight very hard against debasement and isolation. It is the responsibility of the Artist perpetually to question the zealous State and the narcoticized Society. Or—bearing in mind that, for the most part, it is the poor and the helpless who are incarcerated while the able and affluent fly away—it may be time to suggest that if the State depended less heavily on criminals, the Society would be burdened with fewer prisoners.

Then we, as society with a small s, might be enabled to reassume our real responsibilities for each other and for all our children and tear down those incarcerations which we have built for others and in which we strangle, daily, on our own vomit.

(1983)

On Being White . . . and Other Lies

THE CRISIS OF LEADERSHIP in the white community is remarkable—and terrifying—because there is, in fact, no white community.

This may seem an enormous statement—and it is. I'm willing to be challenged. I'm also willing to attempt to spell it out.

My frame of reference is, of course, America, or that portion of the North American continent that calls itself America. And this means I am speaking, essentially, of the European vision of the world—or more precisely, perhaps, the European vision of the universe. It is a vision as remarkable for what it pretends to include as for what it remorselessly diminishes, demolishes, or leaves totally out of account.

There is, for example—at least, in principle—an Irish community: here, there, anywhere; or, more precisely, Belfast, Dublin, and Boston. There is a German community: both sides of Berlin, Bavaria, and Yorkville. There is an Italian community: Rome, Naples, the Bank of the Holy Ghost, and Mulberry Street. And there is a Jewish community, stretching from Jerusalem to California to New York. There are English communities. There are French communities. There are Swiss consortiums. There are Poles: in Warsaw (where they would like us to be friends) and in Chicago (where because they are white we are enemies). There are, for that matter,

Indian restaurants, and Turkish baths. There is the underworld—the poor (to say nothing of those who intend to become rich) are always with us—but this does not describe a community. It bears terrifying witness to what happened to everyone who got here, and paid the price of the ticket. The price was to become "white." No one was white before he/she came to America. It took generations, and a vast amount of coercion, before this became a white country.

It is probable that it is the Jewish community—or, more accurately perhaps, its remnants—that in America has paid the highest and most extraordinary price for becoming white. For the Jews came here from countries where they were not white, and they came here, in part, *because* they were not white; and incontestably—in the eyes of the black American (and not only in those eyes)—American Jews have opted to become white; and this is how they operate. It was ironical to hear, for example, former Israeli prime minister Menachem Begin declare some time ago that "the Jewish people bow only to God" while knowing that the state of Israel is sustained by a blank check from Washington. Without further pursuing the implication of this mutual act of faith, one is nevertheless aware that the Jewish translation into a white American can sustain the state of Israel in a way that the black presence here can scarcely hope—at least not yet—to halt the slaughter in South Africa.

And there is a reason for that.

America became white—the people who, as they claim, "settled" the country became white—because of the necessity of denying the black presence, and justifying the black subjugation. No community can be based on such a principle—or, in other words, no community can be established on so genocidal a lie. White men—from Norway, for example, where they were "Norwegians"—became white by slaughtering the cattle, poisoning the wells, torching the houses, massacring Native Americans, raping black women.

This moral erosion has made it quite impossible for those who think of themselves as white in this country to have any moral authority at all—privately or publicly. The multitudinous bulk of them sit, stunned, before their TV sets, swallowing garbage that they know to be garbage, and—in a profound and unconscious effort to justify this torpor that disguises a profound and bitter panic—pay a vast amount of attention to athletics, even though they know that the football player (the Son of the Republic, *their* son!) is merely another aspect of the moneymaking scheme. They are either relieved or embittered by the presence of the black boy on the team.

I do not know if they remember how long and hard they fought to keep him off it. I know that they do not dare have any notion of the price black people (mothers and fathers) paid and pay. They do not want to know the meaning, or face the shame, of what they compelled—out of what they took as the necessity of being white—Joe Louis or Jackie Robinson or Cassius Clay (aka Muhammad Ali) to pay. I know that they themselves would not have liked to pay it.

There has never been a labor movement in this country, the proof being the absence of a black presence in the so-called father-to-son unions. There are, perhaps, some niggers in the window; but blacks have no power in labor unions.

Just so does the white community, as a means of keeping itself white, elect, as they imagine, their political (!) representatives. No nation in the world, including England, is represented by so stunning a pantheon of the relentlessly mediocre. I will not name names—I will leave that to you.

But this cowardice, this necessity of justifying a totally false identity and of justifying what must be called a genocidal history, has placed everyone now living into the hands of the most ignorant and powerful people the world has ever seen. And how did they get that way? By deciding that they were white. By opting for safety instead of life. By persuading themselves that a black child's life meant nothing compared with a white child's life. By abandoning their children to the things white men could buy. By informing their children that black women, black men, and black children had no human integrity that those who call themselves white were bound to respect. And in this debasement and definition of black people, they debased and defined themselves.

And have brought humanity to the edge of oblivion: because they think they are white. Because they think they are white, they do not dare confront the ravage and the lie of their history. Because they think they are white, they cannot allow themselves to be tormented by the suspicion that all men are brothers. Because they think they are white, they are looking for, or bombing into existence, stable population, cheerful natives, and cheap labor. Because they think they are white, they believe, as even no child believes, in the dream of safety. Because they think they are white, however vociferous they may be and however multitudinous, they are as speechless as Lot's wife—looking backward, changed into a pillar of salt.

However—! White being, absolutely, a moral choice (for there *are* no white people), the crisis of leadership for those of us whose identity has been forged, or branded, as black is nothing new. We—who were not black before we got here, either, who were defined as black by the slave trade—have paid for the crisis of leadership in the white community for a very long time and have resoundingly, even when we face the worst about ourselves, survived and triumphed over it. If we had not survived, and triumphed, there would not be a black American alive.

And the fact that we are still here—even in suffering, darkness, danger, endlessly defined by those who do not dare define, or even confront, themselves—is the key to the crisis in white leadership. The past informs us of various kinds of people—criminals, adventurers, and saints, to say nothing, of course, of Popes—but it is the black condition, and only that, which informs us concerning white people. It is a terrible paradox, but those who believed that they could control and define black people divested themselves of the power to control and define themselves.

(1984)

Blacks and Jews

In 1983 Baldwin was appointed Five College Professor in the W. E. B. DuBois Department of Afro-American Studies of the University of Massachusetts at Amherst. In that position he would teach and lecture at all the schools in the Amherst area—Amherst College, Hampshire College, Mount Holyoke College, Smith College, and the UMass Amherst. A number of African-American writers were teaching at Amherst at the time, including John Edgar Wideman (Homewood Trilogy), Julius Lester (*Black Folktales*)—incidentally, a black man who converted to Judaism—and Michael Thelwell (*The Harder They Come*), who also had been active with SNCC during the 1960s and was one of the founders of the Afro-American Studies program at that school.

Baldwin spoke on the campus of UMass Amherst on February 28, 1984, an election year: former Vice President Walter Mondale was running for the Democratic presidential nomination, as was political activist the Reverend Jesse Jackson, who had founded PUSH (People United to Save Humanity) in the 1970s and the National Rainbow Coalition in the 1980s. In January of that year, he had used the term

"Hymietown" while discussing New York City. "Hymie" is a derogatory
term used for Jews. Jackson later apologized for the remark, but it tar-
nished his campaign. Jackson would back out of the race after winning five primaries.

Though the first twenty seconds of the transcript was lost, the
record of this event contains a great deal of interaction with the students after the body of his talk.

.   .   .

BALDWIN: . . . He comes to collect the rent, so you know him in that role. He
runs the grocery store and he gives you credit, so you know him in that role.
He runs the drugstore and he bandages your wounds, and you know him in
that role. You don't really know him from anybody else, but your father says,
and your aunt says, and the neighbors say, and the cops say, and the cops—
you already know this—are for the most part not Jews, whatever at that
moment in your life a Jew is. Well, time goes on, you deal with it one way or
another.

When I was growing up it was a time, after all, of the Second World War.
My best friends in high school were Jewish. It was a very, very important
moment in my life because it was a time when I realized in a way not at all
biblical, as I wrote somewhere, my friends, who really were my friends, were
not so far from the fiery furnace after all. They were being burned to cinders
across the ocean in a very criminally Christian nation, Germany.

This makes one begin to wonder about the whole life, the whole moral
life of the West, which is too vast a subject to go into right now. Now I want
to go into one thing, which is the relationship of the blacks to Jews in this
society: the alleged relationship and the real relationship. A great deal is
invested in keeping these two people at a division, and a great deal really can
divide us.

In my own time, in my own career, according to the limits of my
own perception and my experience, the most difficult thing, the most
treacherous thing, I would hazard, about being an American white man who
is of Jewish inheritance, the most difficult thing, I would think, would be to
accept that inheritance, which is a mighty one, as distinguished from and as
opposed to the American inheritance. Because the most awful thing about
the black American relationship to Jews, to the American Jew, is that the
black American singles out the American Jew because so much of the black
inheritance comes from the Old and New Testament—so much of our

imagery: "Let my people go," all of those legends black people have lived with and made real up until this hour—and that means that unconsciously a black person tends to expect more from a Jewish person than he expects from anybody else. And because the American Jew in this country is essentially a white man, this expectation is always defeated with a resulting accumulation of bitterness, because the American Jew is acting on the minor inheritance and rejecting the major one.

You will observe that in the American inheritance—and you will presently turn the tables on me, correct me if you think I'm wrong—but in the American inheritance insofar as I have been able to read it, and insofar as I've had to make it my own, there is no suggestion of morality. The American inheritance is essentially an inheritance which is called opportunity; and in execution of this opportunity, it doesn't matter what principle or what human being is in the way.

When I was younger, when I was young, then, many of my friends—I began my career, as the Moral Majority seems to have discovered, on what we call the left, even the far left—that is to say, I was an anticommunist when America and Russia were allies. And many of my friends, black—but there were not many black kids or black survivors in the time that I was beginning to grow up—those who had preceded me were silent or dead, and my generation was already being decimated, I had already run into familiar faces, so there I was without a [inaudible]. But my point is not there. My point is that in the intervening time, people's names you would recognize had moved from where we were, my youthful comrades, when, for better or for worse and as very young people, we were trying to do something to alter the state of the world, trying to be faithful to some kind of vision, some kind of idea of what America could become, what a man and a woman could become. These people who are now my age, of course, give or take a year, have with almost no exceptions become what they call the neoconservatives: a polite word for a peculiarly vindictive form of American neofascism. It is quite incredible to me, as I watch it with my own eyes, but it also illustrates something of what I mean when I say that a black man does not expect from an American white man what he expects from an American Jew, and when that expectation is defeated, a certain bitterness ensues. I might feel very differently about my ex–running buddies if in fact they were all Calvinists, if they were people like William Buckley, from whom obviously I expect nothing. [Laughter from audience.]

But these are people from whom I did expect something at one time in my life. And I thought they were better than that. I thought that they knew more than that. I thought that they could be clearer than that. What is behind it, in another way, has to do with something else—something else which no one ever wishes to discuss. And that is the actual role in the Middle East of the state of Israel. Whenever Israel is mentioned one is required, it appears sometimes to me, to maintain a kind of pious silence. Well, why? It is a state like other states. It has come into existence in a peculiar way. But it does not, does not, become a state because people who wrote the Balfour Declaration, or Winston Churchill, or for that matter anyone in Europe, or in the Western world, really cared what happened to the Jews. I wish I could say differently, but I would be lying if I did—it came into existence as a means of protecting Western interests at the gate of the Middle East. The British promised land back and forth, depending on which horse would be in the lead, to the Arabs and to the Jews. The English, as you will have heard, have an expert, have a policy which they are experts at, and the policy is called "divide and rule." Sometimes I think the British may be the authors of twentieth-century racism. They certainly codified it. In any case, in order to be a Zionist, it is not necessary to love the Jews. I know some Zionists who are definitely anti-Semitic. And to be a Jew is not necessarily to be a Zionist. I'm putting it to you this way in the attempt to clarify something which is happening all around us. All of this is triggered by the incipient attack on Jesse Jackson, who allegedly made, or has confessed to having made, an anti-Semitic remark in a private conversation, while a reporter was listening. There is something about the whole anecdote which rubs me the wrong way, something that—I smell a rat somewhere, it doesn't seem entirely—can we use the word?—kosher. [*Laughter from audience.*] Be that as it may, the press, the media, to which we owe so much, which is so enlightening for us all, is now saddling Jesse Jackson with the label or the suggestion of being anti-Semite, of being an anti-Semite. I think I know Jesse well enough to say that that seems to me exceedingly unlikely. But what does impress me is the uses to which this anecdote is being put.

Yes, sir?

STUDENT: Didn't the Jewish Anti-Defamation League publish a paper or article on why Jews should not vote for Jesse Jackson?

BALDWIN: I don't know, did they?

STUDENT: Yes, they did. They alleged that he was anti-Semitic and that they had [*inaudible*].

BALDWIN: I would like to read it, but on what basis do they say he is anti-Semitic?

STUDENT: I only heard about it last night. Someone in my class was telling me about it. I'll bring it for you.

BALDWIN: I would like to read it. Yes, sir?

STUDENT: Can you explain "anti-Semitic" and "anti-Semite"? Someone told me that even Arabs are Semites.

BALDWIN: What?

STUDENT: Can you explain "Semite," how it came to be recognized today as anti-Jewish? And I'm not clear about it here. Arabs are also "Semites" in language. The Arabic language is [*inaudible*] is Semite? Can you explain that?

BALDWIN: Can I explain how does it happen that when someone is called anti-Semitic he is only considered to be anti-Jewish, because Arabs are also Semites, and what you are saying is that you cannot call a pro-Arab an anti-Semite? Well, I cannot answer your question really, because your logic, you know, is true. For example, obviously I am not an anti-Semite, not only because I am pro-Arab but because I am not anti-Jewish, either. I have my quarrel with the idea of Zion, but it has nothing to do with the entity called Jewish and still less with the entity called Arab. What has happened in the Western world is, I think, probably because so much of the Western world is incipiently or actually anti-Semitic and very dishonest about it; therefore, because they are so dishonest about it, if one takes a position vis-à-vis the state of Israel which is not the popular one, or points out that the black boys and the Puerto Rican boys pushing trucks in the Garment Center are pushing those trucks for American industry and their bosses are Jews, but the fact that their bosses are Jews is absolutely unimportant, what is important is that they are pushing those trucks, what is crucial, what is terrible about it, is that when you turn, you know, pushing the trucks, and accuse your boss of doing what you know he's doing, and he says "I can't be doing that because I'm a Jew," then you begin to hate him and that's when you're called an anti-Semite. And no one is called an anti-Semite because he dislikes Arabs. Most Americans dislike Arabs too, insofar as they know they exist. But you see what I mean; we are talking about the Western piety, we are talking about a form of hypocrisy. Come on, don't stop now! [*Laughter from audience.*]

I think the whole Jesse Jackson thing that I've watched in the paper is dangerous in that it confirms or tends to confirm deep suspicions within the breasts of both groups, the Jew and the black American. And there are reasons for this suspicion. And it is true that for the most part the American

Jew is simply, in the black person's life, nothing but another white American, who goes to church on Saturday instead of Sunday. I hate to put it that way, but it would be true if I didn't say so; and it is something I think one has to try to deal with, to look at. It is an attempt, the attack on Jesse—as I read it, and bear in mind I haven't read the paper yet—an attempt to set us at another division, obviously an attempt to discredit Jesse, but to prevent the possibility of a certain kind of coalition. Not only between blacks and Jews but between . . . The importance of Jesse's campaign, I thought, was perhaps to create a possibility of a coalition between people who stopped voting quite some time ago. People overlook how few, how small a percentage of the American public vote at all. What I myself may think of Mr. Jackson, Reverend Jackson, in the privacy of my own house has nothing to do with this possibility, and he's the only candidate which offers us this possibility. And it would seem to be a pity if it can be destroyed by this ancient red herring of anti-Semitism which I've seen drag through so many discussions with such disastrous results over so many years. But if that should happen, and I think it very well may happen, then all of us have to figure out something else, because it is not the end of the road.

And I've brought up the discussion at liberty this morning in a way to clear the air, because once this question is in the public print, once it is on television, it's going to be in everybody's mind in one way or another, and nobody wants to talk about it because it's unpleasant, and it's dangerous too, and you lose friends too, yet what's in the record book is in the record book. And the American Jew faces the same moral choice, is in the same moral dilemma, as any other white American, perhaps compounded by the Jewish inheritance, but it's the same moral dilemma as any other white American, which is: whether he wants your safety or your honor. That may seem a grandiose way to put it, but that is what the choices are. White people have opted for safety in the generality, which means they have no honor in the generality, and consider that they have given me, Sambo, more than I deserve and as much as they are ever going to give me. There is a fatal lack of logic to this line of reasoning, but it is the American line of reasoning. It is what Americans really feel about black people and about themselves. And they really think that they have something to give, which is even more astounding.

But let us turn the tables, I think I talked enough, perhaps even too much. Tell me what is on your minds. Yes, sir?

STUDENT: Don't you think a little bit of the whole Jackson thing is a little bit, is "time manipulation" of the press? I mean things like James Watt, where it is the same sort of thing that comes out of a little article from two weeks past, and all of a sudden right before you make big decisions this whole hour-and-a-half television [program] on it at night and then the Jackson thing comes out three or four days before the primary, the thing is printed two weeks ago, the twenty-third line of a little article, and all of a sudden they bring that out. We don't even know, because we are unaware of what the press doesn't want to show us. Maybe Mondale . . . I'm not saying he did, but maybe he said something four or five weeks ago, a little off-color remark that got printed in Topeka, Kansas, news that if the press decided that they wanted to put that in the front line, that could destroy his whole campaign. They decide what little things are going to . . . who is going to get the votes and who isn't based on what they decide to print as the big news.

BALDWIN: I quite agree with you except that it is not the press alone that makes this decision, you know. The press is part of the society and it has the same options, as I said, safety or honor, which may be a grandiose way to put it, but the press is a part of the system. And if Jesse is now being attacked as anti-Semitic, now at this moment, it is not an act of God, it is a decision on the part of the people who are the press and on the part of the people who own the press, who run the press. It is deliberate. It is not spontaneous. In the, in the . . . Sometimes it is true, I suppose, that something happens which nobody can suppress or interpret quickly enough, but this is not one of those occasions.

STUDENT: I have been working on Mr. Jackson's campaign and I have every intention of voting for him. Part of what bothers me about the whole thing is that he has now said that he let his guard down and made the comment, and I'm not sure what he means by "I let my guard down."

BALDWIN: I know it is a very unfortunate phrase and I'm very worried about it too because what it means, what it can mean, obviously, is that he really is anti-Semitic but never lets it be shown. I have no reason to believe that, but I've never had any reason to think about it until these last few days, these last few hours. It's a very unfortunate way to put it. That's the best that can be said for him, and it's going to cost him and us a great deal. I'm only trying to get us to be clear about it. I don't know if he's anti-Semitic. I doubt it, but he may be. The trouble is that all the candidates suffer from one kind of affliction, racially speaking or socially speaking, or another, because all of them are Americans. Jesse is singled out for particular reasons, and it will have a particular effect. It will have a disastrous effect on the campaign, because it questions his moral veracity—therefore, your intelligence. Do you see what I'm saying?

STUDENT 1: Would you say that the allegations of Jesse Jackson being antichoice as far as abortion is concerned is another example of that, of people who have a vested interest in preventing a rainbow coalition from forming, as another example of that?

BALDWIN: I wasn't aware, I have not followed his campaign very closely. What is his stand on abortion? Antichoice?

STUDENT 2: No, he's not. [*Multiple responses.*] He's prochoice and on a personal level antiabortion. He's also against the Hite amendment and for poor people's and everybody's choice. [*Several students*] Stand up!

STUDENT 1: I said that he wasn't antichoice, and he's antiabortion on a personal level.

BALDWIN: Are you still talking?

STUDENT 1: What he says is right, but I think he's been accused and allegations have been made that he is antichoice, and I was wondering if you think that is an example of the same sort of thing.

BALDWIN: Well, if that's true, yes, it would be. But as she [the other student?] interprets his position it sounds coherent to me to be prochoice and not to want your wife or your sister to have an abortion. That's a coherent position, I'm saying. But no matter what position Jesse takes, it could be used against us.

STUDENT: Excuse me, speaking as president of the Students for Jesse Jackson on the UMass campus [*laughter from audience*], I'd like to say that I hear a lot of misinterpretation from the press and the media, and I don't think that is the fault of any of us, it is the fault of the media. I would like to say that for those people who are interested in finding out exactly what Mr. Jackson's stands [are] on such rights as abortion, as nuclear proliferation, as student [*inaudible*] financial aid, we now have a table set up in the Campus Center concourse right this very moment, and we are giving information on exact quotes from Mr. Jackson himself, so that you might better be aware of his stands on the issues. In terms of the media fest on Mr. Jackson, I would just like to say that in terms of last week's caucus you will notice that Mr. Jackson only had what the media presented him to only have 3 percent of the vote, while John Glenn had 5 percent of the vote. May I interject with this piece of information: Jesse Jackson was not even on the ballot and he got 3 percent of the vote. The media did not present that fact. Okay, if you notice in today's New Hampshire primary, okay, they are playing up Gary Hart, they are playing up John Glenn, but they are not mentioning Jesse Jackson's stand in terms of New Hampshire votes. I will give you this piece of information. A group of us students went to New Hampshire two weekends ago, where we met face to face with people from Keene State College, people from UMass and people from Manchester, most of those people were very pro-Jackson. I will say this to you, if you are interested in finding out more about Jackson's issues, finding out about his side of the argument, as opposed to the *New York Times* or *Boston Globe* or [*inaudible*] or in the various news commentators, I suggest you come down to the table, find out information, come to one of our meetings, find out the information. And then make your own decision. And I ask you to vote.

BALDWIN [*laughs*]: Thank you, sir. [*Audience applause.*]

STUDENT: I just wanted to clarify something for myself, talking about the role of Jews as the kind of businessmen of the Garment District and stuff like that. I just wanted to know how, politically, has the role of Jews in that sense, the liberal kind of role, do you see that as a kind of contradiction to the businessman role, or do you see that as something separate?

BALDWIN: Well, it depends on . . . How do we repeat your question? Your question essentially being—you are talking about the black relationship to Jews, actually? You are talking about the black relationship to Jews?

STUDENT: Yeah.

BALDWIN: And is there a contradiction between the Garment Center boss and the Jewish liberal? In action, no. In terms of the effect it has on the daily life of a black person, no. In some ways, to put it very brutally, the liberal image can be used in the sense to nullify the reality of the Garment Center. In any case, it's not enough to be a liberal—Christian or Jew. That is something that people have a great deal of difficulty with. But it is not enough to be a liberal, to have the right attitudes and even to give money to the right causes. You have to know more than that. You have to be prepared to risk more than that. I am telling you this because I have watched what happened to many of my liberal friends when the civil rights movement was in Alabama, let us say, in the Deep South, and they were [*inaudible*] very indignant. And then I watched what happened imperceptibly but fatally when that same movement moved north to Brooklyn, to Pittsburgh, Detroit, and New York. And their attitudes changed. I really hate to put it to you that way, but that is what happened. Their attitudes changed because they began to feel more and more threatened, and a liberal facade or even a liberal attitude was not enough to deal with the speed with which the movement was moving and the complications of American life as revealed in the fact by the interracial tensions in every major city, and being liberal was no defense against that and no interpretation of that. Do you see what I mean?

STUDENT: Can you see a similar problem happening—

BALDWIN: Beg your pardon?

STUDENT: Can you see a similar problem happening when blacks start making their way up into the business world? Themselves? [*Laughter from audience.*]

BALDWIN: When the blacks start making their way up into the business world, where would the similar problem be? You're talking about the moral choices again.

STUDENT: Their relation to the workers whether they be blacks themselves.

BALDWIN: Their relation to whom?

STUDENT: Workers. Whether they be blacks themselves?

BALDWIN: Oh! I see what you are saying. Well, for the moment, the question is more or less academic. Blacks are not making their way in great numbers up the corporate ladder. And I will repeat what I have said often: you cannot tell a black man by the color of his skin, either. But the particular danger that we are speaking of when we are talking about American or Jewish liberals is not yet a danger for black Americans; we are not yet anywhere near that situation.
    Yes?

STUDENT: In talking about Israel before, you said that Israel wasn't set up because anyone else [cared] about the Jews, but you implied it was set up to protect oil interests in that area. And I would argue that point and say that I think after centuries of despoil that there was a bit of that, [but] that this was an area that the Jews did deserve as their homeland, and I just find it hard to accept that it was set up to protect oil interests.

BALDWIN: I said to protect the vital interests of the Western world, and I don't mean to be sardonic or cynical, but I would be lying to you and lying by my own experience if I said to you that the Europeans—the English, the Dutch, the Germans, the French—impressed me as having any very vivid concern for Jews. The French are still anti-Semitic, so are the British, so are the Dutch, so are the Poles, so are the French. They'll probably be anti-Semitic until the nation disappears.

STUDENT: That's not my . . . I won't argue with that. I'm saying that, well, if they're anti-Semitic, why do they think that the Jews are going to protect Western interests and Israel doesn't even have the oil?

BALDWIN: Oh! Yeah, I know that. I didn't say oil, I said the vital interests of the Western world. Part of the hazard of being a Jew, historically and actually, and part of precisely the danger I was talking about when I began about the way a Jew intrudes himself on a black person's attention because he is the only white man you see. But then part of the hazard, actually, morally, historically, of the Jewish . . . of being a Jew, is finding yourself doing the Christian's dirty work. You see what I'm saying? It's not a condemnation; it's simply a fact. So it is in that sense to say that Israel is useful to the Western interests.

STUDENT: [*inaudible*]

BALDWIN: The Christian's dirty work?

STUDENT: Yes.

BALDWIN: The people who own Harlem, for example, never arrive to collect the rent. The people who really are responsible for the misery all up and down those streets do not run the pawnshop. The people responsible for the horror are not in the liquor store, the people responsible for all the horror, if you really want to find out . . . When I was running up and down Manhattan trying to find a place to live, it was not the landlord I had to deal with; it was the man who owned the building. And he was in Croton-on-Hudson. Or it was Columbia University. The people who own anything, who really own it in the ghetto, are not to be found in the ghetto. The middleman is in the ghetto doing, in fact, the Christian's dirty work. Is that clear? [*Applause from audience.*]

STUDENT: You said that the liberal facade is not enough.

BALDWIN: I can't hear you.

STUDENT: You said that the liberal facade and being a liberal is not enough. Well, what is? What is necessary?

BALDWIN: Commitment. That is what is necessary. You mean it or you don't.

PROFESSOR MICHAEL THELWELL: I'd like to speak to that [*inaudible*]. [*Laughter and applause from audience.*] And I'm here, brother, because for the first time I'm not quite satisfied with an answer you gave. The young man who asked a question initially about Jewish liberals, I'm afraid, defined the question in such a way that the answer did not satisfy me. I'm not in the habit of speaking publicly and personally at the same time, but I'm going to do that. When I worked . . . when I was a young man in the civil rights movement, there was a set of alliances in this country, and the young black movement—and it was very young, in terms of age, in terms of capability, in terms of resources—made alliances with professional Jewish organizations in the sense that they sought us out and they became our allies. And they are formidable allies. I mean, they are capable, and they fight, and are incredible allies to have. By the same token they are incredible enemies to have also, as Jesse Jackson is finding out. But if we say "What about the Jewish liberal?," by the imposition of that term, "liberal," you distort the argument, because liberals of all stripes suffer from the disabilities that you have attributed to them. But it wasn't liberalism that we were experiencing. There is a quality which comes out of Judaism—that is to say, the Jewish faith and experience. And what we experienced, there were some groups which were liberal, there were some groups which were professional kinds, Zionist groups—so the alliance ruptured very easily the moment black people raised the question of the Middle East. But if we say that and leave it there, then the situation is significantly distorted. Because what there is in the traditions of Judaism is, number one, a genuine sense of social justice which, as Jimmy says, frequently comes up against the impositions of American reality. But there does seem to be a real stream which characterizes the people, a sense of struggle and a sense of distrust of power and an outrage at injustice, a quality of morality, codified in the Bible and coming down . . . and a tradition of social struggle. And that, it seems to me, is a very strong element of Judaism quite separate from American liberalism or anything else; and if we don't recognize that, then the situation is distorted, because there were people acting less out of a sense of American liberalism, but out of . . . I got the sense of . . . a tradition going far back, of a kind of spontaneous struggle, a kind of spontaneous joining hands with the afflicted and the weak, and that is a real element of Judaism about which, I think, every Jewish person should be very proud and, also, should think very carefully about how they preserve and strengthen. [*Applause.*] Thank you. And which is why it is so distressing, because the consequences of this very disastrous thing with Jesse is that there is going to be a further rift driven between the two most visible of the minority and oppressed communities in this country, because when American racism or the American state is pressured, that expresses itself in either anti-Semitism or racism. We both know that. And that is why the alliance has to be preserved, and we've got to go beyond this very temporary thing.

BALDWIN: Thank you, Mike. Yes?

STUDENT: I have a question on anti-Semitism and Israelis or Jews doing America's dirty work. Has Jackson made any censorious remarks about Israeli arms sales to South Africa? And could you maybe talk about how Jackson might take a position on Israel and arm sales to South Africa?

BALDWIN: As far as I know, Jesse has said nothing about arms sales to South Africa, and I don't think he will, you know. The arms sales to South Africa on the part of Israel are again an example of the traditional role that Jews have often played in Christendom. It is, uh . . . After all, the state of Israel, as a state, that is to say, in terms of who is responsible for it, where the money comes from, is a—what is a polite word we use?—it is a Western state, it is a Western creation, it is a Western responsibility, isn't it? And Israel selling arms to Israel, selling arms . . . I mean, South Africa, well, we all know that. I think it would serve very little purpose to single out Israel as the supplier of arms to South Africa when the real supplier of arms, not only to South Africa but to many, many other parts of the world, is not the state of Israel, but France, England, this country above all—you see what I'm saying? The state of South Africa, the state of Johannesburg, cannot be blamed on Israel—you see what I'm saying?

STUDENT: Yes, I [*inaudible*] the accusation of anti-Semitism [*inaudible*].

BALDWIN: I think it would be a red herring; I think it would be a false trail— you see what I'm saying? It is not important in the context in which I am speaking that Israel can be accused of selling arms to [South Africa]. It is a distraction. In fact, the Western world is involved with selling arms not only to South Africa but to various other parts of the globe to keep, to maintain, the status quo. And Israel is simply a part of that structure. Where was I? Yes, ma'am?

STUDENT: I just wanted to say that when you said [*inaudible*].

BALDWIN: I can't hear you. I'm sorry.

STUDENT: I'm sorry. I don't know your name, but the professor—

THELWELL: Mike Thelwell.

STUDENT: What you said was very important, but the one thing that he did say was that also the Jews could be the blacks' worst enemy.

BALDWIN: He said what?

STUDENT: He said that the Jews also could be the blacks' worst enemies.

BALDWIN: He said they could be formidable enemies also.

THELWELL: I said that the Jewish organizations could be formidable allies and could make formidable enemies.

STUDENT: Formidable enemies, okay. I'm sorry, I don't think I understand . . . But this seems to be something that is just influenced or brought down by the American system when we choose, as you said, to make a distinction between the true safety over honor, and I think this is something that is influenced by the American system and that this is where the distinction comes, where the system itself is the instrumental factor which separates minorities and we've been able to cause that . . .

BALDWIN: Well, the system is made for that. That is what it intends to do.

STUDENT: Yeah, and it just weakens the structural or the pattern [*inaudible*] by Jews and blacks together as a whole. I know on a personal level that it is obvious that the similarities are there but on a political level we seem to always see the separation that is trying to be, or how they are trying to separate us . . . the whole case with Jesse Jackson [*inaudible*] expounding on it.

BALDWIN: On the political level your options are, in principle at least, very different from mine. On the political level your options are white, you know, and it's up to you.

STUDENT: What do you mean by that?

BALDWIN: Well, you are legally white in this country. I mean, I don't know if you are white, but legally you're white, and your political options, your social options, are, at least in principle, very different from that of any black person—you see what I mean? And the system knows that very well, and plays on that very well. It is very hard for a person to give up safety. The system knows that very well, and it can divide us and keep us both in the same place forever as long as we go for it, as long as we don't see what they are doing. As long as you don't see or I don't see—you see what I'm saying?

STUDENT: Right, but I would think it's also a fact that legally . . . I'm legally a woman, so these things come into play also.

BALDWIN: Yeah, of course, but you are the one who has to make the choice concerning these realities.

STUDENT: Right. [*inaudible*]

STUDENT: If you think that her political priorities are white—

BALDWIN: I don't know what they are. I said the system assumes that they are white.

STUDENT: Okay, that is the question.

BALDWIN: Okay, wait a minute. You first, Okay.

STUDENT: If we accept that the essential character of the American heritage is immoral, do you then attribute to the elements of the civil rights movement which used these organs of immorality to achieve their aims—

BALDWIN: What do you mean, "organs of immorality"?

STUDENT: The courts and the political system established by the American heritage—do we consider them then as legitimizing or contributing to the immorality of the system?

BALDWIN: Well, no, I wouldn't put it that way. I think what the movement had to do, had no choice but to do, was to challenge.

STUDENT: But challenge through the system or challenge by repudiating it?

BALDWIN: One does both at the same time. You cannot take—I cannot take, you know—a blanket position, because you move according to where you can move. Of course, we had to begin with the courts, the legal system. And it is, you know . . . a proof of its immorality was the fact that it had to be attacked. The fact that it is immoral doesn't mean that it cannot change. It doesn't mean that human beings cannot change it. If you see what I mean. In fact we—What?

STUDENT: Transcendence [*inaudible*].

BALDWIN: Well, one is not obliged to be at the mercy of the institution. You made it and you can unmake it. You made it and you can remake it.

STUDENT: We didn't make it. We used it.

BALDWIN: So it's a way of trying to make it serve a human purpose. Isn't that the aim?

STUDENT: I'm not questioning that we did have a positive effect. I'm just asking whether or not you see that as again reaffirming an essentially immoral system by using it in that way, by using it as an organ of change.

BALDWIN: But all systems—for the sake of my argument, anyway, and in my experience—all systems are immoral, you know. Every system, social system, because it involves human beings in order to be made useful, has to be attacked and endlessly changed—you see what I'm saying? Where am I? I'll begin way in the back and move forward.

STUDENT: Okay, let me see if I've got your message so far. If you go into a black neighborhood being the middleman and the media ploy—

BALDWIN: The what?

STUDENT: —the media ploy on the Jesse Jackson issue, trying to divide and conquer, and the event was the creation of the federal state. How else could Jews [inaudible] in response to the possibility of what would happen if the Jews stopped being the middlemen—

BALDWIN: The Jews stopped being middlemen . . .

STUDENT: —and somehow form an alliance with all the other people who are being oppressed by this system? What do you think about that, is there that possibility?

BALDWIN: Well, you've asked me an absolutely impossible question. If American Jews, or Polish Jews for that matter, if such an alliance could be— well, let's leave it to America, let's limit it to America. If the American Jew joined forces with the Native American, the so-called American Indian, and the blacks and Hispanics, which is not impossible, it would be bringing New Jerusalem much closer, but it is not very likely to happen. It is not likely to happen for a great many reasons, one of them being the American inheritance, one of them being the difficulty of turning your back on . . . and also a certain confusion, even a certain modesty. Some people in the civil rights movement were very hesitant about trying to—and this is in the best sense—were very hesitant about trying to intrude on the black experience. They were not only afraid of it in a negative sense, but afraid of seeming to be impertinent, afraid of seeming to be presumptuous. There is that too. But it is unlikely that such a coalition will be formed very soon. People form coalitions of that kind when they cannot do anything else.

Yes, ma'am.

STUDENT 1: I don't know whether I can explain this in the way I want to—

STUDENT 2: Please stand.

BALDWIN: Please stand.

STUDENT 1: I don't know whether I can explain this in the way I want to, but I think a major misconception in all the ideas that are going around here is that all Jews have money and are capable—

BALDWIN: Have money?

STUDENT 1: —have money and are capable in general of being middlemen. I know as a Jew, there are a hell of a lot of poor Jews in the United States, and I think that most Jews realize that if they had dark skin or if they had corns or something, they'd be just as oppressed as anybody else and it's just because they are white and because we've been able to change our names from something really Jewish-sounding that we've been able to have the ability to succeed. So I, as a Jew and as a woman, tend to vote for people who are . . . support all people who support blacks, because I am black-oriented, and I don't see myself as being a middleman or being rich or anything else.

BALDWIN: Well, I wasn't accusing all Jews of being middlemen, and I certainly wasn't accusing them of being rich.

STUDENT 1: No, that's not what I meant. It's the whole idea here . . .

BALDWIN: What's the idea?

STUDENT 1: I don't know . . . that Jews do realize, I hope, more of them than a lot of people think, do realize they are minorities, but I hope that they do vote along the same lines that any other minority votes.

BALDWIN: Well, I would hope so too. But I will tell you something else, which is . . . I will tell you very briefly: if you weren't already a minority, you don't really want to be part of another one. [*Laughter from audience.*] There is that, too.

STUDENT 1: But you can form an alliance with—

BALDWIN: You can form an alliance, but it is always at the mercy of another option.

STUDENT 1: Yeah. Okay.

STUDENT: Do you mind if I just answer that gentleman's question back there—

BALDWIN: Please stand up.

STUDENT: Do you mind if I discuss a bit that question of that man back there about Jews and blacks and other minorities? Does Jesse Jackson's Rainbow Coalition include Jews?

BALDWIN: Of course. How could it not?

STUDENT: In light of what he said . . .

BALDWIN: In light of what he said . . . ?

STUDENT: . . . about Jews.

BALDWIN: In light of what he's allegedly said about Jews. What did he say about Jews?

STUDENT: He called them "Hymies" and New York City "Hymietown."

BALDWIN: Yes.

STUDENT: How should that be construed to mean . . . ?

BALDWIN: I can't answer that. I know that the Rainbow—

STUDENT: What does he then think about Jews being part of the Rainbow Coalition?

BALDWIN: Well, until, until he said that, I had no reason to wonder about it; neither did you. Now that he has made an anti-Semitic remark, one has the right to question everything. It is a . . . it's a very serious event, maybe a disastrous event. I can't answer the question otherwise.
     Yes, man.

STUDENT: Yes. As far as I am concerned, I'd like to speak up, I'd like to express my life, my experience, growing up in Philadelphia, and from my experience I see alliance with a Jewish group very difficult because of the experience I had. That is, the apartment that my family lives in, which has dozens of fire violations, is owned by a minority real estate lawyer. He knows this. The first lawyer, the first owner who was also there, he moved out. He moved out. He sold the building to another dude [*inaudible*]. And the violations still kept continuing, the fire violations. After three fires in one week [*inaudible*] still nothing happened. The fourth fire, we saw the people hanging out the windows screaming, almost to the point of jumping out and [*inaudible*]. Then the following day after the fire [*inaudible*], a very serious fire [*inaudible*] because, in fact, the next day the owners come around, they look around, they pull up in their Mercedes-Benz, then they look around and they leave. And then the building manager comes up, he doesn't even live in the building, he comes up and he says to me, "Oh, it's not that bad—the fire wasn't that bad." He had no idea. I wanted right then to shoot that man. I would have . . . When these kinds of situations occur, it's no way of getting around it [*inaudible*].

PROFESSOR JOHN BRACEY:* I don't think this is going to get anywhere, but we've got one announcement from Ernie. But what's remarkable to me in here is there's a room full of white people and black people in a tremendously tense situation that has tremendous social ramifications, and people are sitting here trying to work out ways to make some sense out of it. Twenty years ago there would have been a fight breaking out. Black people would have said "To hell with it," white people would have said . . . "I'm going back home to have some supper." And what you have here is a rather remarkable attempt for people to actually make a coalition work. I think you ought to congratulate yourselves. [*Applause.*] Nobody said any kind of rainbow was going to be formed without some thunderstorms. [*Applause.*]

(1984)

*A UMass Amherst professor of Afro-American studies since 1972.

To Crush a Serpent

Why do the heathen rage, and the people imagine a vain thing?
—PSALMS 2:1

I WAS A YOUNG EVANGELIST, preaching in Harlem and other black communities for about three years: "young" means adolescent. I was fourteen when I entered the pulpit and seventeen when I left.

Those were very crucial years, full of wonder, and one of the things I most wondered about was the fellowship of Christians in the United States of America.

My father and I were both black ministers working exclusively in black churches, which was due primarily to the fact that white Christians considered black people to be less human than themselves and certainly unqualified to deliver God's Word to white ears. (This fact was more vivid for my father than for me—at least in the beginning.)

Mountains of blasphemous rhetoric have been written to deny or defend this fact, but the white message comes across loud and clear: Jesus Christ and his Father are white, and the kingdom of heaven is no place for black people to start trying on their shoes.

White people justified this violation of the message of the Gospel by quoting Scripture (the Old Testament curse laid on the sons of Ham—

which curse, even if conceivable, had been obliterated by the blood of Christ) and the Pauline injunction concerning servants' obeying their masters.

It was impossible not to sense in this a self-serving moral cowardice. This caused me to regard white Christians and, especially, white ministers with a profound and troubled contempt. And, indeed, the terror that I could not suppress upon finally leaving the pulpit was mitigated by the revelation that now, at least, I would not be compelled—allowed—to spend eternity in their presence. (And I told God this—I was young enough for that and wondered where He would be.)

Adolescence, as white people in this country appear to be beginning to remember—in somewhat vindictive ways—is not the most tranquil passage in anybody's life. It is a virgin time, *the* virgin time, the beginning of the confirmation of oneself as *other.* Until adolescence, one is a boy or a girl. But adolescence means that one is becoming *male* or *female,* a far more devastating and impenetrable prospect.

Until adolescence, one's body is simply there, like one's shadow or the weather. With adolescence, this body becomes a malevolently unpredictable enemy, and it also becomes, for the first time, appallingly *visible.* Everybody sees it. *You* see it, though you have never taken any real notice of it before. You begin to hear it. And it begins to sprout odors, like airy invisible mushrooms. But this is not the worst. Other people also see it and hear it and smell it. You can scarcely guess what they see and hear and smell— can guess it dimly, only from the way they appear to respond to you.

But you are scarcely able to respond to the way people respond to you, concentrated as you are on the great war being waged in that awkward body, beneath those clothes—a secret war, as visible as the noonday sun.

It is not the best moment to be standing in the pulpit. Though, having said that, I must—to be honest—add that my ministry almost certainly helped me through my adolescence by giving me something larger than myself to be frightened about. And it preserved, as it were, an innocence that, in retrospect, protected me.

For, though I had been formed by sufficiently dire circumstance and moved in a severely circumscribed world, I was also just another curious, raunchy kid. I was able to see, later, watching other kids like the kid I had been, that this combination of innocence and eagerness can be a powerful aphrodisiac to adults and is perhaps the key to the young minister's force.

Or, more probably, only one of many keys. Certainly the depth of his belief is a mighty force; and when I was in the pulpit, I believed. The personal anguish counts for something, too: it was the personal anguish that made me believe that I believed. People do not know on what this anguish feeds, but they sense the anguish and they respond to it. My sexuality was on hold, for both women and men had tried to "mess" with me in the summer of my fourteenth year and had frightened me so badly that I found the Lord. The salvation I was preaching to others was fueled by the hope of my own.

I left the pulpit upon the realization that *my* salvation could not be achieved that way.

But it is worth stating this proposition in somewhat harsher terms.

An unmanageable distress had driven me to the altar, and once there, I was—at least for a while—cleansed. But at the same time, nothing had been obliterated: I was still a boy in trouble with himself and the streets around him. Salvation did not make time stand still or arrest the changes occurring in my body and my mind. Salvation did not change the fact that I was an eager sexual potential, in flight from the inevitable touch. And I knew that I was in flight, though I could not, then—*to save my soul!*—have told you from what I was fleeing.

And, at the same time, the shape of my terror became clearer and clearer: as hypnotic and relentless as the slow surfacing of characters written in invisible ink.

I threw all my anguish and terror into my sermons and I thus learned nearly all there was to know concerning my congregations. They trusted me because they sensed my anguish—and my anguish was the key to my love. I think I hoped to love them more than I would ever love any lover and, so, escape the terrors of this life.

It did not work out that way. The young male preacher is a sexual prize in quite another way than the female; and congregations are made up of men and women.

So, in time, a heavy weight fell on my heart. I did not want to become a liar. I did not want my love to become manipulation. I did not want my fear of my own desires to transform itself into power—into power, precisely, over those who feared and were therefore at the mercy of their own desires.

In my experience, the minister and his flock mirror each other. It demands a very rare, intrepid, and genuinely free and loving shepherd to challenge the habits and fears and assumptions of his flock and help them enter into the freedom that enables us to move to higher ground.

I was not that shepherd. And rather than betray the ministry, I left it.

It can be supposed, then, that I cannot take seriously—not, at least, as

Christian ministers—the present-day gang that calls itself the Moral Majority or its tongue-speaking relatives, such as follow the Right Reverend Robertson.

They have taken the man from Galilee as hostage. He does not know them and they do not know him.

Nowhere, in the brief and extraordinary passage of the man known as Jesus Christ, is it recorded that he ever upbraided his disciples concerning their carnality. These were rough, hard-working fishermen on the Sea of Galilee. Their carnality can be taken as given, and they would never have trusted or followed or loved a man who did not know that they were men and who did not respect their manhood. Jesus made wine at the wedding, for example, by way of a miracle or otherwise—anyone who has been to a black fish fry knows how miraculously wine can appear. He appears not to have despised Mary Magdalene and to have got on just fine with other ladies, notably Mary and Martha, and with the woman at the well. Not one of the present-day white fundamentalist preachers would have had the humility, the courage, the sheer presence of mind to have said to the mob surrounding the woman taken in adultery, "He that is without sin among you, let him first cast a stone," or the depth of perception that informs "Neither do I condemn thee: Go, and sin no more."

It is scarcely worth comparing the material well-being—or material aspirations—of these latter-day apostles with the poverty of Jesus. Whereas Jesus and his disciples were distrusted by the state largely because they respected the poor and shared everything, the fundamentalists of the present hour would appear not to know that the poor exist.

They are aided enormously in this blindness by the peculiar self-deception the American poor white applies to his own poverty. His poverty afflicts him with an eerie and paralyzing self-contempt, but he denies it: poverty is meant for niggers. And, at the same time, he is aware that the ministers he sees on TV and to whom he sends his nickels and dimes were once no better off than he: he recognizes each as kin, so to speak.

These ministers, however, are of no interest in themselves—at least of no more intrinsic interest than any Deep South sheriff. And, indeed, the ministers remind me of sheriffs and deputies I have encountered: the same lips, the same flat, slatelike eyes, the same self-righteous voices.

Now, I find it somewhat disturbing to mention the minister and the sheriff in the same breath, but I am black and they entered my life in the same breath. Both the white fundamentalist minister and the deputy are Christians—hard-core Christians, one might say. Both believe that they are

responsible, the one for divine law and the other for natural order. Both
believe that they are able to define and privileged to impose law and order;
and both, historically and actually, know that law and order are meant to
keep me in my place.

Or I can put it another way, make another suggestion. Race and religion, it has been remarked, are fearfully entangled in the guts of this
nation, so profoundly that to speak of the one is to conjure up the other.
One cannot speak of sin without referring to blackness, and blackness
stalks our history and our streets. Therefore, in many ways, perhaps in the
deepest ways, the minister and the sheriff were hired by the Republic to
keep the Republic white—to keep it free from sin. But sin is no respecter of
skin: Sin stains the soul. Therefore, again and again, the Republic is con-
vulsed with the need for exorcism—sin has not only come to town but is in
bed with us, churning out white niggers.

So something must be done. And what must be done, each time, is to
attack the sexual possibility, to make the possibility of the private life as
fugitive as that of a fleeing nigger.

The fundamentalist ministers remind me of my time in the pulpit, of
ministers I have known, and of my own choices. In some of my encounters
with ministers, I found myself dealing with people from whose lives all
possibility of earthly joy had fled. Joy was not even, to judge from the endless empty plain behind their eyes, a memory. And they could recognize, in
others, joy or the possibility of joy only as a mighty threat—as something,
as they put it, obscene.

The very first time I saw this—without knowing what I was seeing—
was shortly after my conversion. I was not yet in the pulpit, so I was still
thirteen.

The deacon of the church in which I had been converted was leaving to
go to another church. This deacon's youngest son was my best friend, and
this family had become my second family. They had been accused by the
elders of the church of "walking disorderly." I had no idea what this meant,
but I was told that if I did not stop seeing these people, I, too, would be
walking disorderly. I concluded that walking disorderly meant that I had to
choose between my friends and this particular church, and so I decided to
walk disorderly and leave with my friends.

As I was leaving the church that night, the pastor's aide, a woman from
Finland and the only white woman in our church, grabbed my arm as I
started down the steps. She was standing just above me, leaning on the railing, dressed in white.

I was standing at the top of a steep flight of steps, and she had me off balance.

I knew that she knew this.

Her face and her eyes seemed purple. I could not take my eyes from hers. Her lips seemed to be chewing and spitting out the air. She told me of the eternal torment that awaited boys like me. And, all the time, her grip on my arm tightened. She was hurting me, and I wanted to ask her to stop.

But, of course, she knew that she was hurting me. I wonder if she *knew* she knew it. She finally let me go, consigning me to perdition, and I grabbed the banister, just in time.

Quite a collision between a thirteen-year-old black boy and an aging, gaunt white woman—all in the name of Jesus and with my salvation as the motive.

But Jesus had nothing to do with it. Jesus would never have done that to me, nor attempted to make my salvation a matter for blackmail. The motive was buried deep within that woman, the decomposing corpse of her human possibilities fouling the air.

I was in love with my friend, as boys indeed can be at that age, but hadn't the faintest notion of what to do about it—not even in my imagination, which may suggest that the imagination is kicked off by memory. Or perhaps I simply refused to allow my imagination to wander, as it were, below the belt.

Judging from my experience, I think that all of the kids in the church were like that, which is certainly why a couple of us went mad. Others simply backslid—went "back into the world." One relentless and realistic matron, a widow, determined to keep her eighteen-year-old athlete in the flock, in the pulpit, and in his right mind, took him South and found him a bride and brought the son and the girl—who scarcely knew each other— back home. The entire operation could not have taken more than a week.

We went to see the groom one morning, and as we left, my friend yelled, "Don't do anything *we* wouldn't do!"

The groom responded, with a lewd grin, "You all better not be doing what *I'm* doing!"

Which suggests that we endured our repression with a certain good humor, at least for a time.

The Bible is full of prohibitions, tribal, domestic, practical, profound, or seemingly useless; so the way of the transgressor is hard, is it? Thanks a lot.

We are not told that the way of the transgressor is *wrong,* nor are we told what a transgression is.

This means that I was challenged to discover for myself the meaning of the word "transgressor": or the meaning of the Word. This challenge became the key to my journey through the Bible.

For example, it seemed to me that those people in Hitler's Germany who opposed the slaughter of, among others, the Jews, were transgressors. So was Mrs. Rosa Parks in Montgomery, Alabama, on the day she refused to surrender her seat on the bus to a white man. Where were the white Christian ministers then? (Christ was there. Mrs. Parks will tell you so.) A transgressor was the one white woman out of a white multitude who sat on the bus-stop bench in Charlotte to console the lone black girl whose life had been threatened by a mob of white Christians because she wanted to go to school. The South African horror was perceived and confronted by very few people: the Christian church cannot be numbered among those few. The Christian ministers who perceived the moral and actual horror of apartheid were transgressors. So are certain Catholic priests today, and so, for that matter, was the late Dr. Martin Luther King Jr.

The Bible is not a simple or a simple-minded book, and it is not to be reduced to a cowardly system of self-serving pieties.

The most crucial and celebrated biblical prohibition, "Thou shalt not kill," is observed by virtually no one, either in or out of the Bible; and Christ recognizes—in ways having nothing to do with his desire or intention—that he brings "not . . . peace, but a sword."

In other words, you can glide through the Bible and settle for the prohibitions that suit you best.

The prohibitions that suit the fundamentalists best all involve the flesh.

And here I must, frankly, declare myself handicapped, even, or perhaps especially, as a former minister of the Gospel.

Salvation is not precipitated by the terror of being consumed in hell: this terror itself places one in hell. Salvation is preceded by the recognition of sin, by conviction, by repentance. Sin is not limited to carnal activity, nor are the sins of the flesh the most crucial or reverberating of our sins. Salvation is not flight from the wrath of God; it is accepting and reciprocating the love of God. Salvation is not separation. It is the beginning of union with all that is or has been or will ever be.

It is impossible to claim salvation and also believe that, in this life or in any life to come, one is better than another.

Or let me try to put it another way. Salvation is as real, as mighty, and as impersonal as the rain, and it is yet as private as the rain in one's face. It is never accomplished; it is to be reaffirmed every day and every hour. There is absolutely no salvation without love: this is the wheel in the middle of the wheel. Salvation does not divide. Salvation connects, so that one sees oneself in others and others in oneself. It is not the exclusive property of any dogma, creed, or church. It keeps the channel open between oneself and however one wishes to name That which is greater than oneself. It has absolutely nothing to do with one's fortunes or one's circumstances in one's passage through this world. It is a mighty fortress, even in the teeth of ruin or at the gates of death. It protects one from nothing except one thing: one will never curse God or man.

Salvation repudiates condemnation, since we all have the right, for many reasons, to condemn one another. Condemnation is easier than wonder and obliterates the possibility of salvation, since condemnation is fueled by terror and self-hatred. I am speaking as the historical victim of the flames meant to exorcise the terrors of the mob, and I am also speaking as an actual potential victim.

Those ladders to fire—the burning of the witch, the heretic, the Jew, the nigger, the faggot—have always failed to redeem, or even to change in any way whatever, the mob. They merely epiphanize and force their connection on the only plain on which the mob can meet: The charred bones connect its members and give them a reason to speak to one another, for the charred bones are the sum total of their individual self-hatred, externalized. The burning or lynching or torturing gives them something to talk about. They dare no other subject, certainly not the forbidden subject of the bloodstained self. They dare not trust one another.

One of them may be next.

And this accounts for the violence of our TV screen and cinema, a violence far more dangerous than pornography. What we are watching is a compulsive reliving of the American crimes; what we are watching with the Falwells and Robertsons is an attempt to exorcise ourselves.

This demands, indeed, a simple-mindedness quite beyond the possibilities of the human being. Complexity is our only safety and love is the only key to our maturity.

And love is where you find it.

(1987)

PROFILES

The Fight: Patterson vs. Liston

Floyd Patterson (1935–2006) was twice world heavyweight boxing champion—the youngest to win the title (in 1956) and the first ever to lose and (in 1960) regain it. Sonny Liston (1932–1970) took the championship from Patterson by knockout. His nickname was the "Big Bear" and he was known for his powerful punches and jabs. The famous match had originally been scheduled to take place in New York City, but due to Liston's criminal record the event had to be moved to Chicago, Illinois, and took place on September 25, 1962.

On February 25, 1964, Liston would lose his crown to the twenty-two-year-old Cassius Clay. The next day Clay changed his name to Cassius X; a week later, to Muhammad Ali.

．　　．　　．

WE, THE WRITERS—A WORD I am using in its most primitive sense—arrived in Chicago about ten days before the baffling, bruising, an unbelievable two minutes and six seconds at Comiskey Park. We will get to all that later. I know nothing whatever about the Sweet Science or the Cruel

Profession or the Poor Boy's Game. But I know a lot about pride, the poor boy's pride, since that's my story and will, in some way, probably, be my end.

There was something vastly unreal about the entire bit, as though we had all come to Chicago to make various movies and then spent all our time visiting the other fellow's set—on which no cameras were rolling. Dispatches went out every day, typewriters clattered, phones rang; each day, carloads of journalists invaded the Patterson or Liston camps, hung around until Patterson or Liston appeared; asked lame, inane questions, always the same questions; went away again, back to those telephones and typewriters; and informed a waiting, anxious world, or at least a waiting, anxious editor, what Patterson and Liston had said or done that day. It was insane and desperate, since neither of them ever really *did* anything. There wasn't anything for them *to* do, except train for the fight. But there aren't many ways to describe a fighter in training—it's muscle and sweat and grace, it's the same thing over and over—and since neither Patterson nor Liston were doing much boxing, there couldn't be any interesting thumbnail sketches of their sparring partners. The "feud" between Patterson and Liston was as limp and tasteless as British roast lamb. Patterson is really far too much of a gentleman to descend to feuding with anyone, and I simply never believed, especially after talking with Liston, that he had the remotest grudge against Patterson. So there we were, hanging around, twiddling our thumbs, drinking Scotch, and telling stories, and trying to make copy out of nothing. And waiting, of course, for the Big Event, which would justify the monumental amounts of time, money, and energy which were being expended in Chicago.

Neither Patterson nor Liston has the *color,* or the instinct for drama, which is possessed to such a superlative degree by the marvelous Archie Moore and the perhaps less marvelous, but certainly vocal, and rather charming, Cassius Clay. In the matter of color, a word which I am not now using in its racial sense, the press room far outdid the training camps. There were not only the sportswriters, who had come, as I say, from all over the world: there were also the boxing greats, scrubbed and sharp and easygoing, Rocky Marciano, Barney Ross, Ezzard Charles, and the King, Joe Louis, and Ingemar Johansson, who arrived just a little before the fight and did not impress me as being easygoing at all. Archie Moore's word for him is "desperate," and he did not say this with any affection. There were the ruined boxers, stopped by an unlucky glove too early in their careers, who seemed to be treated with the tense and embarrassed affection

reserved for faintly unsavory relatives, who were being used, some of
them, as sparring partners. There were the managers and trainers, who, in
public anyway, and with the exception of Cus D'Amato, seemed to have
taken, many years ago, the vow of silence. There were people whose functions were mysterious indeed, certainly unnamed, possibly unnamable,
and, one felt, probably, if undefinably, criminal. There were hangers-on
and protégés, a singer somewhere around, whom I didn't meet, owned by
Patterson, and another singer owned by someone else—who couldn't sing,
everyone agreed, but who didn't have to, being so loaded with personality—and there were some improbable-looking women, turned out, it
would seem, by a machine shop, who didn't seem, really, to walk or talk,
but rather to gleam, click, and glide, with an almost soundless meshing of
gears. There were some pretty incredible girls, too, at the parties, impecca-
bly blank and beautiful and rather incredibly vulnerable. There were the
parties and the postmortems and the gossip and speculations and recollec-
tions and the liquor and the anecdotes, and dawn coming up to find you
leaving somebody else's house or somebody else's room or the Playboy
Club; and Jimmy Cannon, Red Smith, Milton Gross, Sandy Grady, and A. J.
Liebling; and Norman Mailer, Gerald Kersh, Budd Schulberg, and Ben
Hecht—who arrived, however, only for the fight and must have been left
with a great deal of time on his hands—and Gay Talese (of the *Times*), and
myself. Hanging around in Chicago, hanging on the lightest word, or
action, of Floyd Patterson and Sonny Liston.

I am not an aficionado of the ring, and haven't been since Joe Louis lost
his crown—*he* was the last great fighter for me—and so I can't really make
comparisons with previous events of this kind. But neither, it soon struck
me, could anybody else. Patterson was, in effect, the *moral* favorite—people *wanted* him to win, either because they liked him, though many people
didn't, or because they felt that his victory would be salutary for boxing
and that Liston's victory would be a disaster. But no one could be said to be
enthusiastic about either man's record in the ring. The general feeling
seemed to be that Patterson had never been tested, that he was the champion, in effect, by default; though, on the other hand, everyone attempted
to avoid the conclusion that boxing had fallen on evil days and that Patterson had fought no worthy fighters because there were none. The desire to
avoid speculating too deeply on the present state and the probable future
of boxing was responsible, I think, for some very odd and stammering talk
about Patterson's personality. (This led Red Smith to declare that he didn't
feel that sportswriters had any business trying to be psychiatrists, and that

he was just going to write down who hit whom, how hard, and where, and the hell with why.) And there was very sharp disapproval of the way he has handled his career, since he has taken over most of D'Amato's functions as a manager, and is clearly under no one's orders but his own. "In the old days," someone complained, "the manager told the fighter what to do, and he did it. You didn't have to futz around with the guy's *temperament*, for Christ's sake." Never before had any of the sportswriters been compelled to deal directly with the fighter instead of with his manager, and all of them seemed baffled by this necessity and many were resentful. I don't know how they got along with D'Amato when he was running the entire show—D'Amato can certainly not be described as either simple or direct— but at least the figure of D'Amato was familiar and operated to protect them from the oddly compelling and touching figure of Floyd Patterson, who is quite probably the least likely fighter in the history of the sport. And I think that part of the resentment he arouses is due to the fact that he brings to what is thought of—quite erroneously—as a simple activity a ter- rible note of complexity. This is his personal style, a style which strongly suggests that most un-American of attributes, privacy, the will to privacy; and my own guess is that he is still relentlessly, painfully shy—he lives gal- lantly with his scars, but not all of them have healed—and while he has found a way to master this, he has found no way to hide it; as, for example, another miraculously tough and tender man, Miles Davis, has managed to do. Miles's disguise would certainly never fool anybody with sense, but it keeps a lot of people away, and that's the point. But Patterson, tough and proud and beautiful, is also terribly vulnerable, and looks it.

I met him, luckily for me, with Gay Talese, whom he admires and trusts. I say "luckily" because I'm not a very aggressive journalist, don't know enough about boxing to know which questions to ask, and am simply not able to ask a man questions about his private life. If Gay had not been there, I am not certain how I would ever have worked up my courage to say anything to Floyd Patterson—especially after having sat through, or suffered, the first, for me, of many press conferences. I only sat through two with Patterson, silently, and in the back—he, poor man, had to go through it every day, sometimes twice a day. And if I don't know enough about boxing to know which questions to ask, I must say that the boxing experts are not one whit more imaginative, though they were, I thought, sometimes rather more insolent. It was a curious insolence, though, veiled, tentative, uncertain—they couldn't be sure that Floyd wouldn't give them as good as he got. And this led, again, to that curious resentment I mentioned earlier, for they were forced, perpetually, to speculate about the man instead of the boxer. It doesn't appear to have occurred yet to many members of the press that one of the reasons their relations with Floyd are so frequently strained is that he has no reason, on any level, to trust them, and no reason to believe that they would be capable of hearing what he had to say, even if he could say it. Life's far from being as simple as most sportswriters would like to have it. The world of sports, in fact, is far from being as simple as the sports pages often make it sound.

Gay and I drove out, ahead of all the other journalists, in a Hertz car, and got to the camp at Elgin while Floyd was still lying down. The camp was very quiet—bucolic, really—when we arrived: set in the middle of small, rolling hills; four or five buildings; a tethered goat, the camp mascot; a small green tent containing a Spartan cot; lots of cars. "They're very car-conscious here," someone said of Floyd's small staff of trainers and helpers "Most of them have two cars." We ran into some of them standing around and talking on the grounds, and Buster Watson, a close friend of Floyd's, stocky, dark, and able, led us into the press room. Floyd's camp was actually Marycrest Farm, the twin of a Chicago settlement house, which works, on a smaller scale but in somewhat the same way, with disturbed and deprived children, as does Floyd's New York alma mater, the Wiltwyck School for Boys. It is a Catholic institution—Patterson is a converted Catholic—and the interior walls of the building in which the press conferences took place were decorated with vivid mosaics, executed by the children in colored beans, of various biblical events. There was an extraordinarily effective crooked cross, executed in charred wood, hanging high on one of the walls. There were two doors to the building in which the two press agents worked, one saying "Caritas," the other saying "Veritas." It seemed an incongruous setting for the life being lived there, and the event being prepared, but Ted Carroll, the Negro press agent, a tall man with white hair and a knowledgeable, weary, gentle face, told me that the camp was like the man. "The man lives a secluded life. He's like this place— peaceful and faraway." It was not all that peaceful, of course, except naturally; it was otherwise menaced and inundated by hordes of human beings, from small boys who wanted to be boxers to old men who remembered Jack Dempsey as a kid. The signs on the road pointing the way to Floyd Patterson's training camp were perpetually carried away by souvenir hunters. ("At first," Ted Carroll said, "we were worried that maybe they were carrying them away for another reason—you know, the usual hassle— but no, they just want to put them in the rumpus room.") We walked about with Ted Carroll for a while and he pointed out to us the house—white, with green shutters, somewhat removed from the camp and on a hill—in which Floyd Patterson lived. He was resting now, and the press conference had been called for three o'clock, which was nearly three hours away. But he would be working out before the conference. Gay and I left Ted and wandered close to the house. I looked at the ring, which had been set up on another hill near the house, and examined the tent. Gay knocked lightly on Floyd's door. There was no answer, but Gay said that the radio was on. We sat down in the sun, near the ring, and speculated on Floyd's training habits, which kept him away from his family for such long periods of time.

Presently, here he came across the grass, loping, rather, head down, with a small, tight smile on his lips. This smile seems always to be there when he is facing people and disappears only when he begins to be comfortable. Then he can laugh, as I never heard him laugh at a press conference, and the face which he watches so carefully in public is then, as it were, permitted to be its boyish and rather surprisingly zestful self. He greeted Gay, and took sharp, covert notice of me, seeming to decide that if I were with Gay, I was probably all right. We followed him into the gym, in which a large sign faced us, saying, "So we being many are one body in Christ." He went through his workout, methodically, rigorously, pausing every now and again to disagree with his trainer, Dan Florio, about the time—he insisted that Dan's stopwatch was unreliable—or to tell Buster that there weren't enough towels, to ask that the windows be closed. "You threw a good right hand that time," Dan Florio said; and, later, "Keep the right hand *up. Up!*" "We got a floor scale that's no good," Floyd said, cheerfully. "Sometimes I weigh two hundred, sometimes I weigh 'eighty-eight." And we watched him jump rope, which he must do according to some music in his head, very beautiful and gleaming and faraway, like a boy saint helplessly dancing and seen through the steaming windows of a storefront church.

We followed him into the house when the workout was over, and sat in the kitchen and drank tea; he drank chocolate. Gay knew that I was somewhat tense as to how to make contact with Patterson—my own feeling was that he had a tough enough row to hoe, and that everybody should just leave him alone; how would *I* like it if I were forced to answer inane questions every day concerning the progress of my work?—and told Patterson about some of the things I'd written. But Patterson hadn't heard of me, or read anything of mine. Gay's explanation, though, caused him to look directly at me, and he said, "I've seen you someplace before. I don't know where, but I know I've seen you." I hadn't seen him before, except once, with Liston, in the commissioner's office, when there had been a spirited fight concerning the construction of Liston's boxing gloves, which were "just about as flat as the back of my hand," according to a sportswriter, "just like wearing no gloves at all." I felt certain, considering the number of people and the tension in that room, that he could not have seen me *then*—but we do know some of the same people, and have walked very often on the same streets. Gay suggested that he had seen me on TV. I had hoped that the contact would have turned out to be more personal, like a mutual friend or some activity connected with the Wiltwyck School, but Floyd now remembered the subject of the TV debate he had seen—the race problem, of course—and his face lit up. "I *knew* I'd seen you somewhere!" he said, triumphantly, and looked at me for a moment with the same brotherly pride I felt—and feel—in him.

By now he was, with good grace but a certain tense resignation, preparing himself for the press conference. I gather that there are many people who enjoy meeting the press—and most of them, in fact, were presently in Chicago—but Floyd Patterson is not one of them. I think he hates being put on exhibition, he doesn't believe it is real; while he is terribly conscious of the responsibility imposed on him by the title which he held, he is also afflicted with enough imagination to be baffled by his position. And he is far from having acquired the stony and ruthless perception which will allow him to stand at once within and without his fearful notoriety. Anyway, we trailed over to the building in which the press waited, and Floyd's small, tight, shy smile was back.

But he has learned, though it must have cost him a great deal, how to handle himself. He was asked about his weight, his food, his measurements, his morale. He had been in training for nearly six months ("Is that necessary?" "I just like to do it that way"), had boxed, at this point, about 162 rounds. This was compared to his condition at the time of the first fight with Ingemar Johansson. "Do you believe that you were overtrained for that fight?" "Anything I say now would sound like an excuse." But, later, "I was careless—not overconfident, but careless." He had allowed himself to be surprised by Ingemar's aggressiveness. "Did you and D'Amato fight over your decision to fight Liston?" The weary smile played at the corner of Floyd's mouth, and though he was looking directly at his interlocutors, his eyes were veiled. "No." Long pause. "Cus knows that I do what I want to do—ultimately, he accepted it." Was he surprised by Liston's hostility?

No. Perhaps it had made him a bit more determined. Had he anything against Liston personally? "No. I'm the champion and I want to remain the champion." Had he and D'Amato ever disagreed before? "Not in relation to my opponents." Had he heard it said that, as a fighter, he lacked vicious-ness? "Whoever said that should see the fights I've won without being vicious." And why was he fighting Liston? "Well," said Patterson, "it was my decision to take the fight. You gentlemen disagreed, but you were the ones who placed him in the number-one position, so I felt that it was only right. Liston's criminal record is behind him, not before him." "Do you feel that you've been accepted as a champion?" Floyd smiled more tightly than ever and turned toward the questioner. "No," he said. Then, "Well, I have to be accepted as the champion—but maybe not a good one." "Why do you say," someone else asked, "that the opportunity to become a great champion will never arise?" "Because," said Floyd, patiently, "you gentle-men will never let it arise." Someone asked him about his experiences when boxing in Europe—what kind of reception had he enjoyed? Much greater and much warmer than here, he finally admitted, but added, with a weary and humorous caution, "I don't want to say anything derogatory about the United States. I am satisfied." The press seemed rather to flinch from the purport of this grim and vivid little joke, and switched to the sub-ject of Liston again. Who was most in awe of whom? Floyd had no idea, he said, but, "Liston's confidence is on the surface. Mine is within."

And so it seemed to be indeed, as, later, Gay and I walked with him through the flat midwestern landscape. It was not exactly that he was less tense—I think that he is probably always tense, and it is that, and not his glass chin, or a lack of stamina, which is his real liability as a fighter—but he was tense in a more private, more bearable way. The fight was very much on his mind, of course, and we talked of the strange battle about the boxing gloves, and the commissioner's impenetrable and apparent bias toward Liston, though the difference in the construction of the gloves, and the possible meaning of this difference, was clear to everyone. The gloves had been made by two different firms, which was not the usual procedure, and, though they were the same standard eight-ounce weight, Floyd's gloves were the familiar, puffy shape, with most of the weight of the padding over the fist, and Liston's were extraordinarily slender, with most of the weight of the padding over the wrist. But we didn't talk only of the fight, and I can't now remember all the things we *did* talk about. I mainly remember Floyd's voice, going cheerfully on and on, and the way his face kept changing, and the way he laughed; I remember the glimpse I got of him then, a man more complex than he was yet equipped to know, a hero for many children who were still trapped where he had been, who might not have survived without the ring, and who yet, oddly, did not really seem to belong there. I dismissed my dim speculations, that afternoon, as sentimental inaccuracies, rooted in my lack of knowledge of the boxing world, and corrupted with a guilty chauvinism. But now I wonder. He told us that his wife was coming in for the fight, against his will, "in order," he said, indescribably, "to *console* me if—" and he made, at last, a gesture with his hand, downward.

Liston's camp was very different, an abandoned racetrack in, or called, Aurora Downs, with wire gates and a uniformed cop, who lets you in, or doesn't. I had simply given up the press conference bit, since they didn't teach me much, and I couldn't ask those questions. Gay Talese couldn't help me with Liston, and this left me floundering on my own until Sandy Grady called up Liston's manager, Jack Nilon, and arranged for me to see Liston for a few minutes alone the next day. Liston's camp was far more outspoken concerning Liston's attitude toward the press than Patterson's. Liston didn't like most of the press, and most of them didn't like him. But I didn't, myself, see any reason why he *should* like them, or pretend to— they had certainly never been very nice to him, and I was sure that he saw in them merely some more ignorant, uncaring white people, who, no matter how fine we cut it, had helped to cause him so much grief. And this impression was confirmed by reports from people who *did* get along with him—Wendell Phillips and Bob Teague, who are both Negroes, but rather rare and salty types, and Sandy Grady, who is not a Negro, but is certainly rare, and very probably salty. I got the impression from them that Liston was perfectly willing to take people as they were, if they would do the same for him. Again, I was not particularly appalled by his criminal background, believing, rightly or wrongly, that I probably knew more about the motives and even the necessity of this career than most of the white press could. The only relevance Liston's—presumably previous—associations should have been allowed to have, it seemed to me, concerned the possible effect of these on the future of boxing. Well, while the air was thick with rumor and gospel on this subject, I really cannot go into it without risking, at the very least, being sued for libel; and so, one of the most fascinating aspects of the Chicago story will have to be left in the dark. But the Sweet Science is not, in any case, really so low on shady types as to be forced to depend on Liston. The question is to what extent Liston is prepared to cooperate with whatever powers of darkness there are in boxing; and the extent of his cooperation, we must suppose, must depend, at least partly, on the extent of his awareness. So that there is nothing unique about the position in which he now finds himself and nothing unique about the speculation which now surrounds him.

I got to his camp at about two o'clock one afternoon. Time was running out, the fight was not more than three days away, and the atmosphere in the camp was, at once, listless and electric. Nilon looked as though he had not slept and would not sleep for days, and everyone else rather gave the impression that they wished they could—except for three handsome Negro ladies, related, I supposed, to Mrs. Liston, who sat, rather self-consciously, on the porch of the largest building on the grounds. They may have felt as I did, that training camps are like a theater before the curtain goes up, and if you don't have any function in it, you're probably in the way.

Liston, as we all know, is an enormous man, but surprisingly trim. I had already seen him work out, skipping rope to a record of "Night Train," and, while he wasn't nearly, for me, as moving as Patterson skipping rope in silence, it was still a wonderful sight to see. The press has really maligned Liston very cruelly, I think. He is far from stupid; is not, in fact, stupid at all. And, while there is a great deal of violence in him, I sensed no cruelty at all. On the contrary, he reminded me of big, black men I have known who acquired the reputation of being tough in order to conceal the fact that they weren't hard. Anyone who cared to could turn them into taffy.

Anyway, I liked him, liked him very much. He sat opposite me at the table, sideways, head down, waiting for the blow: for Liston knows, as only the inarticulately suffering can, just how inarticulate he is. But let me clarify that: I say "suffering" because it seems to me that he has suffered a great deal. It is in his face, in the silence of that face, and in the curiously distant light in the eyes—a light which rarely signals because there have been so few answering signals. And when I say "inarticulate," I really do not mean to suggest that he does not know how to talk. He is inarticulate in the way we all are when more has happened to us than we know how to express; and inarticulate in a particularly Negro way—he has a long tale to tell which no one wants to hear. I said, "I can't ask you any questions because everything's been asked. Perhaps I'm only here, really, to say that I wish you well." And this was true, even though I wanted Patterson to win. Anyway, I'm glad I said it, because he looked at me then, really for the first time, and he talked to me for a little while.

And what had hurt him most, somewhat to my surprise, was not the general press reaction to him, but the Negro reaction. "Colored people," he said, with great sorrow, "say they don't want their children to look up to me. Well, they ain't teaching their children to look up to Martin Luther King, either." There was a pause. "I wouldn't be no bad example if I was up there. I could tell a lot of those children what they need to know—because—I passed that way. I could make them *listen.*" And he spoke a little of what he would like to do for young Negro boys and girls, trapped in those circumstances which so nearly defeated him and Floyd, and from which neither can yet be said to have recovered. "I tell you one thing, though," he said, "if I was up there, I wouldn't bite my tongue." I could certainly believe that. And we discussed the segregation issue, and the role in it of those prominent Negroes who find him so distasteful. "I would never," he said, "go against my brother—we got to learn to stop fighting among our own." He lapsed into silence again. "They said they didn't want me to have the title. They didn't say that about Johansson." "They" were the Negroes. "*They* ought to know why I got some of the bum raps I got." But he was not suggesting that they were *all* bum raps. His wife came over, a very pretty woman, seemed to gather in a glance how things were going, and sat down. We talked for a little while of matters entirely unrelated to the fight, and then it was time for his workout, and I left. I felt terribly ambivalent, as many Negroes do these days, since we are all trying to decide, in one way or another, which attitude, in our terrible American dilemma, is the most effective: the disciplined sweetness of Floyd or the outspoken intransigence of Liston. *If I was up there, I wouldn't bite my tongue.* And Liston is a man aching for respect and responsibility. Sometimes we grow into our responsibilities and sometimes, of course, we fail them.

I left for the fight full of a weird and violent depression, which I traced partly to fatigue—it had been a pretty grueling time—partly to the fact that I had bet more money than I should have—on Patterson—and partly to the fact that *I* had had a pretty definitive fight with someone with whom I had hoped to be friends. And I was depressed about Liston's bulk and force and his twenty-five-pound weight advantage. I was afraid that Patterson might lose, and I really didn't want to see that. And it wasn't that I didn't like Liston. I just felt closer to Floyd.

I was sitting between Norman Mailer and Ben Hecht. Hecht felt about the same way that I did, and we agreed that if Patterson didn't get "stopped," as Hecht put it, "by a baseball bat," in the very beginning—if he could carry Liston for five or six rounds—he might very well hold the title. We didn't pay an awful lot of attention to the preliminaries—or I didn't; Hecht did; I watched the ballpark fill with people and listened to the vendors and the jokes and the speculations; and watched the clock.

From my notes: Liston entered the ring to an almost complete silence. Someone called his name, he looked over, smiled, and winked. Floyd entered, and got a hand. But he looked terribly small next to Liston, and my depression deepened.

My notes again: Archie Moore entered the ring, wearing an opera cape. Cassius Clay, in black tie, and as insolent as ever. Mickey Allen sang "The Star-Spangled Banner." When Liston was introduced, some people booed—they cheered for Floyd, and I think I know how this made Liston feel. It promised, really, to be one of the worst fights in history.

Well, I was wrong; it was scarcely a fight at all, and I can't but wonder who on earth will come to see the rematch, if there is one. Floyd seemed all right to me at first. He had planned for a long fight, and seemed to be feeling out his man. But Liston got him with a few bad body blows, and a few bad blows to the head. And no one agrees with me on this, but at one moment, when Floyd lunged for Liston's belly—looking, it must be said, like an amateur, wildly flailing—it seemed to me that some unbearable tension in him broke, that he lost his head. And, in fact, I nearly screamed, "Keep your head, baby!" but it was really too late. Liston got him with a left, and Floyd went down. I could not believe it. I couldn't hear the count, and though Hecht said, "It's over," and picked up his coat and left, I remained standing, staring at the ring, and only conceded that the fight was really over when two other boxers entered the ring. Then I wandered out of the ballpark, almost in tears. I met an old colored man at one of the exits, who said to me, cheerfully, "I've been robbed," and we talked about it for a while. We started walking through the crowds, and A. J. Liebling, behind us, tapped me on the shoulder and we went off to a bar, to mourn the very possible death of boxing, and to have a drink, with love, for Floyd.

(1963)

Sidney Poitier

THE FIRST TIME I MET SIDNEY, I walked up to him at an airport. He didn't know me, but I admired him very much, and I told him so. I've never done that with anyone, before or since, and Sidney looked at me as though he thought I was crazy, but he was very nice about it. Some years later, I really met him. We were both in Philadelphia. He was doing *A Raisin in the Sun*, and I was working with Kazan in *Sweet Bird of Youth*, and we hit it off.

Then, of course, years passed. Things happened to Sidney; things happened to me. All artists who are friends have a strange relationship to each other; each knows what the other is going through, even though you may see each other only briefly, at functions, at benefits, at airports; and this is especially true, I think, for black artists in this country, and especially over the last several years. It's ironical indeed, but it's only the black artists in this country—and it's only beginning to change now—who have been called upon to fulfill their responsibilities as artists and, at the same time, insist on their responsibilities as citizens. As Ruby Dee once said to me, when we were working on the Christmas boycott campaign following the murder of the four little girls in Birmingham, "Soon, there won't be enough colored people to go around." She wasn't joking—I might add that that statement has, today, a rather sinister ring.

As the years passed, and given the system in which all American artists, and especially all American actors, work, I began to tremble for Sidney. I must state candidly that I think most Hollywood movies are a thunderous waste of time, talent, and money, and I rarely see them. For example, I didn't think *Blackboard Jungle* was much of a movie—I know much more than *that* about the public-school system of New York—but I thought that Sidney was beautiful, vivid, and truthful in it. He somehow escaped the film's framework, so much so that until today, his is the only performance I remember. Nor was I overwhelmed by *Cry, the Beloved Country,* but Sidney's portrait, brief as it was, of the young priest was a moving miracle of indignation. That was the young Sidney, and I sensed that I was going to miss him, in exactly the same way I will always miss the young Marlon of *Truckline Cafe* and *Streetcar Named Desire.* But then, I miss the young Jimmy Baldwin, too.

All careers, if they are real careers—and there are not as many of these occurring as one might like to think—are stormy and dangerous, with turning points as swift and dizzying as hairbreadth curves on mountain roads. And I think that America may be the most dangerous country in the world for artists—whatever creative form they may choose. That would be all right if it were also exhilarating, but most of the time, it isn't. It's mostly sweat and terror. This is because the nature of the society isolates its artists so severely for their vision; penalizes them so mercilessly for their vision and endeavor; and the American form of recognition, fame and money, can be the most devastating penalty of all. This is not the artist's fault, though I think that the artist will have to take the lead in changing this state of affairs.

The isolation that menaces all American artists is multiplied a thousand times, and becomes absolutely crucial and dangerous, for all black artists. "Know whence you came," Sidney once said to me, and Sidney, his detractors to the contrary, *does* know whence he came. But it can become very difficult to remain in touch with all that nourishes you when you have arrived at Sidney's eminence and are in the interesting, delicate, and terrifying position of being part of a system that you know you have to change.

Let me put it another way: I wish that both Marlon and Sidney would return to the stage, but I can certainly see why they don't. Broadway is almost as expensive as Hollywood, is even more hazardous, is at least as incompetent, and the scripts, God knows, aren't any better. Yet I can't but feel that this is a great loss, both for the actor and the audience.

I will always remember seeing Sidney in *A Raisin in the Sun.* It says a great deal about Sidney, and it also says, negatively, a great deal about the regime under which American artists work, that that play would almost certainly never have been done if Sidney had not agreed to appear in it. Sidney has a fantastic presence on the stage, a dangerous electricity that is rare indeed and lights up everything for miles around. It was a tremendous thing to watch and to be made a part of. And one of the things that made it so tremendous was the audience. Not since I was a kid in Harlem, in the days of the Lafayette Theatre, had I seen so many black people in the theater. And they were there because the life on that stage said something to them concerning their own lives. The communion between the actors and the audience was a real thing; they nourished and re-created each other. This hardly ever happens in the American theater. And this is a much more sinister fact than we would like to think. For one thing, the reaction of that audience to Sidney and to that play says a great deal about the continuing and accumulating despair of the black people in this country, who find nowhere any faint reflection of the lives they actually lead. And it is for this reason that every Negro celebrity is regarded with some distrust by black people, who have every reason in the world to feel themselves abandoned.

I ought to add, for this also affects any estimate of any black star, that the popular culture certainly does not reflect the truth concerning the lives led by white people, either; but white Americans appear to be under the compulsion to dream, whereas black Americans are under the compulsion to awaken. And this fact is also sinister.

I am not a television fan, either, and I very much doubt that future generations will be vastly edified by what goes on on the American television screen. TV commercials drive me up the wall. And yet, as long as there is *that screen* and there are *those commercials,* it is important to tip the American people to the fact that black people also brush their teeth and shave and drink beer and smoke cigarettes—though it may take a little more time for the American people to recognize that we also shampoo our hair. It is of the utmost importance that a black child see on that screen *someone who looks like him.* Our children have been suffering from the lack of identifiable images for as long as our children have been born.

Yet, there's a difficulty, there's a rub, and it's precisely the nature of this difficulty that has brought Sidney under attack. The industry is compelled, given the way it is built, to present to the American people a self-perpetuating fantasy of American life. It considers that its job is to entertain the American people. Their concept of entertainment is difficult to distinguish from the use of narcotics, and to watch the TV screen for any length of time is to learn some really frightening things about the American sense of reality. *And the black face, truthfully reflected, is not only no part of this dream, it is antithetical to it.* And this puts the black performer in a rather grim bind. He knows, on the one hand, that if the reality of a black man's life were on that screen, it would destroy the fantasy totally. And on the other hand, he really has no right *not* to appear, not only because he must work, but also for all those people who need to see him. By the use of his own person, he must smuggle in a reality that he knows is not in the script. A celebrated black TV actor once told me that he did an entire show for the sake of *one line.* He felt that he could convey something very important with that *one line.* Actors don't write their scripts, and they don't direct them. Black people have no power in this industry at all. Furthermore, the actor may be offered dozens of scripts before anything even remotely viable comes along.

Sidney is now a superstar. This must baffle a great many people, as, indeed, it must baffle Sidney. He is an extraordinary actor, as even his detractors must admit, but he's been that for a long time, and that doesn't really explain his eminence. He's also extraordinarily attractive and winning and virile, but that could just as easily have worked against him. It's something of a puzzle. Speaking now of the image and not of the man, it has to do with a quality of pain and danger and some fundamental impulse to decency that both titillates and reassures the white audience. For example, I'm glad I didn't write *The Defiant Ones,* but I liked Sidney in it very much. And I suppose that his performance has something to do with what I mean by smuggling in reality. I remember one short scene, in close-up, when he's talking about his wife, who wants him to "be nice." Sidney's face, when he says, "She say, 'Be nice. Be nice,' " conveys a sorrow and humiliation rarely to be seen on our screen. But white people took that film far more seriously than black people did. When Sidney jumps off the train at the end because he doesn't want to leave his buddy, the white liberal people downtown were much relieved and joyful. But when black people saw him jump off the train, they yelled, "Get back on the train, you fool." That didn't mean that they hated Sidney: they just weren't going for the okey-doke. And if I point out that they were right, it doesn't mean that Sidney was wrong. That film was made to say something to white people. There was really nothing it *could* say to black people—except for the authority of Sidney's performance.

Black people have been robbed of everything in this country, and they don't want to be robbed of their artists. Black people particularly disliked *Guess Who's Coming to Dinner,* which I made a point of seeing, because they felt that Sidney was, in effect, being used against them. I'm now on very delicate ground, and I know it, but I can't really duck this issue, because it's been raised so often. I can't pretend that the movie meant anything to me. It seemed a glib, good-natured comedy in which a lot of able people were being wasted. But, I told myself, this movie wasn't made for *you*. And I really don't know the people for whom it *was* made. I moved out of their world, insofar as this is ever possible, a long time ago. I remember the cheerful English lady in a wine shop in London who had seen this movie and adored it and adored the star. She was a nice lady, and certainly not a racist, and it would simply have been an unjust waste of time to get angry with her for knowing so little about black people. The hard fact is that most people, of whatever color, don't know much about each other, because they don't care much about each other. Would the image projected by Sidney cause that English lady to be friendly to the next West Indian who walked into her shop? Would it cause her to *think*, in any real way, of the *reality*, the presence, the simple human *fact* of black people? Or was Sidney's black face simply, now, a part of a fantasy—the fantasy of her life, precisely—which she would never understand? This is a question posed by the communications media of the twentieth century, and it is not a question anyone can answer with authority. One is gambling on the human potential of an inarticulate and unknown consciousness—that of the people. This consciousness has never been of such crucial importance in the world before. But one knows that the work of the world gets itself done in very strange ways, by means of very strange instruments, and takes a very long time. And I also thought that *Guess Who's Coming to Dinner* may prove, in some bizarre way, to be a milestone, because it is really quite impossible to go any further in that particular direction. The next time, the kissing will have to start.

I thought of something else, something very difficult to convey. I remember a night in London, when Diana Sands was starring in *The Owl and the Pussycat*. There were about four or five of us, walking to some discotheque, and with us was a very angry, young, black cat. Across the street from us was Sidney's name in lights in some movie I've not seen. Now, I understand the angry, young, black cat, and he was right to be angry. He was not angry at Sidney, but at the world. But I knew there was no point in saying that, at the time I was born, the success of a Sidney Poitier or a Diana Sands was not to be imagined. I don't mean to congratulate the American people on what they like to call progress, because it certainly isn't. The careers of all black artists in this country prove that. Time passes and phenomena occur in time. The *presence* of Sidney, the precedent set, is of tremendous importance for people coming afterward. And perhaps that's what it's really all about—just that.

Sidney, as a black artist, and a man, is also up against the infantile, furtive sexuality of this country. Both he and Harry Belafonte, for example, are sex symbols, though no one dares admit that, still less to use them as any of the Hollywood he-men are used. In spite of the fabulous myths proliferating in this country concerning the sexuality of black people, black men are still used, in the popular culture, as though they had no sexual equipment at all. This is what black men, and black women, too, deeply resent.

I think it's important to remember, in spite of the fact we've been around so long, that Sidney is younger than I, and I'm not an old man yet. It takes a long time in this business, if you survive in it at all, to reach the eminence that will give you the power to change things. Sidney has that power now, to the limited extent that *anyone* in this business has. It will be very interesting to see what he does with it. In my mind, there's no limit to what he might become.

But Sidney, like all of us, is caught in a storm. Let me tell you one thing about him, which has to do with how black artists particularly need each other. Sidney had read *Another Country* before it came out. He liked it, and he knew how frightened I was about the book's reception. I'd been in Europe, and I came back for the publication because I didn't want anyone to think I was afraid to be here. My publisher gave a party at Big Wilt's Smalls Paradise in Harlem. Sidney came very early. I was ready to meet the mob, but I was scared to death, and Sidney knew it, and he walked me around the block and talked to me and helped me get myself together. And then he walked me back, and the party was starting. And when he realized that I was all right, he split. And I realized for the first time that he had only come for that. He hadn't come for the party at all.

And the following may also make a small, malicious point. There's speculation that the central figure of my new novel, who is a black actor, is based on Sidney. Nothing could be further from the truth, but people naturally think that, because when they look around them, Sidney's the only black actor they see. Well, that fact says a great deal more about this country than it says about black actors, or Sidney, or me.

(1968)

LETTERS

Letters from a Journey

When this selection of letters was published in the May 1963 issue of *Harper's* magazine, it was introduced by Baldwin's agent, Robert P. Mills, to whom these letters were largely addressed. Baldwin had been working on *Another Country* for five years when the editor of *The New Yorker* enticed Baldwin to travel to Africa and write about it. (He was also completing the essay "Down at the Cross," which would become a major part of *The Fire Next Time*.) Baldwin departed in September 1961, accompanied by his sister Paula, whom he would leave with friends in Paris. As a guest of the government, he first made a stop in Israel, a place which, according to Mills, Baldwin looked upon as a gateway to Africa. But due to time pressures he first made a detour to Turkey to finish his novel. He had also agreed to be a literary judge for the Prix International des Éditeurs sponsored by Grove Press, thus forcing him to be in Mallorca in late April of the following year.

. . .

Paris, September 15, 1961

I feel very strange and naked, but I guess that's good. Appetite seems to be returning, and I'm able to work. And Paris is still beautiful, in spite of its danger and sorrow and age.

Pray for me.

Israel, October 5

This is almost the only night I've had since I got here when it's been possible to write letters. Being a guest of the government really involves becoming an extremely well-cared-for parcel post package. But the visit seems, so far, to have been a great success: Israel and I seem to like each other. I've been trying, as usual, to do too many things at once and I've been keeping a diary of sorts of things as they happen—places I've been, people I've talked to—every night, when I come home. But I come home late and I get up early (the phone rings, and it's the hotel manager informing me that "my" car has arrived) and off I and the government go—tomorrow morning, for example, to the Negev and the Dead Sea. I am always worried about wearing out my welcome, and imagined I'd be gone by now: but no, they keep saying "Please don't hurry." Still, I'm leaving Monday morning.

I must say, it's rather nice to be in a situation in which I haven't got to count and juggle and sweat and be responsible for a million things that I'm absolutely unequipped to do. All I'm expected to do is observe, and, hopefully, to write about that which I've observed. This is not going to be easy; and yet, since this trip is clearly my prologue to Africa, it has become very important to me to assess what Israel makes me feel. In a curious way, since it really *does* function as a homeland, however beleaguered, you can't walk five minutes without finding yourself at a border, can't talk to anyone for five minutes without being reminded first of the mandate (British), then of the war—and of course the entire Arab situation, outside the country, and, above all, within, causes one to take a view of human life and right and wrong almost as stony as the land in which I presently find myself—well, to bring this thoroughly undisciplined sentence to a halt, the fact that Israel *is* a homeland for so many Jews (there are great faces here; in a way the whole world is here) causes me to feel my own homelessness more keenly than ever. (People say, "Where are you from?" And it causes me a tiny and resentful effort to say "New York"—what did *I* ever do to deserve so ghastly a birthplace?—and their faces fall.)

But just because my homelessness is so inescapably brought home to me, it begins, in some odd way, not only to be bearable, but to be a positive opportunity. It must be, must be made to be. My bones know, somehow, something of what waits for me in Africa. That is one of the reasons I have dawdled so long—I'm afraid. And, of course, I am playing it my own way, edging myself into it; it would be nice to be able to dream about Africa, but once I have been there, I will not be able to dream anymore. The truth is that there is something unutterably painful about the end of oppression—not that it *has* ended yet, on a black-white basis, I mean, but it *is* ending—and one flinches from the responsibility, which we all now face, of judging black people solely as people. Oh, well. I think of the poor Negroes of the U.S. who identify themselves with Africa, or imagine that they identify themselves with Africa—and on what basis? It would seem to be clear, but it is not: Africa has been black a long time, but American Negroes did not identify themselves with Africa until Africa became identified with power. This says something about poor human nature which indeed one would rather not be forced to see—enough of this. And at the same time, the continuing situation of the black people of this world, my awareness of the blandness with which white people commit and deny and defend their crimes, fill me with pain and rage. Well. This promises to be an extremely valuable journey.

Israel, October 8
Stood on a hill in Jerusalem today, looking over the border: the Arab-Israeli border. There is really something frightening about it. There is something insane about it, something which breaks the heart. I've been wandering up and down Israel for a couple of weeks now, have stayed in a kibbutz near the Gaza Strip, have been in an art colony near Haifa, wandered through bazaars; and indeed all of this, all I have seen, is Jewish—if you like. But it is really the Middle East, it has that spice and stink and violence and beauty, and it is not Jewish so much as it is Semitic; and I am very struck by the realization that the Semites were nomads and this is still, somehow, the atmosphere of the entire country.

What *is* a Jew? An old question, I know, but it presents itself to one with great force once one is in this country. Jehovah, Christ, and Allah all came out of this rocky soil, this fragile handkerchief at the gate of the Middle East. And the people—the Jews—of this beleaguered little country are united, as far as I can tell, by two things only (and perhaps "united" is too strong a word). One is the experience of the last world war and the memory of the six million—which is to say that they are united by the evil that is in the world, that evil which has victimized them so savagely and so long. But is this enough to make a personality, to make an identity, to make a religion? (And *what*, precisely, is a religion? And how dreary, how disturbing, to find oneself asking, now, questions which one supposed had been answered forever!) But one is forced to ask these kindergarten questions because the only other thing which unites the Jews here is the resurrection of the Hebrew language.

The most religious—or, in any case, the most orthodox—people here are the Yemenites, who are also the most lively, and who seem to produce the only artists—well, that is not quite true; but it is almost true: they produce the only artists who can be said to be working out of the Jewish or Semitic or nomadic past. They are also at the bottom of the social ladder, coming from the most primitive conditions—having been, in fact, only yesterday transported from the twelfth century. Well. In spite of the fact that the nation of Israel cannot afford, and is far too intelligent, to encourage any form of social discrimination, the fact remains that there is a tremendous gap between a Jew from Russia or France or England or Australia and a Jew but lately arrived from the desert. Is the resurrection of the language enough to bridge this gap? And one cannot help asking—*I* cannot help asking—if it is really desirable to resurrect the Jewish religion. I mean, the Jews themselves do not believe in it anymore: it was simply one of the techniques of their survival—in the desert. Lord, I don't know. One cannot but respect the energy and the courage of this handful of people: but one can't but suspect that a vast amount of political cynicism, on the part of the English and the Americans, went into the creation of this state; and I personally cannot help being saddened by the creation, at this late date, of yet another nation—it seems to me that we need fewer nations, not more: the blood that has been spilled for various flags makes me ill.

Perhaps I would not feel this way if I were not on my way to Africa: what conundrums await one there! Or perhaps I would not feel this way if I were not helplessly and painfully—most painfully—ambivalent concerning the status of the Arabs here. I cannot blame them for feeling dispossessed; and in a literal way, they have been. Furthermore, the Jews, who are surrounded by forty million hostile Muslims, are forced to control the very movements of Arabs within the state of Israel. One cannot blame the Jews for this necessity; one cannot blame the Arabs for resenting it. *I* would—indeed, in my own situation in America, I do, and it has cost me—costs me—a great and continuing effort not to hate the people who are responsible for the societal effort to limit and diminish me.

Someone said to me the other day that the real trouble between Arabs and Jews has to do with the fact that their idea of a nation—the Arab idea, the Jewish idea—is essentially religious. For the word "religious," I read "tribal." Is it not possible to hope that we can begin, at long last, to transcend the tribe? But I will think about this more another day. Whether I want to or not.

Anyway—Jerusalem, God knows (!), *is* golden when the sun is shining on all that yellow stone. What a blue sky! What a beautiful city—you remember that song? "Oh, What a Beautiful City!" Well, that's the way Jerusalem makes one feel. I stood today in the upper room, the room where Christ and his disciples had the Last Supper, and I thought of Mahalia and Marian Anderson and "Go Down, Moses" and of my father and of that other song my father loved to sing: "I want to be ready / To walk in Jerusalem / Just like John." And here I am, far from ready, in one of the homelands which has given me my identity and on my way to another. To ask oneself "What is a Jew?" is also, for me, to ask myself "What is a black man?" And what, in the name of heaven, *is* an American Negro? I have a gloomy feeling that I won't find any answers in Africa, only more questions.

Turkey, October 20

In great haste, far from my own desk. A virus, Mideastern, & trouble, account for my silence. News from Paris bad, Algerian situation unutterable; & Paula, especially as my sister, much too close to it, & frightened. ("Fear," she says, "is an awful thing.") Well. More of this in a real letter.

I have an awful feeling that I've only moved Paula from a ghetto to a developing *plastique* battleground.

But have been working, steadily, just the same, & will send a batch of stuff, finally, including contracts, before I finally leave here.

Hold on, hold on. Don't be mad at me, if you are, this is a fearful passage.

Turkey, November 20

I am seeing Kenyatta's daughter sometime this week—she is in town; and this encounter, along with the news of the famine in Kenya, may take me out of here at a moment's notice. But I hope not, it would be extremely awkward for me now. I'm barreling ahead with the book, because I want the book in NY before I go to Africa. I dare not predict, again, the time that it will take; but I'm very close to the end.

I am also working on "Down at the Cross." It's my hope that God will be good and that it won't take too long to hammer into its final shape. For I also want *that* in NY before I leave here—I particularly want it to be finished before I try to deal with Africa. The Israeli notes are still disorganized, and the Israeli story—for reasons which have nothing to do with the Israeli character, really—is fairly disheartening. But I must do it. And I am also preparing an essay on Turkey. With these last two, I can only hope to have everything down, and up-to-date, before I take off.

My actor friend's military duties have taken him to the Turkish Siberia, and I'm staying with his sister and brother-in-law. I had meant to move to a hotel, but they all considered this to be an insult. They're very nice people. There's something very sweet, for me, and moving and rare in feeling their impulse to make life as easy as possible for me, so that I can work. I've gained a little weight here and this is taken, apparently, as an enormous justification for Turkey's existence. Well, I exaggerate, of course—but life *has* been, after my prolonged storm, very restful here. The only trouble is that you do not know how you can possibly repay such people. Perhaps it is important to learn that there are some people who don't think of payment—time, perhaps, for me to learn how to take. If you don't learn how to take, you soon forget how to give.

Best to Anne, Alison, Freddie, you. I hope Freddie's having some hard second thoughts about that business of being a writer. But he sounded pretty definite. Your trials with me, dear friend, may prove to be but a weak rehearsal for what's coming.

Love. Write.

Turkey, December

I've just cabled you to send money to me here, so I can get out, and money to meet me in Paris. I thought I had explained to you—but perhaps I didn't, I've been so goddamn swamped and upset—that I am going, now, Saturday, from Paris to Dakar and Brazzaville. I have tem-

porarily eliminated Kenya mainly because I wanted to have my novel finished before I went to Africa (have you received it and have you read it?
anxiety is eating me up); and then because Kenyatta seemed never to be
in Kenya; and finally because Turkish currency regulations do not allow
one to buy traveler's checks or take any money out of Turkey; so that I
would have had to arrange to stop somewhere else, anyway. I first
thought Athens, and then decided on Paris—at first because I thought
Paula was still there, and now because I'm indescribably weary and
depressed and weary of new places. Mary will be in Paris, I'll spend the
holidays with her, and take off at the beginning of the year. I'll be there
a month, and be in NY in February. I'll certainly turn in one, possibly
two, of the *NYorker* articles, and return to Africa in the spring and finish
up their assignment in the summer. Then, back to NY, and the play. (I'm
in correspondence with Gadg [Elia Kazan], he'll be in Athens next
month, but I, alas, will not be.)

This is one of the reasons I jumped at the Grove Press invitation: It
gives me a deadline to get out of NY. For I must say, my dear Bob—
though I am perhaps excessively melancholy today—one thing which
this strange and lonely journey has made me feel even more strongly is
that it's much better for me to try to stay out of the U.S. as much as possible. I really *do* find American life intolerable and, more than that, personally menacing. I know that I will never be able to expatriate myself
again—but I also somehow know that the incessant strain and terror—
for me—of continued living there will prove, finally, to be more than I
can stand. This, like all such decisions, is wholly private and unanswerable, probably irrevocable and probably irrational—whatever that last
word may mean. What it comes to is that I am already tearfully menaced—within—by my vision and am under the obligation to minimize
my dangers. It is one thing to try to become articulate where you are,
relatively speaking, left alone to do so and quite another to make this
attempt in a setting where the terrors of other people so corroborate
your own. I think that I must really reconcile myself to being a transat-
lantic commuter—and turn to my advantage, and not impossibly the
advantage of others, the fact that I am a stranger everywhere. For the
fact won't change. In order for me to make peace with American life, as
it is now lived, I would have to surrender any attempt to come to terms
with my own. And this surrender would mean my death.

In fact, I'm probably suffering from a species of postnatal depression.
Something very weird happens to you when a book is over, you feel old

and useless, and all that effort, which you can't, anyway, remember, seems to have come to nothing. But I'll feel less grim, probably, when I write you again, from Paris, and I'm pushing ahead with the essay and will get it to you before I leave for Dakar.

Loèche-les-Bains, February 1962

Got to Paris, late, as you know, and began tracking down debts and possessions—no easy matter—with the intention of leaving almost at once.

Anyway, partly because I was running around Paris without a winter coat, I came down with the grippe, which rapidly developed into a heavy and painful bronchitis—I thought it was pleurisy, and had visions of pneumonia. The doctor filled me with drugs and told me that, fantastically enough, there was nothing seriously wrong with me, except the bronchitis, but that I was terribly run down and ought not go on to Africa in my exhausted state. I was glad enough to hear this, in a way, I was certainly tired and sad; and so I came here, to the mountains, to the village where I finished my first novel, ten years ago. And Lucien, very much as he did then, came up with me to help me get settled—and he has now gone back on the road (he is a salesman) to feed *his* robins.

So, I meant to write you sooner, but at first I simply could not get myself together enough to do it, and then couldn't stay awake long enough: the French notion of medicine is to knock you out. Then, when I got to the mountains, all I did was sleep—the mountain air, I guess. I feel much better now, ready to start again—though I also feel very still and sad.

This is not quite the tone I meant to strike when writing you, for I know that you tend to worry about me, but it seems to be the only tone I can manage—but please do not worry, everything is much better now. And in fact, Paris was the only really bad spot and that might not have been so bad if I had not fallen ill. Though, in another way, I think that that might have been lucky.

I am again reworking the interminable "Down at the Cross," and will send it off to you as soon as I've sent the rewrites to Jim. You'll see, I imagine, when you read it, why it has been so hard to do, and it probably also illuminates some of the unsettling apprehensions which have so complicated this journey.

Which brings us to the third point: I've kept, as I've told you, a kind of incoherent, blow-by-blow account of this trip, and I intend, before I leave the mountains, to get at least the Israeli section out to you, so that you can send it to [William] Shawn. Again, I think that this will make clearer than any of my letters can, how complex, once I got to Israel, the whole idea of Africa became. It became clear to me at once that I could not hope to manage that confrontation with an exhibition, merely, of journalistic skill. I could deal with it only in an extremely, even dangerously personal way, and try to make the reader ask his own questions and make his own assessments. And this sorrow, if I may call it that, was deepened in Turkey, where the whole somber question of America's role in the world today stared at me in a new and inescapable way; and the question of America's role brings up, of course, the question of what the role of the American Negro is, or can be. Well. I suppose the Israeli piece will cause some people to think I'm anti-Semitic, and God knows what the reaction to the Turkish chapter will be. But they are part of the African book, they must be.

As for Africa, I'd rather like your advice at this point. I, personally, would like to go from here to Dakar at the end of this month—Dakar and Brazzaville—and stay down there until I meet Grove Press in Mallorca at the end of April. In May, I have a tentative rendezvous to meet Elia Kazan in Greece—I saw him just before he left Paris. My own idea was to finish the play during May and June, and then return to Africa, Ghana, Nigeria, and Kenya, and return to New York in the fall. Once I get to Africa, I imagine that I will be extremely busy, particularly with students, and I don't want to stint: it has taken me so long to get there!

The only problem, as far as I can see, involves the American lectures. As you know, I don't have any very clear idea of what that schedule was: but it's my impression that the only firm commitment was Monterey College, sometime in April. If need be, I can fly back for that, since Grove Press, in any case, will fly me out. What do you think? I don't see that there's any great need for me to be home for *Country*'s publication—though I am willing to listen, of course. Finally, though, I must say, I simply dread facing the tigerish Negro press if I return to America without having visited the land which they so abruptly are proud to claim as home. The more particularly as neither *Another Country* nor my report on Africa is likely to please them at all.

This trip has had the effect of opening something in me which I must pursue, and I do not think that I can do that and be a Negro leader, too. And, in any case, my whole attitude toward the fact of color undergoes several melancholy changes: I don't know where they will lead me, but I must buy the time to find out. There is a very grim secret hidden in the fact that so many of the people one hoped to rescue could not be rescued because the prison of color had become their hiding place. I don't know what this means, for me, for us, for the world, for the future of Africa—I don't yet know what color means in Africa (but I *will* know). Life has the effect of forcing you to act on your premises—the only key I can find to my spectacular recklessness—and I have said for years that color does not matter. I am now beginning to feel that it does not matter *at all,* that it masks something else which *does* matter: but this suspicion changes, for me, the entire nature of reality.

Ah. Bear with me, dear friend. I make my journeys by a radar I must trust, and must pursue and bear my discoveries in the best way I can. I know it's hard on everybody's nerves, and it's certainly hard on mine, but I'm not being frivolous and it is done out of love.

Write me, quickly, please, the morale is wildly fluctuating, I'm always afraid, and I'm pregnant with some strange monster.

(1963)

The International War Crimes Tribunal:

Reader's Forum, *Freedomways*

Bertrand Russell, the 3rd Earl Russell (1872–1970), was a philosopher, mathematician, historian, linguist, and antiwar activist. He
wrote more than seventy books on a vast range of subjects that garnered him the 1950 Nobel Prize in Literature. A student of Wittgen-
stein, he helped establish the field of analytic philosophy. In his later
years he dedicated himself to the eradication of nuclear weapons,
and at the age of ninety-four he established, through his Peace
Foundation, an International War Crimes Tribunal. The goal of the
project was to try Lyndon B. Johnson and his administration for war
crimes against the people of Vietnam. James Baldwin was named a
member of the tribunal. This piece was written for the Reader's
Forum of *Freedomways,* a quarterly review.

.   .   .

MY NAME IS INCLUDED among the members of Lord Russell's War
Crimes Tribunal, and it is imperative, therefore, that I make my position

clear. I do indeed have my own reservation concerning this tribunal. There may be something suspect in the spectacle of Europeans condemning America for a war which America inherited from Europe, inherited, in fact, directly from France. In spite of my somewhat difficult reputation, I have never had any interest in attacking America from abroad. I know too much, if I may say so, concerning the complex European motives, of which envy and fury are not the least. It might be considered more logical, for example, for any European, and especially any Englishman, to bring before an international tribunal the government of South Africa, or the government of Rhodesia, which I would do, if I had the power, at nine o'clock tomorrow morning. No Englishman has suggested this. Neither did Jean-Paul Sartre suggest that France be brought before an international tribunal during the war which we have inherited from France, or during the French-Algerian war. It is possible, in short, to consider the tribunal to be both misguided and inept, and I can see to what extent that this is so. But I can also see why. The tribunal, ideally, wishes to make the conscience of the world aware of the crimes being committed in Southeast Asia by the American government, in the name of the American people; and wishes to do this, not only to bring the horror to an end, but to pull all of us back from the brink of total disaster. But this world can only be the Western world, this conscience can only be the Western conscience, and all the Western world is guilty. If I should make the attempt to accuse the Western powers of the crimes they are now committing in Rhodesia, Angola, South Africa—to leave it at that; or should I attempt to bring to the world's attention the actual intention, and the actual result, of those treaties the Europeans, who were not yet Americans, signed with the American Indian, to say nothing of what happened to the blacks, concerning which we know at once too much and too little; I would certainly encounter from the Western powers the very same opposition that Lord Russell's tribunal has encountered. And for the very same reason: such an attempt not only brings into question the real morality of the Western world, it also attacks what that world considers to be its material self-interest. Such a trial should really be held in Harlem, U.S.A. No one, then, could possibly escape the sinister implications of the moral dilemma in which the facts of Western history have placed the Western world.

I speak as an American Negro. I challenge anyone alive to tell me why any black American should go into those jungles to kill people who are not white and who have never done him any harm, in defense of a people who have made that foreign jungle, or any jungle anywhere in the world, a more desirable jungle than that in which he was born, and to which, supposing that he lives, he will inevitably return. I challenge anyone alive to convince me that a people who have not achieved anything resembling freedom in their own country are empowered, with bombs, to free another people whom they do not know at all, who rather resemble me—whom they do not know at all. I challenge any American, and especially Mr. Lyndon Johnson and Mr. Hubert Humphrey and Mr. Dean Rusk and Mr. Robert McNamara, to tell me, and the black population of the United States, how, if they cannot liberate their brothers—repeat: *brothers*—and have not even learned how to live with them, they intend to liberate Southeast Asia. I challenge them to tell me by what right, and in whose interest, they presume to police the world, and I, furthermore, want to know if they would like their sisters, or their daughters to marry any one of the people they are struggling so mightily to save. And this is by no means a rhetorical challenge, and all the men I have named, and many, many more will be dishonored forever if they cannot rise to it. I want an answer: if I am to die, I have the right to know why. And the nonwhite population of the world, who are most of the world, would also like to know. The American idea of freedom and, still more, the way this freedom is imposed, have made America the most terrifying nation in the world. We have inherited Spain's title: the nation with the bloody footprint.

The American war in Vietnam raises several questions. One is whether or not small nations, in this age of superstates and superpowers, will be allowed to work out their own destinies and live as they feel they should. For only the people of a country have the right, or the spiritual power, to determine that country's way of life. Another question this war raises is just how what we call the underdeveloped countries became underdeveloped in the first place. Why, for example, is Africa underpopulated, and why do the resources of, say, Sierra Leone belong to Europe? Why, in short, does so much of the world eat too little and so little of the world eat too much? I am also curious to know just how a people calling itself sovereign allows itself to be fighting a war which has never been officially declared, and I am curious to know why so few people appear to be worried about the arresting precedent thus established. I am curious indeed to know how it happens that the mightiest nation in the world has been unable, in all these years, to conquer one of the smallest. I am curious to know what happens to the moral fabric, the moral sense, of the people engaged in so criminal an endeavor.

Long, long before the Americans decided to liberate the Southeast Asians, they decided to liberate me: my ancestors carried these scars to the grave, and so will I. A racist society can't but fight a racist war—this is the bitter truth. The assumptions acted on at home are also acted on abroad, and every American Negro knows this, for he, after the American Indian, was the first "Vietcong" victim. We were bombed first. How, then, can I believe a word you say, and what gives you the right to ask me to die for you?

The American endeavor in Vietnam is totally indefensible and totally doomed, and I wish to go on record as having no part of it. When the black population of America has a future, so will America have a future—not till then. And when the black populations of the world have a future, so will the Western nations have a future—and not till then. But the terrible probability is that the Western populations, struggling to hold on to what they have stolen from their captives, and unable to look into their mirror, will precipitate a chaos throughout the world which, if it does not bring life on this planet to an end, will bring about a racial war such as the world has never seen, and for which generations yet unborn will curse our names forever.

I think that mankind can do better than that, and I wish to be a witness to this small and stubborn possibility.

(1967)

Anti-Semitism and Black Power

Written for the Reader's Forum of *Freedomways*, a quarterly review.

.　　.　　.

WE ARE IN THE HIDEOUS CENTER of a mortal storm, which many of us saw coming. Many of us will perish and certainly no one of my generation can hope, honorably, to survive. And, whether or not one agrees with me, I think it is useful to assume that America will not survive this storm, either. Nor should she; she is responsible for this holocaust in which the living writhe; it is American power which makes death an enviable state for so many millions of people. We are a criminal nation, built on a lie, and as the world cannot use us, it will presently find some way of disposing of us. I take this for granted; and the future of this nation, even though it may also be my own, cannot concern me any longer. I am concerned with the living, I am concerned with a new morality, and a new creation. I hope I do not sound literary; in any case, I mean what I say. I really believe that it is possible for human beings to make the world a place in which we all can live.

I think I understand, in spite of my limits—for I know more about my limits than anyone else can know, and no tribunal frightens me; I am my own tribunal—a great deal about the crisis which we, black, in America, are now enduring. The crisis has been produced by the history of Europe and the brutality of the Christian church; and I think it is very important to bear in mind that, whereas we, black, are enduring a crisis, the descendants of Europe and the defenders of the faith are witnessing their doom. Indeed, they are graceless—but they are human. This is hard, hard, hard to remember: I know how hard it is. But if one does not remember it, the battle is for nothing.

I think I know how white America operates to destroy the black integrity—and not by accident, but deliberately. You will observe, I hope, that in doing this, it has also destroyed its own integrity. I hope you will understand me and I hope you will believe me when I say that I would rather die than see the black American become as hideously empty as the majority of white men have become. I would like us to do something unprecedented: to create ourselves without finding it necessary to create an enemy. But since we are surrounded by enemies, I think I should spell that out.

A black high-school dropout in Watts, for example, has every reason to hate the police, the lawyers, the judges, the priests, the teachers, the bosses, the landlords, the mayor, the governor, and Ronald Reagan. I do not shrink from asserting that the human value of these people can only exist in the sight of God, and, happily, I'm not God (who is also, in any case, and not a moment too soon, about to go out of business). But he has no right to hate the governor's child, and no one has a right to teach him to hate. I think that we, human beings, must try to change each other. I am perfectly aware that nothing will ever change Governor Wallace or Senator Eastland. But it is the system which created these people and gave them their power which must be isolated, anatomized, attacked, and destroyed. And I think we must be very clear-headed about this, for no people have ever been in a revolutionary situation so bizarre. It is a revolution which has all the aspects of a civil war; but at the same time, it is happening all over the globe, and America is fighting it all over the globe—using, by no means incidentally, vast numbers of its surplus and despised population. Hopefully, for example, if enough Vietnamese and black Americans are blown into eternity, the world will be made safe—for business. There is a very good reason, after all, why the government which could so severely compromise the Cuban economy can do nothing whatever to intimidate the

South African economy. A revolution in South Africa would have a terrible effect on Wall Street and on the Bank of the Holy Ghost—which latter institution stands, as you know, in Rome: a monument to what is probably the most extensive, successful, murderous, and blasphemous enterprise in the history of mankind. If the Bank of the Holy Ghost should fail, the heathen could no longer be saved. And you remember, I hope, how desperately we heathens longed for salvation.

Well, then: the nature of the enemy is history; the nature of the enemy is power; and what every black man, boy, woman, girl, is struggling to achieve is some sense of himself or herself which this history and this power have done everything conceivable to destroy. But let us try to be clear. Black power is not a mystical or a poetic concept, for example; it is simply a political necessity. It has nothing to do with bad guys or good guys, and it really has nothing to do with color. Black arts has nothing to do with color, either. It is an attempt to create a black self-image which the white Republic could never allow. It is an attempt to tell the truth about black people *to* black people because the American Republic has told us nothing but lies.

But the Republic has told *itself* nothing but lies. If one accepts my basic assumption, which is that all men are brothers—simply because all men share the same condition, however different the details of their lives may be—then it is perfectly possible, it seems to me, that in re-creating ourselves, in saving ourselves, we can re-create and save many others: whosoever will. I certainly think that this possibility ought to be kept very vividly in the forefront of our consciousness. The value of a human being is never indicated by the color of his skin; the value of a human being is all that I hold sacred; and I know that I do not become better by making another worse. One need not read the New Testament to discover that. One need only read history and look at the world—one need only, in fact, look into one's mirror.

The specific reason for this rather long letter is the series of articles concerning the Jew in Harlem (in *Liberator* magazine). I think it is most distinctly unhelpful, and I think it is immoral, to blame Harlem on the Jew. For a man of Editor Dan Watts's experience, it is incredibly naive. Why, when we should be storming capitols, do they suggest to the people they hope to serve that we take refuge in the most ancient and barbaric of the European myths? Do they want us to become better? Or do they want us, after all, carefully manipulating the color black, merely to become white?

(1967)

An Open Letter to My Sister Angela Y. Davis

Alabama-born Angela Yvonne Davis was an assistant professor of philosophy at the University of California-Los Angeles in 1969. She considered herself an activist, a radical feminist, was a member of the Communist Party, and worked with the Black Panther Party. Ronald Reagan, then governor of California, led the call for her termination from the university system, but she was soon rehired.

In 1970 a number of armed black militants, led by Jonathan Jackson, the brother of Soledad Prison inmate George Jackson, took over a Marin County courtroom in an attempt to free three convicts during a trial. Guns were drawn. A judge was held at gunpoint. Ultimately, two of the prisoners were shot dead, as well as Jonathan Jackson; the prosecutor was paralyzed by a policeman's bullet; the judge, Harold Haley, was killed. Angela Davis, who reportedly had purchased the guns used by Jackson and his cohorts, escaped and fled California. She became the third woman ever listed on the FBI's Ten Most Wanted List, charged with conspiracy, kidnapping, and homicide. She was captured two months later in New York, and her 1972 trial became one of the most publicized criminal trials of the 1970s. She was eventually acquitted of all charges, and today is a highly respected professor, author, and activist. Abolishing the death penalty has become one of her key causes.

Baldwin wrote this piece while she was awaiting trial.

.   .   .

Dear Sister:

One might have hoped that, by this hour, the very sight of chains on black flesh, or the very sight of chains, would be so intolerable a sight for the American people, and so unbearable a memory, that they would themselves spontaneously rise up and strike off the manacles. But no, they appear to glory in their chains; now, more than ever, they appear to measure their safety in chains and corpses. And so, *Newsweek*, civilized defender of the indefensible, attempts to drown you in a sea of crocodile tears ("it remained to be seen what sort of personal liberation she had achieved") and puts you on its cover, chained.

You look exceedingly alone—as alone, say, as the Jewish housewife in the boxcar headed for Dachau, or as any one of our ancestors chained together in the name of Jesus, headed for a Christian land.

Well. Since we live in an age in which silence is not only criminal but suicidal, I have been making as much noise as I can, here in Europe, on radio and television—in fact, have just returned from a land, Germany, which was made notorious by a silent majority not so very long ago. I was asked to speak on the case of Miss Angela Davis, and did so. Very probably an exercise in futility, but one must let no opportunity slide.

I am something like twenty years older than you, of that generation, therefore, of which George Jackson ventures that "there are no healthy brothers—*none at all.*" I am in no way equipped to dispute this speculation (not, anyway, without descending into what, at the moment, would be irrelevant subtleties), for I know too well what he means. My own state of health is certainly precarious enough. In considering you, and Huey, and George, and (especially) Jonathan Jackson, I began to apprehend what you may have had in mind when you spoke of the uses to which we could put the experience of the slave. What has happened, it seems to me, and to put it far too simply, is that a whole new generation of people have assessed and absorbed their history and, in that tremendous action, have freed themselves of it and will never be victims again.

This may seem an odd, indefensibly impertinent and insensitive thing to say to a sister in prison, battling for her life—for all our lives. Yet, I dare to say it, for I think that you will perhaps not misunderstand me, and I do not say it, after all, from the position of a spectator.

I am trying to suggest that you—for example—do not appear to be your father's daughter in the same way that I am my father's son. At bottom, my father's expectations and mine were the same, the expectations of his generation and mine were the same; and neither the immense difference in our ages nor the move from the South to the North could alter these expectations or make our lives more viable. For, in fact, to use the brutal parlance of that hour, the interior language of that despair, he was just a nigger—a nigger laborer preacher, and so was I. I jumped the track, but that's of no more importance here, in itself, than the fact that *some* poor Spaniards become rich bullfighters, or that *some* poor black boys become rich—boxers, for example. That's rarely, if ever, afforded the people more than a great emotional catharsis, though I don't mean to be condescending about that, either. But when Cassius Clay became Muhammad Ali and refused to put on that uniform (and sacrificed all that money!) a very different impact was made on the people and a very different kind of instruction had begun.

The American triumph—in which the American tragedy has always been implicit—was to make black people despise themselves. When I was little I despised myself; I did not know any better. And this meant, albeit unconsciously, or against my will, or in great pain, that I also despised my father. *And* my mother. *And* my brothers. *And* my sisters. Black people were killing each other every Saturday night out on Lenox Avenue, when I was growing up; and no one explained to them, or to me, that it was *intended* that they should; that they were penned where they were, like animals, in order that they should consider themselves no better than animals. Everything supported this sense of reality, nothing denied it: and so one was ready, when it came time to go to work, to be treated as a slave. So one was ready, when human terrors came, to bow before a white God and beg Jesus for salvation—this same white God who was unable to raise a finger to do so little as to help you pay your rent, unable to be awakened in time to help you save your child!

There is always, of course, more to any picture than can speedily be perceived and in all of this—groaning and moaning, watching, calculating, clowning, surviving, and outwitting—some tremendous strength was nevertheless being forged, which is part of our legacy today. But that particular aspect of our journey now begins to be behind us. The secret is out: we are men!

But the blunt, open articulation of this secret has frightened the nation to death. I wish I could say "to life," but that is much to demand of a disparate collection of displaced people still cowering in their wagon trains and singing "Onward, Christian Soldiers." The nation, *if* America is a nation, is not in the least prepared for this day. It is a day which the Americans never expected or desired to see, however piously they may declare their belief in progress and democracy. Those words, now, on American lips, have become a kind of universal obscenity: for this most unhappy people, strong believers in arithmetic, never expected to be confronted with the algebra of their history.

One way of gauging a nation's health, or of discerning what it really considers to be its interests—or to what extent it can be considered as a nation as distinguished from a coalition of special interests—is to examine those people it elects to represent or protect it. One glance at the American leaders (or figureheads) conveys that America is on the edge of absolute chaos, and also suggests the future to which American interests, if not the bulk of the American people, appear willing to consign the blacks. (Indeed, one look at our past conveys that.) It is clear that for the bulk of our (nominal) countrymen, we are all expendable. And Messrs Nixon, Agnew, Mitchell, and Hoover, to say nothing, of course, of the *Kings Row* basket case, the winning Ronnie Reagan, will not hesitate for an instant to carry out what they insist is the will of the people.

But what, in America, is the will of the people? And who, for the above-named, *are* the people? The people, whoever they may be, know as much about the forces which have placed the above-named gentlemen in power as they do about the forces responsible for the slaughter in Vietnam. The will of the people, in America, has always been at the mercy of an ignorance not merely phenomenal, but sacred, and sacredly cultivated: the better to be used by a carnivorous economy which democratically slaughters and victimizes whites and blacks alike. But most white Americans do not dare admit this (though they suspect it), and this fact contains mortal danger for the blacks and tragedy for the nation.

Or, to put it another way, as long as white Americans take refuge in their whiteness—for so long as they are unable to walk out of this most monstrous of traps—they will allow millions of people to be slaughtered in their name, and will be manipulated into and surrender themselves to what they will think of—and justify—as a racial war. They will never, so long as their whiteness puts so sinister a distance between themselves and their own experience and the experience of others, feel themselves sufficiently human, *sufficiently worthwhile,* to become responsible for themselves, their leaders, their country, their children, or their fate. They will perish (as we once put it in our black church) in their sins—that is, in their delusions. And this is happening, needless to say, already, all around us.

Only a handful of the millions of people in this vast place are aware that the fate intended for you, Sister Angela, and for George Jackson, and for the numberless prisoners in our concentration camps—for that is what they are—is a fate which is about to engulf them, too. White lives, for the forces which rule in this country, are no more sacred than black ones, as many and many a student is discovering, as the white American corpses in Vietnam prove. If the American people are unable to contend with their elected leaders for the redemption of their own honor and the lives of their own children, we, the blacks, the most rejected of the Western children, can expect very little help at their hands; which, after all, is nothing new. What the Americans do not realize is that a war between brothers, in the same cities, on the same soil, is not a *racial* war but a *civil* war. But the American delusion is not only that their brothers all are white but that the whites are all their brothers.

So be it. We cannot awaken this sleeper, and God knows we have tried. We must do what we can do, and fortify and save each other—*we* are not drowning in an apathetic self-contempt; we *do* feel ourselves sufficiently worthwhile to contend even with inexorable forces in order to change our fate and the fate of our children and the condition of the world! We know that a man is not a thing and is not to be placed at the mercy of things. We know that air and water belong to all mankind and not merely to industrialists. We know that a baby does not come into the world merely to be the instrument of someone else's profit. We know that democracy does not mean the coercion of all into a deadly—and, finally, wicked—mediocrity but the liberty for all to aspire to the best that is in him, or that has ever been.

We know that we, the blacks, and not only we, the blacks, have been, and are, the victims of a system whose only fuel is greed, whose only god is profit. We know that the fruits of this system have been ignorance, despair, and death, and we know that the system is doomed because the world can no longer afford it—if, indeed, it ever could have.

And we know that, for the perpetuation of this system, we have all been mercilessly brutalized, and have been told nothing but lies, lies about ourselves and our kinsmen and our past, and about love, life, and death, so that both soul and body have been bound in hell.

The enormous revolution in black consciousness which has occurred in your generation, my dear sister, means the beginning or the end of America. Some of us, white and black, know how great a price has already been paid to bring into existence a new consciousness, a new people, an unprecedented nation. If we know, and do nothing, we are worse than the murderers hired in our name.

If we know, then we must fight for your life as though it were our own—which it is—and render impassable with our bodies the corridor to the gas chamber. For, if they take you in the morning, they will be coming for us that night.

Therefore: peace.

Brother James
November 19, 1970

A Letter to Prisoners

ARTISTS AND PRISONERS have more in common with each other than have the servants of the State. Put it another way: the warden of the prison is not expected, still less required, to answer to his conscience; he is expected (and required) to execute the will of the State. (How he explains this to his children is, cunningly enough, no concern of the State, which has every reason to believe that the son will grow up to be like the father.) Or, to put it in yet another way, the artist, insofar as the State is compelled to consider this inconvenient creature at all, is nothing more—and also nothing less—than a potential prisoner. The artist is the prisoner at large who has so far escaped his just deserts by means of his private cunning and the liberal bleeding-heart public cowardice.

What artists and prisoners have in common is that both know what it means to be free.

Now, this is a thoroughly unattractive paradox which I, like many another, would like to be able to avoid. But it is impossible not to recognize that the people who are endlessly boasting of their freedom—*we're the best because we're free!*—loathe the very suggestion of such a possibility for anyone other than themselves. They are forever stitching flags, making and threatening and dropping bombs, creating instruments of torture and torture chambers and overseers and deputies and detention centers. Their notion of freedom is so strenuously calisthenic, not to say defensive, that freedom becomes a matter of keeping everybody else out of your backyard. Or bomb shelter: there are none, by no means incidentally, in the ghetto. (If I happen to be wrong about ghetto bomb shelters, I would love to be corrected.)

A vast amount of energy (the word is not yet obsolete) and an indefensible proportion of the public treasury—this government is spending *our* money, after all—go into endeavors which have as their single intention and concrete purpose and effect that no one be so rash as to act, or to dream of acting, on his or her right to be.

I have suggested that the connection between the artist and the prisoner is an unattractive paradox. But it is more than that. I have called it an unattractive paradox because it would seem to indicate that, in general, we value freedom, or find ourselves compelled to attempt to define it, only when it is arbitrarily limited, or menaced: when another *human* power has the right to tell us when and where to stand or sit or move or live or make love or have (or claim) our children—or bow mighty low, or die. We do not feel this way about the rain, the snow, the thunder, or the earthquake, or death. These have no reason to consider our hope, or anguish. The thunder which deafens me or the water which drowns me is not a man like me, is not compelled to hear my cry or answer my plea.

But we are compelled to hear each other: knowing perfectly well how little can be done, one discovers how to do some things.

This may be part of the definition, or pride or price of freedom, for this apprehension necessarily involves a real recognition of, and respect for, the other and for the condition of the other. The other is no longer other and is indeed, as the song puts it, closer than a brother—the other is oneself.

There is absolutely nothing, in my experience, more painful, more devastating, than this revelation. One can scarcely live with it, but one can certainly not begin to live without it. It is this perception, as I begin more and more to believe, which gives the person the energy—the passion—to break the chains which bind him. Or, to be accurate, the chains which bind us. The unattractive paradox is that it is this danger, this action, this recognition of what it means to love one another, which defines freedom, which brings it to being, which makes it as real as the Word become flesh, to dwell among us.

Brethren, please remember, especially in this speechless time and place, that in the beginning was the Word. We are in ourselves much older than any witness to Carthage or Pompeii and, having been through auction, flood, and fire, to say nothing of the spectacular excavation of our names, are not destined for the rubble.

(1982)

The Fire This Time: Letter to the Bishop

When this open letter was published in the *New Statesman* in August 1985, Desmond Mpilo Tutu (b. 1931), then the Anglican bishop of Johannesburg, had recently been awarded the Nobel Peace Prize. In 1986 Tutu was made the archbishop of Cape Town, making him the first black person to lead the Anglican Church in South Africa. He had been deeply involved in the fight against apartheid—and for human rights around the world—for most of his adult life.

.   .   .

THOUGH I AM NOT a religious or, more precisely, a churchgoing man, I, like all black Americans, come out of the church—the black church, for we were not allowed to be members of the white one. I can, therefore, use an image which is part of my inheritance and say that you and I, who have never met on earth (but who may meet in that kingdom that you are struggling to make real), have already met: in hell. And a more felicitous dwelling place has a very precise meaning for those who meet in hell.

But this is a very particular and peculiar hell. It is not built foursquare. It is hard to convey the quality of the inhabitants. Every system involves a hierarchy, so perhaps I could suggest a system of this hell by observing that those who meet there manage to meet because they know where they are. The others—the minority in your country, the majority in mine—never meet, because they imagine that hell is a place for others. They also imagine that they control this system.

It will be considered offensive—unpatriotic—to compare the South African situation to the American situation: nor will I, in fact, make such a comparison, because I do not know enough about your country (I may not know enough about my own). Yet, you must have sometimes been struck, as I have been, by the vehemence of the Western leaders (my own nominal representative in France *en tête*) concerning global freedom and democracy: deep concern over Polish freedom, the determination of the American government to bring freedom to South America and the Philippines by any means whatever, and the ineffable gallantry of the British prime minister's insistence on freedom for the islands off Argentina.

But none of this bellicosity is exhibited in the case of South Africa.

To backtrack, and in order to make my point clear: I am certainly concerned about the freedom of the Poles in Warsaw; but the Poles in Chicago are whites who hate blacks. I am certainly concerned about Ireland: but the Irish in Boston are whites who hate niggers. I may be ambivalent concerning the physical purposes of the state of Israel, but American Jews are, in the main, indistinguishable from American white Christians: and I would not like to be an Arab in Jerusalem. And Israel is, also, an ally of South Africa—which Western nation, indeed, is not? (And it is worth pointing out that the ANC [African National Congress] is as homeless as the PLO, for the same reasons.)

And finally, to discuss—I dismiss—"the Russian menace": I have known very few black Communists; black Americans, on the whole, are far less romantic than white Americans. The Russian menace has been invented by the West in order to distract attention from the moral and actual chaos in the West. People one day ahead of death by starvation do not huddle before their campfires (assuming that they have any fire at all) reading Marx or arguing about dialectical materialism. And it is worth pointing out that my country, which accuses Cuba of exporting revolution, is the most notorious exporter of revolution of this century. Neither Havana nor

Moscow has the remotest interest in each other—why on earth should they have? What could they have hoped to do for each other? No. It was expected that the U.S.A., "the last best hope of earth," a country itself born of a revolution, would be their hope and their friend.

But there are revolutions and revolutions—to leave it at that. They are glorified in the past. They are dreaded and, insofar as possible, destroyed in the present.

Now, I do not know if what is happening in South Africa is a revolution (but perhaps each revolution redefines the word), but I do know this: the moral pretensions of the West are being tested and exposed, and the real meaning of the "civilizing mission" revealed.

You are, yourself, incontestably, one of the products of this mission, and so was the late Dr. Martin Luther King Jr., and so was Harry Belafonte, and my mother and myself. Yet, we do not owe our presence to the Civilized. We are here in spite of the Civilized. And nowhere is this clearer than in South Africa now, and in the reaction of the Civilized to this slaughter. We are not white, we are black, and we exist therefore, in this system, this hierarchy, on another, quite literally unspeakable level.

No one wishes to admit this, for it would be to admit something else. Africa fed itself, for generations, long before the Civilized arrived. As of that moment, Africa was forced to feed the world. There is not a single diamond mine, as far as I know, in England; nor, as it turns out, enough coal to keep the English warm. My grandfather, perfectly capable of feeding his family and keeping them warm, was forced instead to pick cotton to keep white families warm. The wealth of England and my country, the wealth of the Western world, in short, is based on slave labor, and the intolerable guilt thus engendered in hearts and minds of the Civilized is the root of what we call racism. From this root spring the legends concerning—proving—the inferiority of black people. One must justify the appalling action of turning a man into a thing. To turn a human being into a moneymaking beast of burden and, by this action, believe—or make oneself believe—that one is "civilizing" this creature is to have surrendered one's morality and imperiled one's sense of reality.

"The problem of the twentieth century," [said] W. E. B. DuBois, in 1903, "is the problem of the color line." And this problem begins to arrive now in an unanswerable dénouement, in Africa, where white men—or perhaps white power—began it.

Finally, it is exceedingly hypocritical for the West to pretend that it will not apply sanctions against South Africa, nor disinvest, because this would hurt black people. This pretension is scarcely worth noting, much less answering. The morality of the West and its economic self-interest are allied, as they always were. Now, as the dungeon in which we were meant to be used forever shakes, one sees how little the free world trusts the possibility of freedom.

But you believe in this possibility—and so do I. Our assassinations and our funerals testify to the absolute truth that the world's present social and economic arrangements cannot serve the world's needs: and racism is the cornerstone and principal justification of these arrangements. And I am sure that you believe, with me, this paradox: black freedom will make white freedom possible. Indeed, *our* freedom, which we have been forced to buy at so high a price, is the only hope of freedom that they have.

Till we meet, then, sir, and with my deepest respect,

Yours in the faith,

(1985)

FOREWORDS AND AFTERWORDS

A Quarter-Century of Un-Americana

A Quarter-Century of Un-Americana, 1938–1963: A Tragico-Comical Memorabilia of HUAC is a scrapbook of sorts, chronicling and critiquing the United States House of Representatives' House Committee on Un-American Activities (HUAC). The committee was renamed the House Committee on Internal Security in 1969; a vestige of this committee still remains as the House Judiciary Committee. The committee concerned itself with investigating everything from Communist activity to Nazis in America to the Ku Klux Klan. It had a hand in the World War II internment of Japanese-Americans and the Hollywood blacklists. HUAC is often confused with Senator Joseph McCarthy's Permanent Subcommittee on Investigations, which, perforce, was a part of the Senate. Both organizations were criticized by former President Harry Truman as being "the most Un-American thing in the country today" in 1959.

. . .

WE ARE LIVING THROUGH the most crucial moment of our history, the moment which will result in a new life for us, or a new death. I am not being in the least metaphorical about this. When I say "a new life," I mean a new vision of America, a vision which will allow us to face, and begin to change, the facts of American life; and when I say "death," I mean Carthage. This seems a grim view to take of our situation, but it is scarcely grimmer than the facts. Our honesty and our courage in facing these facts is all that can save us from disaster. And one of these facts is that there has always been a segment of American life, and a powerful segment, too, which equated virtue with mindlessness.

In this connection, the House Un-American Activities Committee is one of the most sinister facts of the national life. It is not merely that we do not need this committee; the truth is, we cannot afford it. It always reminds me of a vast and totally untrustworthy bomb shelter in which groups of frightened people endlessly convince one another of its impregnability, while the real world outside—by which, again, I mean the facts of our private and public lives—calmly and inexorably prepares their destruction. It is perhaps because I am an American Negro that I have always felt white Americans, many if not most of them, are experts in self-delusion—they usually speak as though I were not in the room. "I," here, does not refer so much to the man called Baldwin as it does to the reality which produced me, a reality with which I live, and from which most Americans spend all their time in flight. People in flight never can grow up, which means they can never, really, become citizens—and we simply must not surrender this great country to those people. We must not allow their fear to control us, and, indeed, we must not allow it to control them. Rather, we should attempt to release them from their panic and their unadmitted sorrow. We ought to try, by the example of our own lives, to prove that life is love and wonder and that that nation is doomed which penalizes those of its citizens who recognize and rejoice in this fact. We must dare to take another view of majority rule, disengaging it from anything resembling a popularity contest; taking it upon ourselves to become the majority by changing the moral climate. For it is upon this majority that the life of any nation really depends.

Speaking as a man, as a Negro, as a citizen, it has seemed to me for a long time now that the really dreadful agony confronting Americans is this: the time has come for us to grow up. A man grows up when he looks back, *realizes* what has happened to him, accepts it all, and begins to change himself. He cannot grow up until he reaches this moment and passes it. We are now at the end of our extraordinarily prolonged adolescence. A very great poet, an American, Miss Marianne Moore, wrote, many years ago, the following description of our terrors: "The weak overcomes its menace. The strong overcomes itself."

That self-knowledge which matures a nation as well as a man presupposes free men and free minds. This book opens with a drawing by the great American artist Art Young, depicting Jesus Christ as wanted for sedition. It recalled for me another Christ—the "Black Christ" of Countee Cullen:

> Men may not bind the summer sea,
> Nor set a limit to the stars;
> The sun seeps through all iron bars;
> The moon is ever manifest.
> And more than this (and here's the crown)
> No man, my son, can batter down
> The star-flung ramparts of the mind.

(1963)

Memoirs of a Bastard Angel: A Fifty-Year Literary and Erotic Odyssey by Harold Norse

Harold Norse (1916–2009) was a poet and writer often associated with the Beat poets, a friend and contemporary of Allen Ginsberg, William Burroughs, Gregory Corso, Tennessee Williams, William Carlos Williams, and many others. He was openly gay, a native New Yorker, and a friend of James Baldwin. He lived abroad in Europe and North Africa from the early 1950s until 1968, when he moved to the West Coast. The author of many volumes of poems, he wrote of his relationship with Baldwin in his 1989 *Memoirs of a Bastard Angel: A Fifty-Year Literary and Erotic Odyssey*. The preface for that book was this piece written by Baldwin originally for a special Harold Norse issue of the journal *Ole*.

.   .   .

I'VE KNOWN HAROLD NORSE so long that I don't remember when I met him. It was many years ago, anyway, in Greenwich Village, in New York.

It's my impression that Harold was living then on Perry Street; the good Lord knows where I was living. We were quite incredibly, monstrously young, insanely confident—we were destined to do such things! Time passed—perhaps no time in the history of the world has passed so swiftly and so hideously—time passed, testing our assumptions, trying our confidence, breaking our hearts: and forcing us to work. For a very long time we saw each other not at all. But each knew that the other was somewhere around, and, in the peculiar way of poets, and to our peculiar gods, we prayed for each other.

All that I am equipped to recognize in the effort of any poet is whether or not the effort is genuine. The achieved performance, insofar as it is susceptible to contemporary judgment, can only be judged by this touchstone. And by "genuine effort" I do not mean good intentions, or hysterical verbosity, or frantic endeavor: the effort I am suggesting scours the poet's life, reduces him, inexorably, to who he is; and who he is is what he gives us. But he gives us much more than that, for his giving is an example that contains a command: the command is for us to do likewise.

That this example and this command are terrifying is proved by the lives of all poets, and that the example and the command are valid is proved by the terror these evoke. One is commanded to look on each day as though it were the first day, to draw each breath in freedom, and to know that everything that lives is holy. Neither the state nor the church approves of such blasphemy, banks will never knowingly loan it money, and armies trample it underfoot. So be it. It is themselves they are trampling underfoot, their hope, and their continuity: and one day all of us will know this, and be able to love one another and learn to live in peace.

Until that day comes, the poet is in exile, as Harold is now. But if light ever enters the hearts of men, Harold will be one of those who have helped to set it there.

(1965)

The Negro in New York: An Informal Social History, 1626–1940,

edited by Roi Ottley and William J. Weatherby

THE NEGRO IN NEW YORK is an unavoidably sketchy and uneven document, compiled by the Writers' Program of New York City during that very brief period of the WPA when it was recognized that writers existed in our country and had to eat, and even had a certain utility—though, probably, no real value. The curator of the Schomburg Collection of Negro Literature and History, Jean Blackwell Hutson, points out that the material in this book has been sitting in the collection since 1940, with "publication deferred and prevented because information contained in it was too startling for conservative taste." That the information in this book should be startling is an interesting comment on the conservative, that is to say, the prevailing, attitude toward American history. If so many people did not find the information in this book "startling," they might be less at the mercy of their ignorance, and our present situation would be healthier than it is.

The book can be startling only to the brainwashed, in which category, alas, nearly all Americans are presently to be found, and, of course, it would be very hard to use it as a basis for a rousing television series. It strips the Americans of their fig leaves, as it were, and proves that Eden, if it ever existed, certainly never existed here. It proves that anyone who contends that the Northern racial attitudes have not always been, essentially, indistinguishable from those of the South is either lying or is deluded. Of course, one has become deluded when one has believed a lie too long.

It is impossible to read this book and not realize how disastrous has been the effect, in so many millions of lives, of the Industrial Revolution—that same revolution which has been hailed as being so liberating a force. Indeed, it liberated peasants from the land, to say nothing of their lives, small children from their parents, women from their safety, and men from their honor. The tremendous amount of labor needed to cultivate the New World, and the enormous profits to be carried back to Europe as a result of this cultivation, meant that human flesh, any human flesh, became a source of profit. And there is nothing in European, or subsequent American, history to indicate that any consideration whatever deflected the new conquerors from this goal. Such uneasy consciences as we know to have been were as nothing compared to the heartening—yes, the virtuous—sound of money being made and of money making money. The Dutch, who ruled this city, and the Europeans who traded in this harbor, sought one freedom only, the freedom to make money, and in searching for this freedom they did not hesitate to use women and small children, as well as thieves and pirates and murderers. The poor Irish, God knows, fared no better at the hands of the industrialists than any captive African. The Irish situation began to change only after it was no longer necessary, or politic, to use the poor Irish laborer to cow the Negro laborer, or vice versa: no doubt, many Irishmen will find this information startling indeed. (But it is no more startling than the fact that during the potato famine of 1845, their English masters allowed the Irish to starve, in order to protect British merchants. This unhappy circumstance has produced many a virtuous, self-righteous Irish cop, as well as the winning folklore of, say, *The Bells of St. Mary's*.)

The rise of Northern industry, and the consolidation of this power, caused the racial lines of the North to be drawn up very differently, but not less severely, than those in the South: where the poor white, until this hour, has yet to comprehend what his bosses have always understood very well—that any coalition of himself and the black will destroy the system which has kept both black and white in ignorance and peonage for so long. And a marvelous foreshadowing of the scapegoat role the black was to play in American life is contained in Peter Stuyvesant's explanation of his surrender to the British. The city could not withstand the British siege, he explained, because three hundred slaves, brought in just before the British arrived in the harbor, had eaten all the surplus food. Scarcely any American politician has since improved on this extraordinarily convincing way of explaining American reverses.

What the Negro did in New York, and how, is the subject of the book before you, and not the subject of this foreword. But: "[The British] regulated servitude with the thoroughness of modern business methods— every step necessary for its protection and preservation was taken. Blacks were therefore set apart from whites on the theory that to permit them to mingle freely with white people would endanger the chances of keeping them enslaved. This policy was carried out in every straining detail; so much so that a law was passed 'that no Negro shall be buried in Trinity church-yard.' " Nor would some of our more conservative political leaders find the following proclamation, issued in 1706 by Governor Lord Cornbury, the cousin of Queen Anne, in the least startling:

> Requiring and commanding [all officers] to take all proper methods for the seizing and apprehending of all such Negroes as shall be found to be assembled—and if any of them refuse to submit, then fire upon them, kill or destroy them, if they cannot otherwise be taken—I am informed that several Negroes in Kings County [Brooklyn] have assembled themselves in a riotous manner, which if not prevented may prove of ill consequence.

Then, as now, Negroes were in the streets—and this is before the American War of Independence; then, as now, white people professed not to know the reason why; then, as now, it was the slave who was the wrongdoer and not the system which had made him a slave. And then, as now, the Negro's hopes were used with the utmost cynicism by those who could use these hopes to perpetuate their own dominance. Thus, the Declaration of Independence terrified the slave owners, and they would never have armed their slaves if the British had not done so first, promising freedom to any Negro who joined the British lines. Thereupon, the soon-to-be-Americans armed two regiments of blacks, promising freedom to all who served three years, or who were honorably discharged (two interesting stipulations). That this cynical and treacherous pattern has not altered from that day to this is scarcely worth mentioning: but it is worth observing that whereas Americans profess not to know what the Negro wants, they always know what to promise him whenever they need his body.

And here, during the Depression, is a member of the New York City Realty Board: "I believe a logical section for Negro expansion in Manhattan is East Harlem. At present this district has reached such a point of deterioration that its ultimate residential pattern is most puzzling.—An influx of Negroes into East Harlem would not work a hardship on the present population of the area, because its present residents could move to any other section of New York without the attendant racial discrimination which the Negro would encounter if he endeavored to locate in other districts."

Well, we know how the "puzzling" residential pattern of East Harlem eventually resolved itself: into a pattern which changes not. And we will not even discuss the shameful and brutal role played in all this by the churches, by the labor unions, and by revered corporations and utilities. Nor will we—in order to avoid startling our readers—observe that the economic pattern to be discerned in the pages which follow is so brutal, so utterly blind and selfish, and so irresponsible that Russian roulette, by comparison, seems safer than playing jacks.

Here is what Mayor La Guardia's commission had to say about the Harlem race riot of 1935: "As a population of low income, [it] suffered from conditions that affected low income groups of all races, but the causes that kept Negroes in this class did not apply with the same force to whites. These conditions were underscored by discrimination against Negroes in all walks of life. The rumor of the death of a boy which spread throughout the community had *awakened the deep-seated sense of wrongs and denials and even memories of injustices in the South.*" (Italics mine: the pot is calling the kettle black.) The riot's cause was "the smouldering resentments of the people of Harlem against racial discrimination and poverty in the midst of plenty." The riot was "a spontaneous and an incoherent protest by Harlem's population against a studied neglect of its critical problems."

At least, no one said that the riot was Communist inspired. And what was done? "The Board of Education promoted Mrs. Gertrude E. Ayer to the principalship of Public School No. 24, Manhattan, in 1936, and she became the first Negro woman to advance to such a position." (Also, as far as I know, and certainly until very lately, the last. That was my school, and my principal, and I loved and feared the lady—for she really was a lady, and a great one—with that trembling passion only twelve-year-olds can feel.) But let us continue this progress report:

That same year, the Department of Hospitals appointed Dr. John West . . . the director of the new Central Harlem Health Center which had been built at a cost of $250,000. At the same time, the Mayor reported that 435 buildings were torn down in the Harlem slum area. New schools, a housing project, a large recreational center, with a swimming pool, sports fields, tennis courts, and a band concert stadium known as the Colonial [!] Recreation Center, situated at 145th Street on Bradhurst Avenue, have been part of the city's acknowledgment of the needs of the Negro people . . . Throughout his long American history, the Negro's faith has been in the ultimate triumph of democracy. At no time has his goal been as visible as it is today.

The last words were written just before our entry into World War II. If—for those of you who are not too hopelessly startled—the show seems familiar, it is because the show has been running a very long time, and most of the actors have had no choice but to speak the lines and make the moves assigned to them. There is a rumor—striking terror and chaos in the heart of the box office—that some people have become so weary of the spectacle that they have sent for a new show, which is presently on the road. But not until the wheels of those wagons are on our children's necks will we consider reading or revising or throwing away this script.

In the meantime, ladies and gentlemen, after a brief intermission—time out for one or two committee reports, time out for an antipoverty pep talk, time out to make a Vietnamese child an orphan and then lovingly raise him to love all our works, time out for a White House conference, time out to brief and augment the police forces, time out to buy some Negroes, jail some, club some, and kill some—after a brief intermission, ladies and gentlemen, the show begins again in the auction room. And you will hear the same old piano, playing the blues.

(1967)

Daddy Was a Number Runner by Louise Meriwether

I RECEIVED A QUESTIONNAIRE the other day—democracy prides itself on its questionnaires, just as it is endlessly confirmed and misled by its public opinion polls—and the first question was "Why do you continue to write?" Writers do not like this question, which they hear as "Why do you continue to breathe?" but sometimes one can almost answer it by pointing to the work of another writer. There! one says, triumphantly. Look! *That's* what it's about—to make one see—to lead us back to reality again.

The streets, tenements, fire escapes, the elders, and the urgent concerns of childhood—or, rather, the helpless intensity of anguish with which one watches one's childhood disappear—are rendered very vividly indeed by Louise Meriwether, in her first novel, *Daddy Was a Number Runner*. We have seen this life from the point of view of a black boy growing into a menaced and probably brief manhood; I don't know that we have ever seen it from the point of view of a black girl on the edge of a terrifying womanhood. And the metaphor for this growing apprehension of the iron and insurmountable rigors of one's life are here conveyed by that game known in Harlem as the numbers, the game which contains the possibility of making a "hit"—the American dream in blackface, Horatio Alger revealed, the American success story with the price tag showing! Compare the heroine of this book—to say nothing of the landscape—with the heroine of *A Tree*

Grows in Brooklyn and you will see to what extent poverty wears a color—and also, as we put it in Harlem, arrives at an *attitude*. By this time, the heroine of *Tree* (whose name was also Francie, if I remember correctly) is among those troubled Americans, that silent (!) majority which wonders what black Francie wants, and why she's so unreliable as a maid.

Shit, says Francie, sitting on the stoop as the book ends, looking outward at the land of the free, and trying, with one thin bony black hand, to stem the blood which is beginning to rush from a nearly mortal wound. That monosyllable resounds all over this country, all over the world: it is a judgment on this civilization rendered the more implacable by being delivered by a child. The mortal wound is not physical; the book, so far from being a melodrama, is very brilliantly understated. The wound is the wound made upon the recognition that one is regarded as a worthless human being, and, further, in the case of this particular black girl, upon the recognition that the men, one's only hope, have also been cut down and cannot save you. Louise Meriwether wisely ends her book before confronting us with what it means to "jump the broomstick!"—to have a black man and a black woman jump over a broomstick is the way slave masters laughingly married their slaves to each other, those same white people who now complain that black people have no morals. At the heart of this book, which gives it its force, is a child's growing sense of being one of the victims of a collective rape—for history, and especially and emphatically in the black-white arena, is not the past, it is the present. The great, vast, public, historical violation is also the present, private, unendurable insult, and the mighty force of these unnoticed violations spells doom for any civilization which pretends that the violations are not occurring or that they do not matter or that tomorrow is a lovely day. People cannot be—and, finally, will not be—treated in this way. This book should be sent to the White House, and to our earnest attorney general, and to everyone in this country able to read—which may, however, alas, be a most despairing statement. We love—the white Americans, I mean—the notion of the little woman behind the great man: perhaps one day, Louise Meriwether will give us *her* version of *What Every Woman Knows*.

Until that hoped-for hour, because she has so truthfully conveyed what the world looks like from a black girl's point of view, she has told everyone who can read or feel what it means to be a black man or woman in this country. She has achieved an assessment, in a deliberately minor key, of a major tragedy. It is a considerable achievement, and I hope she simply keeps on keeping on.

(1970)

A *Lonely Rage* by Bobby Seale

Bobby Seale (b. 1936) cofounded the Black Panther Party along with Huey P. Newton in 1966. Raised largely in Oakland, California, he would spend three years in the Air Force before receiving a dishonorable discharge for disobeying orders. He met Newton while at the Oakland City College after joining the Afro-American Association. They both were looking for more radical civil rights involvement. Seale became the first chairman of the Black Panther Party. He would become involved in two famous trials, one as a member of the 1968 Chicago Eight (where, famously, he was bound and gagged for outbursts in the courtroom), and again in 1970 in New Haven, Connecticut, where nineteen-year-old Alex Rackley, a suspected FBI informant, had been killed by fellow members of the Panther Party. Seale stood accused of having ordered the "execution." The trial became a cause célèbre, centering around Yale University and the courthouse, where literally thousands descended, including famous radical celebrities; the spectacle turned into an indictment of the Nixon administration, the FBI, the notorious Counter-Intelligence Program (COINTELPRO), and J. Edgar Hoover. The trial ended in a hung jury.

A *Lonely Rage* was Seale's second memoir, after *Seize the Time* (1970).

Eldridge Cleaver (1935–1998)—who joined the Panthers after being released from prison in 1966, after serving nine years for rape and intent to commit murder—possessed conflicted and complicated feelings about Baldwin. On one hand he championed Baldwin's work as an inspiration, but he would go on to say demeaning and homophobic things against him, particularly in his 1968 memoir, *Soul on Ice.* Nonetheless, Baldwin always seemed to treat him with respect.

.   .   .

I WISH I'D KEPT MY NOTES concerning Bobby Seale and Huey Newton and Eldridge Cleaver, so many years ago. It was, actually, only a little over ten years ago, but it seems much longer than that. Everyone was so young— except Eldridge, there was always something of the deacon about that one. Huey was the dedicated poet, and strategist. Bobby was the firebrand.

I first met Huey in San Francisco, but don't remember meeting either Bobby or Eldridge then. My first recollection of Eldridge is in Hollywood, at the Beverly Hills Hotel; he was part of the Black Panther escort for Betty Shabazz. As for Bobby Seale, I first met him, if memory serves, with Marlon Brando, in Marlon's hotel suite, in Atlanta, the day of Martin Luther King Jr.'s funeral. He had been sleeping, was still groggy—was as tense and quiet as the air becomes when a storm is about to break. This was certainly due, in part, to the climate of that momentous day, but it was also due to a kind of intelligence of anguish living behind Bobby's smoky eyes.

This intelligence is unsparing—Bobby certainly does not spare Bobby— and informs this modest, restrained, and passionate book. I feel completely inept, almost presumptuous, in attempting to write a foreword to it. I did not go through what Bobby, and his generation, went through. The time of my youth was entirely different and the savage irony of hindsight allows me to suggest that the time of my youth was far less hopeful. I speak of this savage irony because the political and spiritual currents of my very early youth involved a return to Africa, or a rejection of it; either choice would lead to suicide, or madness, for, in fact, neither choice was possible. Though the American Communist Party, as it was then constituted, anyway, never made any very great impact on the bulk of the black population; its presence, strategies, and mercurial shifts in moral judgment disseminated, at the very least, confusion. Our most visible heroes were

Father Divine and Joe Louis—we in the ghetto then knew very little about Paul Robeson. We knew very little about anything black, in fact, and this was not our fault. Those of us who found out more than the schools were willing to teach us did so at the price of becoming unmanageable, isolated, and, indeed, subversive.

The South was simply the hell which our parents had survived, and fled. Harlem was our rat-and-roach-infested haven: *Nigger Heaven,* a vastly successful novel about Harlem, was published around the time that I was born.

I have suggested that Bobby's time was more hopeful than my own: but I do not wish to be misunderstood concerning the nature, the meaning, and the cruelty of that hope. I do not mean to suggest that the bulk of the American people had undergone a "change of heart" as concerns their relationship to their darker brothers by the time Bobby Seale came down the pike. They hadn't, and it is very much to be doubted that they ever will. Most people cling to their guilts and terrors and crimes, compounding them hour by hour and day by day, and are more likely to be changed from without than from within. No: the world in which we found ourselves at the end of World War II, and, more particularly, the brutal and gratuitous folly with which we ushered in the atomic age, brought into focus, as never before, the real meaning of the American social contract and exposed the self-serving nature of the American dream. And one of the results of this exposure was that the celebrated "Negro problem" became a global instead of a merely domestic matter.

It is in this sense that Seale's era is to be considered more hopeful: in spite of the horrors which he recounts, with such restraint, in these pages. The beacon lit, for his generation, in 1956, in Montgomery, Alabama, by an anonymous black woman, elicited an answering fire from all the wretched, all over the earth, signaled the beginning of the end of the racial nightmare—for it will end; no lie endures forever—and helped Stagolee, the black folk hero Bobby takes for his model, to achieve his manhood. For it is that tremendous journey which Bobby's book is about: the act of assuming and becoming oneself.

(1978)

BOOK REVIEWS

Best Short Stories by Maxim Gorky

IN GORKY'S MASTERWORK, *The Lower Depths,* his greatest gifts shine most clearly: his immense—but not quite profound—perception, his concern for the wretchedness of people, his almost romantic preoccupation with nature. And here, above all, is a carefully controlled rage at the lot of men and an insistence on their noble destiny.

Insofar as one can tell from this translation, however—which, by the way, seems most uneven—he is far from a careful writer and by no means a great one. He is almost always painfully verbose and frequently threatens to degenerate into simple propaganda.

But though this wordiness persists in every story in the book, in such pieces as "Creatures That Once Were Men," in "Cain and Artyom," and in such shorter pieces as "Red," "Twenty-six Men and a Girl," and "Chums," the power of Gorky's sympathy almost succeeds in reducing his flaws to unimportance. There is ironic penetration and great tenderness here which none of the contemporary realists whom Gorky helped to father have yet managed to match. But having said that he is tender, ironic, and observant, and that most of his descendants are not, it must also be admitted that he is also quite frequently sentimental—as are his offspring—and that regardless of how well they succeed as outraged citizens, they are incomplete as artists.

Gorky's range is narrow and in intention and effect alike he can scarcely be called subtle. He reiterates: men can be gods and they live like beasts; this he relates, quite legitimately, indeed necessarily, to a particular and oppressive society. ("And the men, too, the first source of all that uproar, were ludicrous and pitiable: their little figures dusty, tattered, nimble, bent under the weight of goods that lay on their backs, under the weight of cares that drove them hither and thither . . . were so trivial and small in comparison with the colossal iron monsters . . . and all that they had created. Their own creation had enslaved them and taken away their individuality.") This is a disquieting and honest report. Its only limitation, and it is a profound one, is that it remains a report. Gorky does not seem capable of the definitive insight, the shock of identification. Again and again we recognize a *type,* with his human attributes sensitively felt and well reported but never realized. For this reason Gorky's sympathy is often mawkish, his dénouements a brutal and self-consciously sardonic trick. He is concerned, not with the human as such, but with the human being as a symbol; and this attitude is basically sentimental, pitying, rather than clear, and therefore—in spite of the boast of realism—quite thoroughly unreal. There can be no catharsis in Gorky, in spite of the wealth of action and his considerable powers of observation; his people inspire pity and sometimes rage but never love or terror. Finally we are divorced from them; we see them in relation to oppression but not in relation to ourselves. In the short story "The Hermit," the lack of psychological acuteness he brings to a story intended to show the power of virtue (Love) and the roads taken to attain it make for a devastating and characteristic failure.

And yet Gorky was possessed by a rare sympathy for people. Such work as "Cain and Artyom" and even the rather superficial "Red" and the delightful "Going Home" would be impossible if this were not so. But his sympathy did not lead him to that peculiar position of being at once identified with and detached from the humans that he studied. He is never criminal, judge, and hangman simultaneously—and yet indubitably Gorky. His failure was that he did not speak *as a criminal* but spoke *for them;* and operated, consciously or not, not as an artist and a prophet but as a reporter and a judge.

It seems to me that in Gorky's failure can be found the key to the even more dismal failure of present-day realistic novelists. For as a school they do not even have that sympathy which activated Gorky. They do not ever

indicate what Gorky sometimes succeeded in projecting—the unpredictability and the occasional and amazing splendor of the human being. It
is a concept which today—and this is understandable, if alarming—is dismissed as mystic or *unreal*. Without the insight into the mainsprings of
human needs, desperations, and desires, the concern with squalor remains
merely squalid and acts to brutalize the reader rather than to purge him.
If literature is not to drop completely to the intellectual and moral level
of the daily papers, we must recognize the need for further and honest
exploration of those provinces, the human heart and mind, which have
operated, historically and now, as the no-man's-land between us and our
salvation.

(1947)

Mother by Maxim Gorky

MOTHER, ACCORDING TO THE JACKET and the reverent introduction by
Howard Fast, is Maxim Gorky's most notable achievement; the most
beloved of his works in his native Russia, the novel most often and most
widely translated, the novel most reread and treasured by people everywhere. In a word, this is Gorky's best-seller.

And, indeed, though I have not read this book before and am scarcely
likely to enter the fellowship of the faithful now that I have, the reasons for
this resounding popularity are evident on each brave and bitter page. With
some ideological concessions and the proper makeup *Mother* would make
an impressive vehicle for, say, Bette Davis. It is rich in struggle, tears,
courage, and good old-fashioned mother love. Reading it is a little like a
rereading of the beloved, dog-eared classics of our childhood: how musty
it is now, how brave it was then, what a pity we cannot believe it anymore!

Mother, as I gather a great portion of the world's population knows by
now, is that novel dealing with the Russian workers just before the October
Revolution. The story is that of a Russian mother's relationship with her
revolutionary son; and we watch the mother as she becomes "step by step,
a fighter for justice." The characterization of Nilovna is, in fact, done with

a great deal of skill; she is by far the most fully realized character in the book, even though, so accustomed have we become to the proletarian novel, she is entirely predictable, and her development proceeds along lines since grown monotonous. When first written and published, this novel must have had that same splendid fire and impetus characteristic of all battle hymns when people are in the midst of a struggle, and their blood, as the saying goes, is up. Much of the atmosphere of struggle is captured here—the rage, the wretchedness, the heroism—and reading it now, wise after the event, one is also aware of a terrible futility, a sensation of constriction and waste. The battle betrayed becomes, in retrospect, more terrible than the battle itself, the most especially when the betrayal of the battle can be seen to have been caused by those very elements which gave the battle purpose. In the urgency of battle barricades are set up, issues are defined, the intermediate colors disappear. We have instead the verities of our childhood, the contrast of night and day. It is no place for Hamlet.

Gorky, not in the habit of describing intermediate colors, even when he suspected their existence, has in *Mother* written a Russian battle hymn which history has so cruelly and summarily dated that we are almost unwilling to credit it with any reality. In spite of the monstrous sentimentality of this tale, the resolute repetition of words like "truth" and "justice," and the romantic unreality of almost all of its people, there is an ugly, hard truth under it: this did happen, not very long ago; these people really *believed* in a better world and struggled to bring it about. Nilovna's last words have a ring of doom and despair which could hardly have been intended: "You heap up only wrath against yourselves, you unwise ones! It will fall on you—you poor, sorry creatures."

We poor, sorry creatures have not yet, for all our struggle, made this planet a fitting habitation, nor have we learned to live on it at peace with ourselves or with each other. "For us," cries Andrey, "there are only comrades and foes." Indeed; and this formulation, with its implicit challenge to engage in perpetual battle, is not likely to change; nor, on the other hand, is the battle likely to grow any simpler, particularly when the distinction between comrades and foes has become so faint as to reduce us all to a state of incipient schizophrenia.

Fast, in his introduction, makes a good deal of the fact that Gorky never severed himself from the people, that he was active in their cause always and was highly revered by his nation. He was the foremost exponent of the maxim that "art is the weapon of the working class." He is also, probably, the major example of the invalidity of such a doctrine. (It is rather like saying that art is the weapon of the American housewife.) The phrase has always brought to my mind the image of a soldier rushing into battle waving a volume of Shakespeare on the point of a bayonet. Art, to be sure, has its roots in the lives of human beings: the weakness, the strength, the absurdity. I doubt that it is limited to our comrades; since we have discovered that art does not belong to what was once the aristocracy, it does not therefore follow that it has become the exclusive property of the common man—which abstraction, by the way, I have yet to meet. Rather, since it is involved with all of us, it belongs to all of us, and this includes our foes, who are as desperate and as vacuous and as blind as we are and who can only be as evil as we are ourselves.

(1947)

The Amboy Dukes by Irving Shulman

EQUIPPED WITH PERFECTION AND ECONOMY and an impressive narrative power, Irving Shulman tells the story of Frank Goldfarb and the boys who were members of the Amboy Dukes, a street gang in the Brownsville section of Brooklyn during the late spring and summer of 1944. This was when the war hit Brownsville and other slum sections like it with a terrific impact and, suddenly, in the midst of the squalor and congestion, people began making money and spending it, and—remembering the years of Home Relief investigators, food tickets, shabby clothes, and all the incessant humiliations which grind down the poor—grabbing desperately at every chance to work overtime and double time in order to sustain this new solvency for themselves and their children. But the improved financial status, though it brought them more and better food and new clothes and bank accounts, did nothing to release them from the acid, overcrowded ghettos which had conditioned their lives. Rather, this tantalizing, ultimately powerless spending power intensified the violence and frustration contained in their personalities for so long. The children, responding to the complicated drives of adolescence and the electrifying onslaught of global war, were left to their own devices: devices always violent and sometimes lethal, like petty or grand larceny, gang wars, beatings, and rape.

The year that Frank was bar mitzvahed, his family had been too poor to give him anything; but when he was fourteen, in 1942, they made up for it by giving him a beautiful, expensive wristwatch, a symbol of their new prosperity and his new status as a man. Two years later, when the story begins, his membership in the Dukes is of central importance in his life: he has an identity and the security that comes from the knowledge that he is "solid with the right guys." But during the summer he and his sidekick, Benny, in a drunken fight, shoot and kill their high-school teacher, the unendurably goaded and frustrated Mr. Bannon, who has never been able to control the hoodlums in his class and who baits them at the same time that he is forced to realize that they are as helpless as he is himself. Frank and Benny are trapped together now, and neither dares to trust the other. When the alibi they have fashioned is broken, Frank squeals on Benny and tries to escape. But at the last moment he is cornered on his rooftop by a member of the Dukes, the dull-witted, desperate Crazy Sachs, and killed.

It is an unsubtle, ugly story and Mr. Shulman has not attempted, and has certainly not produced, a literary masterpiece. In retrospect I am forced to admit that some of the story devices are contrived (that is, rather transparently contrived), that much of the minor characterization is perfunctory, and that, in one instance, his study of Frank's younger sister, Alice, he succeeds only partially in bringing a potentially significant character to life. But Mr. Shulman, at his best, exhibits a narrative skill that a depressingly large number of his more pretentious colleagues lack, and by some miracle of sympathy he has captured with disturbing accuracy the urgency and restlessness and danger of his locale, the inimitable flavor of speech, and the relentless, inarticulate underache of anguish which culminates in the violence he describes so well. His skill and sensitivity are nowhere more apparent than in his moving sketch of Mrs. Goldfarb, his unfaltering probing of Frank, his realization of the monstrous, sardonic tragedy personified by Crazy Sachs. Here rage is constantly illuminated by pity; even his brutal, shocking climax is saved from being lurid by the painful figure of Crazy shouting, as he pounds Frank's body, "Now I gotcha. I gotcha for everything!"

Mr. Shulman offers no blueprints, no panaceas, which, I imagine, puts him under the stigma of having written a "pessimistic" novel. He does not say, but seems to know, that recreation halls and basketball games, that first resort of the civic-minded, is a procedure about as effective as the application of Vaseline to a syphilitic lesion. The danger and squalor and personal desperation studied in *The Amboy Dukes* is not the peculiar property of displaced, thwarted adolescents. In one sense, at least, it is the inevitable by-product of a way of life which disregards—and therefore violates—the impulse of the individual to dignity and freedom.

(1947)

The Sure Hand of God by Erskine Caldwell

THIS, CALDWELL'S TWENTY-THIRD PUBLISHED VOLUME, is almost impossible to review, largely, I suspect, because it is almost impossible to take it seriously. One wonders why it was done at all. Certainly there is nothing in the book which would not justify the suspicion that Mr. Caldwell was concerned with nothing more momentous than getting rid of some of the paper he had lying about the house, resurrecting several of the tired types on which he first made his reputation, and (incidentally) making a few dollars on the deal.

The story, such as it is, is laid, predictably, in the South, and to no one's surprise it concerns some poor whites struggling to get along. We have the blowsy, aging prostitute, Molly; her carelessly spawned daughter, Lilly, sixteen, and growing swiftly into a willowy and blindly attractive aphrodisiac; a notably uninspired Jeeter Lester type, here named Jethro; a minister and his sex-starved wife; sex, of course, overlaid with squalor and shot through with what here becomes a curiously revolting humor and a snobbish kind of love. For a story line we have the recently widowed Molly's attempt to find a man and to make money and keep Lilly pure until she finds a good husband for her. Hoping, perhaps, to have this described as a tragicomedy,

Mr. Caldwell thwarts his characters at every turn. The story stops where it began and in the same key. Lilly, to be sure, is no longer a virgin, but no one expected that she would be.

Still, this is a curious book; curious because of its effortless tone and absolute emptiness. Mr. Caldwell, it would appear, knows these people so well that he is no longer even interested in them. He sets them up and they strut their stuff and go back into darkness until it is time for another book. Here, the sure hand of Mr. Caldwell is everywhere apparent. He has not written a single sloppy sentence (nor a single interesting one) nor created (within his own familiar framework) a single unlikely character. This must be fun for Mr. Caldwell, and there is no reason why it cannot go on forever.

It is something of a pity, though. Mr. Caldwell's gifts may never have been profound, but he was once—as in *God's Little Acre* and in some of the short stories, notably "Kneel to the Rising Sun," and in the honest, well-controlled rage pervading *You Have Seen Their Faces*—far more valid, far more concerned with human beings and the terrible circumstances of their lives. Mr. Caldwell's strength lay in his skill as a storyteller, which—and almost regrettably—he has not lost; his concern with and knowledge of one of the unlovelier aspects of the Southern scene, which has become mechanical; and his passion, which to all evidence has died. His career is almost a study in the slow conquest of immobility. Unless we hear from him again in accents more individual, we can leave his bones for that literary historian of another day who may perhaps define and isolate that virus in our organism which has thus far proved so deadly to the growth of our literature in general and our writers in particular.

(1947)

The Sling and the Arrow by Stuart Engstrand

THE SLING AND THE ARROW is the carefully documented study of a schizo-phrenic personality. From the first page to the last it is a masterpiece of cor-rect and faintly disturbing detail; the progress of the disease is recorded with cold and merciless accuracy. This novel escapes the grisly gaiety of *The Snake Pit* and is better written and more convincing than *The Fall of Valor*, without, however, being, in any way, a better or more profound piece of work. Mr. Engstrand writes in a curiously flat and bony prose which seems perpetually on the verge of a climax; his characterization is apt even if his people are uniformly uninteresting; his story is very slickly contrived indeed, and Herbert's downfall as final—and as right—as any of our psy-chiatrically conscious millions could wish. To talk of perception here or compassion or eloquence is quite beside the point: the jacket intimates that Mr. Engstrand kept [Wilhelm] Stekel* continually at his elbow and could, presumably, forgo creative intuition for scientific fact.

And Herbert Dawes's case history does, in fact, have a grim and clinical

---

*Wilhelm Stekel (1868–1942) was an Austrian physician and psychologist. He was an early disciple of Sigmund Freud.

interest. When the book begins he is a top West Coast dress designer, seemingly well adjusted and secure, placidly married to a spineless and spectacularly unperceptive girl named Lonna—who, apparently, ceased going to movies shortly before Hollywood discovered Freud. Herbert has molded Lonna into what his neurosis makes him desire in a wife; she is unobtrusive, mannishly dressed, useless about the house, and in their love-making Herbert's passivity has forced her into the dominant role. But the security of this structure is abruptly challenged when Lonna insists on having a child. ("To the male part of you she was a wife," probes the inevitable psychiatrist. "But to the inner female self of you she is your husband—how can a husband become pregnant, nurse a child? Suddenly she had become your enemy.") While swimming Herbert tries to murder his wife with a spear, believing her shadow in the water to be a shark. Even the tranquil Lonna is upset by this and runs off to a psychiatrist, who diagnoses the root of Herbert's trouble as a fiercely repressed homosexuality. This, apparently, is too fantastic for anyone in the book to believe, most of all Herbert. Lonna frets over her childlessness, the while her husband is feverishly spying on the lovemaking of a brawny sailor and his girl. Herbert eventually sleeps with the girl—in lieu of the sailor—and when the sailor deserts her, Herbert deserts her too. But the sailor, meanwhile, has begun an affair with the unhappy, sex-starved Lonna; whereupon Herbert falls in love with Lonna again, trying hard to hide his jubilance at having his lover-by-proxy back. Lonna, prepared to risk their marriage once again, sends the sailor off; Herbert, whose mental battle is breaking through into physical symptoms, becomes sufficiently ill to stay home from the factory, sends Lonna to take his place, does all the housework, and is about to make this precarious adjustment work when Lonna finds she is going to have a child by the sailor. Herbert breaks completely, kills her, is caught trying to escape dressed in a woman's suit with no memory of what he has done. The book ends with him in prison, his fantasy complete, dreaming of a male Lonna about to possess him.

This is done with considerable adroitness; indeed, in the hands of a major novelist, *The Sling and the Arrow* might have been a genuinely moving study. But Mr. Engstrand, for all his skill, never succeeds in cracking the surface of the tragedy or causing, in at least one reader, any sense of identification. His failure is not that his people are unbelievable or his situations unreal. One is simply not interested in his people or in what happens to them. The book reads like a plan—here is a schizophrenic, this is what he does, here is the reason for it. In Herbert's case, the reason, relentlessly tracked down, stems from his relationship with his father, who according to Herbert loved his wife and daughter more than he loved his son, and who rejected Herbert when he was twelve because he found him in homo-sexual play with a young neighbor. Herbert's life was a kind of expiation and flight, an obsession to prove to his dead father that he was masculine entirely and had been cleansed of his sin. Here is a dilemma known to all of us: Herbert's terrible guilt, the compulsion to be accepted, his helpless-ness in the face of the war within him. The contemporary sexual attitudes constitute a rock against which many of us flounder all our lives long; no one escapes entirely the prevailing psychology of the times. Perhaps the failure of *The Sling and the Arrow* can partially be traced to its implicit acceptance of the popular attitude. We are not asked to consider a person-ality but an abnormal psychology, not a study of human helplessness but a carefully embroidered case history. This has, then, ultimately no more reality than any one of the recent spate of films dealing with psychiatric problems. Here is no illumination, no pity, no terror. One closes this neat and empty volume untouched, indifferent, leaving Herbert floundering in his irrelevant hell, knowing that this happens seldom and can never happen to us.

(1947)

Novels and Stories by Robert Louis Stevenson, edited by
V. S. Pritchett; and *Robert Louis Stevenson* by David Daiches

UNTIL THIS NECESSITY I had not read Robert Louis Stevenson since my
childhood. I had read then, and in some corner of my mind remember
with pleasure, *A Child's Garden of Verses, Kidnapped,* and *Treasure Island.* I
especially remembered the poetry, without, of course, ever thinking of
rereading it. It was something designed for my friends' children on their
birthdays. I had, in fact, relegated Stevenson to that dusty and diverse
gallery of my childhood, a gallery which also included Horatio Alger, *Uncle
Tom's Cabin,* and almost all of Dickens. Childhood, I decided, having safely
survived it, was a period of light and sunshine, and in Stevenson these elements were contained in profusion; he was perfect for childhood, because
his stories were so simple and he told them so well.

Thus, rereading Stevenson was something of a shock, almost a betrayal.
It was not that he had become less delightful, but that now there stirred for
me beneath this brave adventure an element faintly disturbing of which I
had not been cognizant before. *Treasure Island,* it is true, remains perhaps
the best boys' book I have ever read; but not even this masterpiece quite
escapes the transformation effected by time.

The most enduring delight offered by Stevenson is contained in his prose; he could write superbly well, a virtue for which we should all be grateful now that the clotheshorse, the fisherman, and nymphomaniac have been equipped with typewriters and entered the world of letters. The admirable study by David Daiches dissects Stevenson's style in some detail and skillfully traces Stevenson from his "sedulous" aping of the styles of other men to the Stevenson who produced *Kidnapped* and *The Beach of Falesa* and the unfinished *Weir of Hermiston*. Daiches does some extremely careful detective work here and achieves a rare effect: he makes Stevenson grow and strengthen before our eyes. Perhaps this is not the definitive study of Stevenson, but it succeeds within its limits perfectly. Whoever attempts such a study hereafter will be greatly in Mr. Daiches's debt.

The Pritchett volume—which is badly printed on bad paper and with an inaccurate table of contents—includes *Weir of Hermiston, Kidnapped, Travels with a Donkey, The Beach of Falesa, The Master of Ballantrae,* and *The Suicide Club,* and contains an introduction by Mr. Pritchett. Pritchett, rather less sympathetic than Mr. Daiches, notes that Stevenson was too mannered and too clever and too vain and was, for much of his life, not so much of an artist as a charming and irresponsible vagrant; and that even *Weir of Hermiston* might never have become the great novel it seems to promise because Stevenson does not, at any other time in his career, seem capable of so sustained an effort on such a mature level. Mr. Daiches, in consideration of this aspect of Stevenson, anatomizes the conflict within Stevenson between a bourgeois and a bohemian morality, a conflict related to his father and accounting in part for his unevenness as an artist and his frequent inability to achieve or sustain adult insights.

Stevenson is always a master storyteller; and his failure, when he fails, is not the inability to tell the story but an inability to handle a theme. It is this failure which mars his two most ambitious efforts for me: the murkiness and indecision and unevenness of characterization in *The Master of Ballantrae* and—in spite of the considerable impressiveness of *Weir of Hermiston* and the sometimes brilliant handling of the father-and-son relationship—a lack of unity in this fragment, which indeed I doubt that Stevenson could have finished.

Stevenson is at his absolute best, however, in a narrative like *Kidnapped,* an exceedingly skillful novel and a far less simple one that I had supposed. (According to Mr. Daiches it is only one-half of the novel its author intended, having been sidetracked midway and become something quite

different. It has a sequel, *David Balfour.*) All of Stevenson's warm brutal
innocence is here, the sensation of light and air, the nervous tension, the
chase, the victory. And the preoccupations he later pursued in more ambitious novels give *Kidnapped* an impetus which makes it a good deal more
than an adventure tale. The story of David Balfour's struggle to attain his
birthright is told with a strange lack of directness and is emphasized by an
indefinable sense of guilt, sometimes almost terror, which makes his victory, when it comes, less than it was in anticipation. He has paid for his victory with himself and has become a different person. The novel, in fact,
ends on a restrained and terrible note of melancholy:

> It was coming near noon when I passed in by the West Kirk and the
> Grassmarket into the streets of the capital. The huge height of the build-
> ings, the foul smells and fine clothes struck me into a kind of stupor of
> surprise so that I let the crowd carry me to and fro; and yet all the time
> what I was thinking of was Alan at Rest-and-be Thankful; and all the
> time (although you would think I would not choose but be delighted
> with these braws and novelties) there was a cold gnawing in my inside
> like a remorse for something wrong.

Again, in *Kidnapped* the relationship of David and Alan, on which much
of the book turns, is far more than a friendship and is certainly not the traditional Anglo-Saxon friendship. Alan is for David a father image, a lover, a
foe, a child, and, over and above all, a symbol of romance. In spite of
Daiches's reservation that the characterization of Alan is not entirely successful, it seems to me that Stevenson exhibits in the relationship of these
two a richness and complexity of insight which does not anywhere—until
Kirstie and Archie in *Hermiston*—characterize his studies of men and
women. Pritchett, observing this, concludes, and I agree, that this does not
at all indicate that Stevenson was homosexual; for Stevenson men were less
of a riddle. They represented no challenge, they were the makers and the
movers of the world and more fitting subjects for romance. Here, probably, is one of the keys to Stevenson's continuing popularity with the young,
and one of the reasons it took him so long to become an artist. He is innocent—or asexual—in the same manner that preadolescent youth is asexual.
In *Treasure Island* as in *Kidnapped,* women and the challenge women represent are only vaguely intimated; it is an element projected into the future
and which allows the protagonists, meanwhile, to live as though this challenge will never have to be met. Later, when the challenge must be taken

up, it is an awkward and unhappy battle; this bright world is darkened and roughly disoriented; at this time David would be almost willing—if he could—to surrender his birthright, to be hunted and threatened all over again if he could thereby return to Alan at Rest-and-be-Thankful.

(1948)

Flood Crest by Hodding Carter

FLOOD CREST, BY HODDING CARTER, is yet another addition to the over-burdened files of progressive fiction concerning the unhappy South. We are asked this time to consider the career and character of Senator Cleve Pikestaff, a most reprehensible old man, who, as is made abundantly clear, is not in the least worthy of his great office. For years his political career has been managed for him by his sharp-witted, strong-willed, seductive daughter, Sudie—who frequently makes Cleve feel bad because she cannot bear his lack of social grace. (Cleve is given to spitting in the fireplace and scratching his bottom in public.) These symbols of corruption are surrounded by various familiar excerpts from the Southern landscape, a landscape which is not, apparently, ever going to change. We have the liberal old Southern professor, fortitudinous and patient, fighting, as one of the more rhetorical characters—perhaps the professor himself—remarks, "to keep change within a channel." In this he is aided by his sharp-witted, strong-willed, seductive daughter, Bethany. They are eventually joined by Sudie's ex-lover Floyd, young, attractive, confused, and—ultimately— Progressive. There are others: a lusty young killer and prison trusty named Clyde; two dreadful Caldwell cretins, Georgie Mae and her man, Pud; and the Mississippi River, which rages fearfully throughout the book, threatening to drown them all—a finale, however, which Mr. Carter avoids, since he is concerned with Progress and flatly opposed to Defeat.

This, like most of its predecessors, effectively resists all attempts at intelligent analysis. It cannot, of course, be criticized in literary terms at all; whatever Mr. Carter's convictions, his notions of trenchant characterization are shallow, not to say antique. The book, presumably, is meant as a study of public corruption feeding on public apathy; its moral is as neat and timely as the subway posters "Freedom Is Everybody's Job." The trouble is not specifically with the moral, which is fine as morals go, but simply with the painful vacuity and indecisiveness of Mr. Carter's story. Mr. Carter manages to say about all of the right things, none of them very strongly, none of them clearly; it is, indeed, made increasingly obvious that he does not quite know *what* to say. Mr. Carter is concerned with Change, which he equates with Progress, and he is against Violence. Progress must, of course, be made; but it must be made neatly, wisely, there must be no messy unforeseen edges to trim. And it must be made in the American Way by all the Common People, acting, as they seldom do, in unison. This metamorphosis demands—naturally—an heroic patience and a fairly transparent condescension towards the Masses. Proving, perhaps, his point, Mr. Carter's Common People—led by the uncommon Floyd—hold back the Mississippi, thus avoiding extinction. Senator Cleve Pikestaff, on the other hand, by a series of wild improbabilities, is assured of re-election, which is, I suppose, the same thing as saying that Rome was not built in a day. Novels and novelists of this genre serve no purpose whatever, so far as I can see, except to further complicate confusion. Mr. Carter knows, I hope, that holding back the Mississippi is not nearly so difficult as striking a bargain with time, which is neither polite nor predictable and refuses to be labeled in advance. And if he means to suggest that there must be men of wisdom and good will in the vanguard, he might also suggest that the wisdom be less vague and the good will less sentimental.

(1948)

The Moth by James M. Cain

A REVIEWER handed a James M. Cain novel to discuss finds himself confronted by several problems, not the least of which is the necessity of
squaring with his conscience the fact that he is discussing Mr. Cain at all.
What, after all, is one to say about such persistent aridity, such manifest
nonsense? Mr. Cain is no novelist: he has, indeed, his first sentence still to
write; he has yet to achieve his first valid characterization. For me, at the
top of his amazingly overrated form, as in *The Postman Always Rings Twice*,
in *Double Indemnity* and *Serenade*, he was, when not downright revolting,
obscurely and insistently embarrassing. Not only did he have nothing to
say, but he drooled, so to speak, as he said it. It seemed much kinder, really,
to take no notice of him, to adopt with him that same fiercely casual,
friendly air, assumed, let us say, when visiting two otherwise harmless people who are, however, shamefully addicted to early-morning drunkenness.

Mr. Cain, of course, strongly resists such treatment; he stands, in the
first place, by no means alone. He has, moreover, a following described by
the publisher's blurb as "vast"; and, what is perhaps more important than
any of this, he is himself convinced of his importance. He writes with the
stolid, humorless assurance of the American self-made man. Rather a

great deal has been written concerning his breathless staccato "pace," his terse, corner-of-the-mouth "style," his significance as a recorder of the seamier side of American life. This is nonsense: Mr. Cain writes fantasies, and fantasies of the most unendurably mawkish and sentimental sort; his pace is simply that of the gangster motion picture; and his style is more pretentious but no more rewarding than that of *Terry and the Pirates.*

The Moth is Mr. Cain's most ambitious novel; the publishers advise that it will "surprise and delight" the aforementioned formidable following, a sentiment endorsed by Mr. Cain himself, who shyly confesses a hankering to tell tales of a "wider implication than those that deal exclusively with one man's relation to one woman"—an ambition which, since I have yet to meet either a man or a woman in Mr. Cain's pages, seems rather premature.

Apparently the great distinction of *The Moth* lies in its exhausting and desperate diversity: it involves boy sopranos, oil wells, oil fires, theft, hoboes, the Depression, the inevitable woman (hard and dangerous), and the inevitable husband (dull and well-meaning). The happy ending is economically assured by an appalling and all-too-likely scheme of frozen dinners shipped to housewives all over the country by a plan known, happily, thus far only to Mr. Cain's hero. The happy ending also involves the culmination of a curious and breathless romance between the hero and an extremely brittle child of twelve, who becomes, at a more seemly age, his wife. This affair, it is worth noting, is not in the least unconvincing; it operates perfectly within Mr. Cain's framework and sums up for me something intrinsically tawdry and ugly, something very literally nasty, which pervades all of his work.

It occurred to me while reading the earlier and less ambitious Mr. Cain that his ruthless protagonists and their fearful sweethearts were actually descendants of the Rover Boys and that the only thing wrong with them was the fact that they were still reeling from the discovery that they were in possession of visible and functioning sexual organs. It was the impact of this discovery that so hopelessly and murderously disoriented them; they were thenceforth at the mercy of their genitalia, the power of which they were endlessly compelled to prove. Mr. Cain surveys these dull, untidy adolescents with a moist, benevolent fascination, betraying in these novels, the novels in which the tradition and jargon of the American tough guy have been pushed to their furthest limit, the hypocrisy, the horror, and the loneliness from which this tradition sprang.

(1948)

The Portable Russian Reader, edited by

Bernard Guilbert Guerney

ONE OF MY CONTINUING and more respectable prejudices has always been, not altogether justly, against anthologies. "Not altogether justly" because an anthology can, I suppose, be very exciting on occasion, and at least as handy as those other indispensables of the earnest middle-brow American, Barlett and Roget's Thesaurus. Anthologies are apparently designed to make life easier for the inveterate sampler and rereader and to fire the neophyte with an urge to more fully discover the authors who have been obligingly edited and presented to him by some zealous editor. It appeals to me usually about as strongly as watered whiskey; but, of course, even watered whiskey is better than none.

Mr. Guerney's watered blend is better than most. His self-avowed determinations to indicate to American readers that Russian literature is not all epileptic melancholia—which hardly seemed likely—and that Russians can be gay as well as gloomy, of which I, for one, received overwhelming evidence from the deluge of Moscow-Sings-Moscow-Dances movies during the recent war. Nevertheless, Mr. Guerney has set out to deliver Russian lit-

erature from under "Dostoevsky's somber cape." This is admirable, perhaps, though of the work printed here (in spite of an occasional, tight,
nightmarish humor), none is precisely lighthearted, and most of it is quite
strenuously grim.

Mr. Guerney apparently feels that of all literary instruments, the Russian language is the mightiest and most profound, a belief which I, naturally, would not dare to challenge; moreover, according to him, almost all
translations from the Russian have been at best weak infidelities or downright profanations. It is something of a blow to discover that one has never
really read Tolstoy or Dostoevsky at all but has been merely titillated by
irresponsible pastel corruptions. Since Mr. Guerney at no point indicates
that he will translate the major works of these men himself, one is left with
the rather despairing alternatives of buying a Linguaphone or sticking
close to Shakespeare. In spite of all this—or quite possibly because of it,
since here each translation has Mr. Guerney's guarantee—*The Portable
Russian Reader* is a moderately fascinating grab bag. It is quite dreadfully
comprehensive, including fables from the eleventh and seventeenth centuries and aphorisms and proverbs from the Lord knows when. More
familiarly, there are short stories and excerpts from Pushkin, Gogol,
Krylov, Garshin, Turgenev, Gorky, Dostoevsky, Tolstoy, and Ehrenburg.
Much of these I have never read before and I am glad to have found them
now; some are slight or so completely Russian idiom that they have little
relevance; later on, with Ehrenburg, for instance, the grim revolutionary
simplicities become rather hard to take. But as a matter of fact, Mr. Guerney's taste, if not irreproachable, is sound, and he has included nothing
which could be called mediocre. There are some things which are unfor-
gettable: Chekhov's "Ward No. 6," for instance, and Dostoevsky's "Grand
Inquisitor" and Garshin's "Four Days." It includes one of Gorky's most
successful sketches, "Birth of a Man," Gogol's "The Overcoat" (there is an
unwritten law, Mr. Guerney claims, that every Russian anthology must
include it), and the understated, bloodcurdling "Specters" by Turgenev.
Mr. Guerney went hog wild, it seemed to me, with the aphorisms and
proverbs, but that is undoubtedly the privilege of an anthologist. In this
book, in spite of Mr. Guerney's irritating tendency to sound as though he
alone understood the Russian psyche, there is evidence of much loving
care, a genuine determination to do the best job possible. But precisely
because it was meant to be both portable and comprehensive, it is pretty
much of a failure. It is never a critical study, though Mr. Guerney sometimes sounds as though he wishes it were; nor yet is it a history, though it

tries to be; and there is no sense of development, though that, presumably, is what Mr. Guerney was aiming at. Since we have no sense of a growing literature, the earlier selections—the fables, etc.—seem charming but irrelevant, conceived in a vacuum. Beyond discovering that it has been going on for a devilishly long time, we do not have any greater understanding of Russian literature than we did before. We have, as I say, a grab bag: diverse, portable, suitable for journeys and after-dinner table conversations.

(1948)

The Person and the Common Good by Jacques Maritain

IT IS DIFFICULT, if not impossible, for anyone not a Catholic to properly comprehend and discuss a Catholic philosopher. The gin-soaked, Benzedrine-ridden children of our violent age are inclined—not without some reason—to hold philosophers in some doubt as being irritatingly serene watchers of a bloodbath; their rules and their conclusions may all be rather impressive, but of what relevance are they, how can these presumably hard-earned precepts do anything to enrich or make more bearable the daily, difficult, urgent life? In addition to the above qualifications one might also add that in the case of Maritain, one would need also to be an impassioned and convinced theologian—and, alas, not many of us are.

In *The Person and the Common Good* Maritain poses, as the title might suggest, some exceedingly pertinent questions; in some ways, the most pertinent questions that there are. It is a pity, then, that at least for this reviewer, the answers are either entirely unacceptable or so obscured by dogma—"revealed" to Maritain but, unhappily, not to me—that this groping with the problems of the human condition becomes, in effect, unintelligible.

The trouble, perhaps, lies in the extreme rigidity of Maritain's definitions. One must agree with him about such concepts as "good," "divine," "absolute," and, of course, "God." It is not possible to extract from this organism sections of the meat and leave the skeleton. Maritain's concepts are as indivisible and as complete within themselves as the peculiarly compelling and circular structure he evolves out of the notion of the personal—or human—and the common good.

The person, informed and cohered by spirit, is ordained, by the fact of its existence, to the absolute and must refer itself and all that it is and has to God, and it is therefore absolutely superior in worth and importance to the temporal society of which it is a part; and at the same time, since it is a part of this temporal society, since in a temporal fashion, it owes all that it is and has to it and, indeed, could not exist without it, it is subordinate, and the needs of the community transcend its human needs. Again, and at the same time, the community has betrayed its responsibility, its raison d'être, so to speak, if it does not everywhere and always respect the human dignity of the person; if, indeed, it is not absolutely devoted—within "numerous restraints"—to the expansion of that dignity. This formulation, if exasperating, is expedient, as almost all of the contradictions attendant upon being alive can be contained within it. Thus, man "finds himself" by subordination to the group, and "the group attains its goal" by a realization of and respect for the great riches of the human spirit. This circle works perfectly, even admirably, within Maritain's framework and prepares us to be told, later on, that it is a crime to kill an innocent man—but who is to judge the guilty?—and that the social body has the right in a "just war" to oblige its citizens to risk their lives in combat; and that, moreover, in this combat, it is as "master of itself" and "as an act of virtue" that the human being faces death. (Maritain does not inquire into the right of the social body to oblige its citizens to murder and is, apparently, quite unconcerned with the problem of what these obliging citizens are to do thereafter with their enormous weight of guilt.)

All of the foregoing, of course, is made possible, even plausible, by Maritain's "here below" ace in the hole. This will be changed up above, and since we are related first to God, that is where we are headed, willy-nilly. (The social body is empowered to make war and punish the guilty, but at no point are we given an inkling as to what the Divine Community is prepared to do with the hopelessly, willfully reprobate.) This by-and-by-it'll-all-be-over exhortation is not likely to deliver many from the dreadful conviction that our life on earth may be quite drastically foreshortened and that it is, in any case, a rather desperate gamble. It is unhelpful indeed to be assured of future angels when the mysteries of the present flesh are so far from being solved.

(1948)

The Negro Newspaper by Vishnu V. Oak;

Jim Crow America by Earl Conrad;

The High Cost of Prejudice by Bucklin Moon;

The Protestant Church and the Negro by Frank S. Loescher;

Color and Conscience by Buell G. Gallagher;

From Slavery to Freedom by John Hope Franklin;

and *The Negro in America* by Arnold Rose

VISHNU V. OAK'S *The Negro Newspaper* is an absurd and hysterical little pamphlet, published—quite justly—at the author's expense, which could easily have been written the day after Booker T. Washington made his "Separate but Equal" speech at the Atlanta Exposition. It is the first volume of a projected series of four concerning Negro business and argues, so far as I can wrest any meaning from Mr. Oak's stammering prose, for a segregated economy. Mr. Oak, apparently, considers this a desirable, if temporary, solution for most problems faced by Negroes, and one which will, in addition, prepare them in some degree for their future splendors and responsibilities when America finally comes of age. He waxes rather petulant concerning the failure of the race to rise—within the limits set by segregation—to that lucrative position Americans so highly esteem; one can almost hear him saying, "They got no git-up, they don't stick together." "They" also have no money; and as to where, in this complex economy, the money for a self-sustaining Negro economy is to come from, Mr. Oak is valiantly vocal but not very lucid. It will—presumably—be donated by philanthropic organizations (who tend anyway to unwise investments) and wealthy Negroes, unsuspected hordes of whom are, at present, pettishly investing their gold in Cadillacs.

One does not learn much about the Negro newspaper from Mr. Oak, either. He discusses the "faults" (sensationalism, political irresponsibility) and the "virtues" (militant race pride) of the Negro press, betraying only the vaguest understanding of the forces dictating their existence. I suppose Mr. Oak, for all his strident good intentions, is betrayed by his astonishingly uncritical acceptance of the status quo and by his admiration for dynamic business methods, no matter how dangerous or how brutal these methods may be. This allows him to say, in answer to the not unreasonable contention that Negro capitalists are no more soft-hearted than white ones, that *the exploitation of a people by some of its own people is less devastating than exploitation by outsiders.*" (The italics are Mr. Oak's.) This—unless such a formidable loyalty is limited to Negroes—would make American labor one vast, happy, if rather sweaty, family, chortling in proud delight each time the boss man acquired a new mansion.

.   .   .

EARL CONRAD, in *Jim Crow America,* is not so fanciful, though he espies at the bottom of the racial squabble the glint of the Yankee dollar. He reduces the problem, therefore, to an essentially economic one, the solution to which will be found in a coalition of black and white in the ranks of American labor. But this attractive hypothesis demands of labor an organization, awareness, and power it does not have; it assumes a homogeneity in this most diverse of nations; and it discounts the profound ambition of the laborer to enter and to assume the loyalties of the middle class. If Mr. Oak writes as though we were living in the 1870s, Mr. Conrad has never, apparently, gotten past the 1930s, a period which was, to say the least, unique for most Americans and which is not likely, if repeated, to be quite so luckily handled. Mr. Conrad tirelessly amasses fact, figure, incident, and even allegory to prove that the status of the Negro and the unendurable legends used to support this status are based on nothing more profound than the lust for gold.

This, in a way, is certainly true, but it is not the whole truth; it leaves too much unaccounted for; nor does it consider, even granting the truth of the hypothesis, how this unethical greed and exploitation have operated on the conscience of the American white or on the psychology of the Negro. Since *Jim Crow America* ignores this complexity and confusion, Mr. Conrad's analysis of the Negro problem is finally superficial, a mere reiteration of the national shame. One is faced with a circular problem: if, on the one hand, Negroes achieved, or were allowed, economic equality, prejudice would vanish; but, on the other hand, despite Mr. Conrad's hopeful or angry pronouncement, this integration will obviously not occur until the bar of prejudice itself has been dissolved.

.   .   .

BUCKLIN MOON, in *The High Cost of Prejudice*, takes up where Mr. Conrad leaves off; he begins by an extremely careful tabulation of what it costs the nation in dollars and cents to maintain this inequitable structure and the circular manner in which this structure feeds on and perpetuates itself. From this, however, he proceeds to consider the deadly and invisible toll in terms of our integrity as individuals and our morality as a nation. This consideration, which might have raised the book to a high level of penetration, is unhappily blunted by easy generalization and compulsive optimism, that national optimism which must find the ray of hope, which must not admit the darkness, be it ever so overwhelming. Hence, his book has a peculiarly muted tone; one closes it wondering why it seems so thin and pale, why all of Mr. Moon's earnestness and all of his dogged probing fail to be either moving or distinguished. This optimism is curious in that it is finally hopeless; one must, very literally, make the best of things, one must not explore anything profoundly. It is, one cannot help feeling, dangerous to do so.

In Mr. Moon's book, therefore, and to a greater or lesser degree in all of these books, however indignant the author may be, the best foot is always in evidence and is finally and firmly put forward; as though, at the end of a fire-and-brimstone sermon, the preacher were to adopt a jovial, almost intimate air and to say: "But all of you—I know you will do better, your hearts are pure—surely, we will meet in heaven." The desperate tremor which accompanies this benediction is wished away; the drunkard, the nymphomaniac, and the sadist, all clothed in the garments of salvation, go home obscurely comforted and thoroughly unchanged. Perhaps the note of hope is struck precisely in order to give people courage, to raise morale, so that the battle will not be lost. But this hopefulness depends on an insistent oversimplification, on platitude and platitudinous speculation, on a happy assumption that the status of the Negro is growing better, whereas it is merely growing more complex.

This complexity whispers in *Color and Conscience* by Buell G. Gallagher and in Frank S. Loescher's *The Protestant Church and the Negro,* in which books the problem of color is attacked from a moral and religious viewpoint. Mr. Loescher's book is the less ambitious and perhaps the more successful: a heavily documented attack on the practical policies of the Protestant church, its systematic betrayal of the first principles of Christianity, its financial and moral support of the status quo. Mr. Loescher is, apparently, one of that unlucky minority who take their Christianity seriously, a hair-splitting refinement which the church has seldom considered necessary and which, indeed, it has frequently and strenuously opposed. The church, to be sure, has made "pronouncements" and is now on the record as being "against" segregation. But this has in no way affected the administration of Protestant-dominated colleges, nor diminished the power of those restrictive covenants held by Protestant institutions; it has rarely led to an interracial church, except in those areas where Negroes (or Mexicans or Orientals) are so few as to be unnoticeable and too few to support a separate church. The decision of the church to be against segregation, which was belated in the first place, means, in practice, nothing; and those sufficiently uncharitable to put these pronouncements to the test—to demand, for instance, that Negro and white sit side by side in the church pew—are not entirely unjustified in concluding that these pronouncements do little more than save face. This cynicism, though, however accurate, is not quite fair, for these pronouncements, like these books, stem from disturbed and frightened consciences.

.   .   .

BUELL G. GALLAGHER'S *Color and Conscience* reiterates Mr. Loescher's thesis. It is vaster in outlook and angrier in tone; one would expect it also to be more penetrating, but this is not the case.

Mr. Gallagher says rather little that Mr. Loescher has not said, though he covers the ground so much more minutely that he seems to; he is concerned with history and the human personality, with time and society and the rigorous demands of conscience: he would make peace with them all. It is hard to assess his failure or give the reasons for it and harder still to say just why I found so much of his book repellent. It is not in what he says but somehow in the manner of his saying it, in what seemed to me to be a shrill and desperate self-righteousness, though Mr. Gallagher early declares his desire to avoid that pit. His book is at once so emotional and so careful, and strives so mightily to be both clear and honest, that it seems almost a blueprint of the advanced and disturbed American conscience; and his failure, with this comparison in mind, seems almost a prophecy of accelerating doom. His is a plea to time to halt for a while that we may make amends; and this is where Mr. Gallagher is defeated, for he does not dare to consider profoundly the independent energy generated by those two implacably interacting forces, history and the human personality. One hesitates to say—anticipating the epithets "mystic" or "defeatist"—that the emphasis is wrong, that there is no panacea, no deliverance, on the strength of good intentions. In a very real sense the Negro problem has become anachronistic; we ourselves are the only problem, it is our hearts only that we must search. It is neither a politic nor a popular thing to say, but a black man facing a white man becomes at once contemptuous and resentful when he finds himself looked upon as a moral problem for that white man's conscience.

.   .   .

JOHN HOPE FRANKLIN'S *From Slavery to Freedom* is an ambitious, top-heavy history beginning in Egypt centuries ago and ending in America of the present day. The title gives the book's tone and intent, but a simple reversal of the key words sums up its unintended effect. For Mr. Franklin, hopeful and painstaking as he is, can only prophesy a great day soon to come and dwell rather wistfully on the splendors past: this heritage and history which have become for the Negro in America, when not outright fantasy, an active source of shame. Mr. Franklin, a Negro and a Negro historian, is aware that there is demanded of him a greater objectivity than might be demanded of other men, and in reaching for this objectivity he becomes very nearly fatuous and persistently shallow. His book—except for the desperate amassing of proof that the Negro is as loyal as any other citizen, has endured much, and deserves that freedom for which he has for so long been exhorted to be patient—is as pallid and platitudinous a performance as those high-school textbooks which we feverishly consulted just before exams. Mr. Franklin, nevertheless, seeks to speak for the enlightened Negro, as Mr. Gallagher speaks for the enlightened white; and if Mr. Gallagher brooks no prejudice, Mr. Franklin harbors no bitterness. But their expressions of goodwill, compulsive on the one hand and strained on the other, are defeated by the very necessity to formulate these expressions on the basis of color. One has the feeling that they protest too much.

.   .   .

ARNOLD ROSE'S *The Negro in America* is a condensation of Gunnar Myrdal's *An American Dilemma,* and is a more astute book than many of its predecessors and more comprehensive than any of them. *An American Dilemma* was impressed most forcibly on my mind long before I read it by a landlord, who, having refused to rent me an apartment, but wishing to assure me of his good intentions, told me he was reading it. I did not, happily, remain homeless long enough to discover what effect this had on his policy; but I am afraid that I brought to Mr. Myrdal's book, when I finally read it, that same impatience the landlord had caused me to feel. This is not, of course, fair to Mr. Myrdal and his associates, and it is certainly not what is called taking the long view.

But it is just the value of this long view that I am beginning to question. Presumably, taking the long view means that one is able to consider and interpret the present in the light of the past; ideally, it leads to that sense of time and history which can operate to make present pain endurable, preventing the disintegration of the person under stress. Nevertheless, this long view, of which we speak so glibly, must be examined: whose long view, and for what purpose, and from what viewpoint?

And the very moment these questions are asked, this long view—which is demanded most vociferously of Negroes—emerges as something less lofty; comes close, indeed, to being nothing more than a system of justification. The American need for justification is a good deal stronger than the American sense of time—which began, as we are inclined to believe, with the Stars and Stripes. Thus, not even Mr. Rose's careful and comprehensive study escapes the pit into which all of these books fall: they record the facts, but they cannot probe the immense, ambiguous, uncontrollable effect. The full story of white and black in this country is more vast and shattering than we would like to believe and, like an unhindered infection in the body, it has the power to make our whole organism sick.

We are sick now, and relations between the races is only one of our symptoms. What is happening to Negroes in this country has been happening for a long time, and it is something quite logical, inevitable, and deadly: they are becoming more American every day.

(1949)

The Cool World by Warren Miller

I CONSIDER IT A TRIBUTE to Warren Miller, whose name was unfamiliar to me, that I could not be certain, when I had read his book, whether he was white or black.* I *was* certain, however, that I had just read one of the finest novels about Harlem that had ever come my way. The author had obviously looked at something very hard. He had felt it very deeply and was trying to tell the truth about it.

The people in his book are Negroes, but they are handled with no condescension and with no self-pity. Because they are seen so clearly and made so real, the drama they act out contains implications which go far beyond the confines of the squalid, claustrophobic world which they inhabit.

This world is a world we have created, we, the American Republic; and its existence gives the lie to every one of the principles in which we say we believe. In fact, the most remarkable and valuable thing about this study of Negro children in Harlem is that it does not leave one thinking about race at all. It leaves one thinking about the moral state of this country.

---

*Mr. Miller (who is white) is a versatile writer. He has published children's books under his own name as well as an adult novel, *The Way We Live Now.* As "Amanda Vail" he is responsible for two spoofs of female boarding-school and college life, *Love Me Little* and *The Bright Young Things.* [This footnote was published with the essay.—Ed.]

I think that there is something suspicious about the way we cling to the concept of race, on both sides of the obsolescent racial fence. White men, when they have not entirely succumbed to their panic, wallow in their guilt, and call themselves, usually "liberals." Black men, when they have not drowned in their bitterness, wallow in their rage, and call themselves, usually "militant." Both camps have managed to evade the really hideous complexity of our situation on the social and personal level.

The Cool World is the story of Richard "Duke" Custis, who lives in a Harlem apartment with his mother and grandmother, and his mother's procession of "husbands." The "husbands," of whom we glimpse, in passing, only one, are a sorry, irresponsible, embittered lot; the mother is not so much indifferent as defeated; and the grandmother has retired into the depths of the Old Testament.

Mr. Miller manages to convey, with a masterful economy, the atmosphere of this dreadful apartment, and the peculiarly desperate apathy which has overtaken this family—if, indeed, it can any longer be called a family. The grandmother can no longer reach her daughter, and neither of them can reach the boy. He has struck out to find his own identity according to the only standards he has ever seen honored: he is the War Lord of the Royal Crocadiles (his spelling), a street gang in mortal competition with the Wolves.

The Wolves have knifed Duke—who has been knifed seven times at the age of fourteen and is proud of it—and killed another member of the Crocadiles, and the Crocadiles are planning a vengeful "rumble." In this "rumble," one Wolf, Angel, and one Crocadile, Cowboy, are killed. Duke is sent away to a Youth Center, from which he tells us his story.

I confess that I do not really believe in his "rehabilitation," there being nothing in the book and very little in my own experience to lead me to believe in it. But this somewhat perfunctory ending cannot really detract from the book's great power.

Mr. Miller tells his story in the argot of the Harlem streets. He appears to be one of the very few people who have ever really listened to it and tried to understand what was being said. In his handling, it is not strange because it is exotic; it is strange, and it is frightening, because it conveys the children's state of mind with such force.

And this state of mind is the American state of mind, seen from a peculiar angle, and in some relief: "Blood got one sister a nurse an a brother at

Fisk University learnin to be a doctor or somethin. Man I dont see it * * *. No point workin like that when they can take it all away from you when ever they feel like it you know."

This frightened and distrustful child has long since ceased believing a word we say—about honor, ideals, equality, hope. He watches what we do. He thinks of the world as a loveless place, of infinite evil, run by thieves and murderers.

Well, we are quick to insist, the world is not like that. We will have to prove this to him, though, for he lives in Harlem, that world we have created but do not have the honesty to visit nor the courage to change. Until we do this, he has no reason to believe us, nor have we the right to expect to be believed.

The "cool" world is a world in which children watch their contemporaries and their elders dying by the hour. And we ignore this world at our own very great peril, for as long as they are dying, we are dying, too.

(1959)

Essays by Seymour Krim

Seymour Krim says at one point in this extraordinary volume: "I was as wrong as you can be, and still live to tell about it." He was, indeed, and so were all of us; not many of us lived; and most of those who lived and tried to tell the tale soon found themselves choked in attitudes, mystiques, and dictions which were not theirs. There is observable, I think, in the work of most of this generation a desire to tell what actually happened—or what it actually feels like to be an American, now; but this desire is perpetually defeated by the spiritual obligation of being an American, which obligation is, simply, never to accept that evil is in the world. I am struck by the variety of ways in which the actual spiritual state of Americans is denied by people who have every reason to know what that state is: our educators, artists, and politicians. It is hard for me to believe, for example, that educators do not know the sorry truth behind the lack of real education here. It seems very clear to me that until the educators themselves believe in what they teach, there is no hope for their students. But the educators cannot accept this, because in order to do so they would have to overhaul every aspect of their private lives, which effort would hurl them forever beyond the bounds of the academic life.

It would hurl them, in fact, into that search and that danger which Krim
has endured and to which he bears witness. I myself believe that it has
never been more difficult to become an individual than it is now, in the
middle of the twentieth century, in the richest and most bewildered country in the Western world, the country which has inherited all the follies and
crimes and contradictions of the West at the very moment that the moral
assumptions of the Western world are proving themselves bankrupt. What
is demanded, if we are to redeem our history, is an unprecedented and violent assault on reality, an overhauling and overturning and undermining of
all the standards by which we imagine ourselves to live. The reason that
this is necessary is that we really do not live by these standards; we cling to
them because we are shipwrecked, and have no other spare, but the awful
gap between our public expectations and our private settlements has precipitated spiritual disaster. To save ourselves, we must re-examine ourselves; and it is probable that never before has so heavy a burden fallen on
so many or been shouldered by so few.

Among these few, alas, most of our elders cannot be included, and Krim
makes this stonily clear in his report on the literary avant-garde life of the
forties ("What's *This* Cat's Story?"). It is the most candid and truthful
record of that time that I have ever read, and I suppose part of its dry effec-
tiveness to come from its total lack of malice. It took perhaps one or two
cocktail parties—those cocktail parties which, since one was present, signaled one's entry into this fabled world—to recognize that one had been
"had." The people with whom one was dealing, so far from being giants,
appeared to be in the literary professions principally because they hated literature. I concluded this from the fact that they placed no more trust in life
than the weariest button merchant, and their timidity, respectability, and
ignorance were made all the more obvious and appalling by the formulas
they adopted to hide these. Their prejudices were precisely those of the
class to which they aspired, or from which they sprang: the property-
owning class (in fact or desire); and I, of course, since I had forced myself
to expect so much more, found it very difficult to forgive them for the
nightmares of tolerance I endured at their hands. But the thing for which I
most scorned them may have been, after all, the most important: they did
not know how to raise their children. They did not trust their own
instincts, or authority, or love, and raised them, as it were, by the book.
And the ill-mannered, tyrannical, anchorless children proved, even more

authoritatively than did the aridity of so much of their elders' work, or lack of conviction when the chips were down, the elders' real vacuity.

Krim is the first person, as far as I know, to bring up, in any responsible fashion, the prevalence of the Jewish intellectual in what we like to call the literary life. I have never really written about Jews, because both culturally and socially, and for better and for worse, I have been too close to them. It is possible that I am afraid of examining whatever tension exists in my mind between the Jewish pawnbrokers and landlords of my childhood, and my friends; though, to tell the truth, in the beginning, for me, all Jews were in the Bible, and all I knew or cared about landlords was that they were white. In short, I think that my hatred of all white people was too incandescent to allow me to see their features. In any case, since the Bible had always been so crucial to me, I concluded that the reason for the prevalence of the Jew in intellectual activity simply resulted from the fact that he was the *only* American who had behind him anything that could be called an intellectual tradition—by which I mean, simply, the *knowledge* that thought and the interior, private life are real. But I did not consider the price that was paid for this—for reasons which are, I suppose, all too obvious; nor did I consider the implications of the fact that the Jewish tradition retained such force because the world did not allow the Jew to escape it. Krim opens up in this book a momentous speculation on how the dreadful Jewish past is yoked to the dreadful American dream, and the dues paid in the Jewish personality. It illuminates for me many of the disasters endured by friends of mine—and also illuminates some of the darker corners in the minds of my present-day friends—and I can only hope that Krim will dig deeper into this question one of these days.

He is also, God bless him, almost the only writer of my generation who has managed to release himself from the necessity of being either romantic or defensive about Negroes. His "Anti-Jazz" essay ought to be required reading by every hipster who can read (on the evidence, there are not many), and its last sentence ought to be engraved on the walls of every jazz point in this country: "It comes from something further down and wayer out than I think you dream of . . . man." Billie Holiday, Charlie Parker, King Oliver, and my mother and my father thank you, baby. Not one of us ever sat in an orgone box, and we've *yet* to hear any singing coming out of *that* cage.

"Ask for a White Cadillac" is more painful and goes much further: but the only hope for the reestablishment of *human* relations in this country, let alone race relations, is for the truth to come out. It can only come out if those who have been there will dare to tell the truth about where they've been—and why.

I have reservations about this book, of course, but I don't know how important they are. Krim's supercharged, locomotive style sometimes drives me mad—I hope he will soon retire from active duty all those monotonous variations on the verb "to swing." I disagree with his estimate of the "Beats," from which so many of his stylistic affections come. On the other hand, since, as Krim says, they "opened me up," I feel that my ground there is rather shot from under me. He has gone far beyond them just the same, in passion and clarity and responsibility, just as he has gone far beyond most of us into that chaos out of which we shall have to rebuild our homes.

(1961)

The Arrangement by Elia Kazan

Was he free? Was he happy? The question is absurd:
Had anything been wrong, we should certainly have heard.
—W. H. AUDEN

MEMORY, ESPECIALLY AS ONE grows older, can do strange and disquieting things. Though we would like to live without regrets, and sometimes proudly insist that we have none, this is not really possible, if only because we are mortal. When more time stretches behind than stretches before one, some assessments, however reluctantly and incompletely, begin to be made. Between what one wished to become and what one *has* become there is a momentous gap, which will now never be closed. And this gap seems to operate as one's final margin, one's last opportunity, for creation. And between the self as it is and the self as one sees it, there is also a distance, even harder to gauge. Some of us are compelled, around the middle of our lives, to make a study of this baffling geography, less in the hope of conquering these distances than in the determination that the distances shall not become any greater. Chasms are necessary, but they can also, notoriously, be fatal. At this point, one is attempting nothing less than the re-creation of oneself out of the rubble which has become one's life: and this is the situation with which Elia Kazan presents us in his first novel, *The Arrangement*.

I am far from certain that anyone can deal with so bleak a situation either to his own or anybody else's satisfaction; and any such attempt is certain to leave one open to the charge of awkwardness. Kazan's book has a certain raw gracelessness which I have not often encountered, and which I find difficult to describe. It is a terribly naked book—not blatantly so, but uncomfortably direct. He does not seem to have invented anything, though obviously he must have, and he seems not so much to have drawn his characters as to have yanked them, bleeding, dismembered, and still in a state of shock, from the scene of their hideous accident. No more than Job's messengers give the impression that they were hoping to become radio announcers does Kazan give the impression that he was trying to write a novel. He is talking. He is trying to tell us something, and not only for his sake—for then *The Arrangement* would be nothing more than an unexpected and arresting tour de force from an eminent man of the theater—but also for ours. The tone of the book is extremely striking, for it really does not seem to depend on anything that we think of as a literary tradition, but on something older than that: the tale being told by a member of the tribe to the tribe. It has the urgency of a confession and the stammering authority of a plea. "I still haven't figured out my accident," the narrator begins; and, in fact, he never does explain it. He doesn't need to. Some accidents can only happen here.

Eddie, Evans, Evangelos—"whatever your name is"—is a big wheel at the advertising firm of Williams and McElroy, where he is known as Indispensable Eddie. He is, he tells us, "solvent, set for life," with a beautiful Beverly Hills house, a swimming pool, "the goddamnedest lawn in that whole area," three cars, a hi-fi, two original Picasso drawings, and a "deep freeze that held thirty-six cubic feet of food." He has been married for twenty-one years to a remarkable woman, named Florence, and they have a daughter, Ellen, of college age. He is indispensable to Williams and McElroy because he is an expert at persuading people to buy trash they don't need and can't use and can't live with. The rewards for this specialty are high indeed in this society—this consumer economy, in which the consumer is both the menace and the prey—and Eddie is very proud of his eminence, his affluence, his skills; which also operate, of course, to get him any girl he wants. His arrangement is all but perfect. But all arrangements depend on the harmony of the elements which make up the arrangement. If any element ceases to function, or begins to function differently, the arrangement is finished. In Eddie's case, the arrangement is menaced and finally destroyed by two elements, one overt and one dormant. The overt element is his relationship to a girl named Gwen, a girl who is a challenge to him, and whom he has really grown to care about. The symptom of his love for her is his need for her respect. But she does not consider him to be better than any of the other whores, in spite of the devastating think pieces he does from time to time for respected intellectual magazines. This, too, is an arrangement: the honesty, or at least the ferocity, of his think pieces is intended to nullify his advertising copy. But Gwen sees this arrangement for exactly what it is, and refuses to be impressed by it, and this brings Eddie's long-buried uneasiness concerning his life, and the manner of his life, to the surface of his troubled mind.

But it is another element altogether which is really responsible for the ruin of all of Eddie's arrangements, an element so long dormant that it would not seem to be part of any arrangement at all. Yet, as Eddie's situation becomes more painful and more grotesque, and as his blind, outrageous, and dangerous decisions multiply, it begins to be clear, both to him and to us, that this element has always contained the germ of the disaster which has so nearly destroyed him. This element is his relationship to his father, his relationship to his past. Seraphaim, his father, is dying. He is dying very loudly, gracelessly, and horribly, disputing death with every stratagem, no matter how base, which cunning and despair can devise.

Seraphaim is a Greek who left Turkey at the end of the century, and somehow managed to bring his entire family to America—where, for a while, they prospered. Eddie—"Evangeleh" to his father—made his father bitter by refusing to go into the family rug business: and it has not helped their relationship that the business subsequently failed, and the family lost all its money in the crash of 1929. Now black sheep Eddie-Evangeleh, once mockingly called "Shakespeare," is the only big shot in the family, and Seraphaim's only hope. For Seraphaim's brothers simply failed to survive the 1929 cataclysm; they literally do not know what hit them, and exist in a carefully cultivated state of semi-idiocy; while all the other members of the family are aggressively respectable and respectably eviscerated. Whatever Eddie is, he is not like these people, who simply wish, at bottom, for Seraphaim to die as quietly and comfortably as possible. But he will not be quiet, and their ideas concerning his comfort strike him—quite rightly, though the poor people have scarcely any other choice—as galling, even dishonest, condescension. On the other hand, there is no possibility whatever that Seraphaim can do what he feverishly demands that Evangeleh help him do: he wants Evangeleh to take him out of the hospital and set him up in business again.

That Seraphaim's intransigence is mad is so clear to everyone that no one listens to him—which increases his madness, of course; only Evangeleh understands, out of his own trouble, that his father is pleading for the chance to live his life again. But Seraphaim would live the same life, only this time more successfully; this time he would not be cheated, this time he would not be ruined. He is completely unable to bear the suspicion that the ruin of his life was caused by factors yet more inexorable than those which brought about the stock market crash. This inability is revealed in the usual way, by the most insanely cruel suspicions of everyone around him, particularly that person he most thoroughly betrayed, his wife. Both Seraphaim and Evangeleh wish to live again: but Eddie-Evangeleh is sickened by the life he has led and has embarked on a semiconscious effort to destroy it, in order to be born again.

The relationship between Seraphaim and Eddie-Evangeleh is amazing in its candor and honesty, and very moving. In an odd, and most un-American, way, it is the source of Evangeleh's strength. It is not based on anything so thin and cerebral as give-and-take, or mutual understanding—which, in practice, nearly always means mutual indifference; it is remote from tolerance, and all the psychoanalytical categories are completely irrelevant to it. This is bloody, brutal, no-holds-barred, father and son mercilessly slugging it out and inflicting real damage on each other. It is not modern, and it is not enlightened, and it is more than a little terrifying; but it is finally affirmative, because the truth of their love for each other, the depth of their involvement with each other, though loudly, theatrically, and endlessly bewailed, is never for an instant denied. It is a relationship so foreign to American life—we imagine ourselves to have gone far beyond it, whereas in truth we have merely fallen far short of it—that it has become nearly impossible to disentangle it from the insane jargon about sado-masochism and Oedipal complexes and penis envy in which it appears now to be breathing its last; but the father-son relationship is one of the most crucial and dangerous on earth, and to pretend that it can be otherwise really amounts to an exceedingly dangerous heresy. There is a terrible fight between Evangeleh and his father after Evangeleh has kidnapped the old man from the hospital, a fight about the past, about their life with each other, about the way the father betrayed the son, about the way the son betrayed the father. It degenerates into the really shattering pettiness of all such quarrels: "... You get your brains from me!" Seraphaim thunders, and the middle-aged Eddie-Evangeleh, shaking like a boy, insists, like a boy, "I became someone in spite of you—I'm not like you, you corrupt and hateful and vicious..." And afterwards, he says, with wonder and remorse, "I thought I'd got over all that." It is to be doubted that any of us ever do, and I think we do ourselves a disservice when we pretend that we have, and substitute the lie of our indifference for the truth of our pain. The truth of our pain is all we have, it is the key to who we are.

But this apprehension is absolutely antithetical to Florence's sense of reality. (I think it is worth noting that Kazan's portrait of the wife is really amazing in that it is so free of that hostility which we have come to take for granted whenever an American woman appears in the pages of American fiction.) Florence's limits are subtle and deadly, but they are the limits of her time and place: her qualities are rare, and her love for her husband is real. She does everything in her power to understand him; she does everything in her power not to parade her suffering, not to whimper, not to cheat, not to lie. Until the very end, she wants Eddie to come back to her, and she never pretends that she wants anything else. She is a really honorable and gallant woman, a lady Henry James's Isabel Archer would certainly have recognized; indeed, if Isabel were living in America now, she would probably, alas, be very much like Florence. No one can possibly blame Florence for being baffled and terrified by the unreadable series of metamorphoses taking place in her husband, who is the center of her life. On the contrary, she is to be saluted for attempting to confront them at all. No one can blame her for being unable to do what none of us can do: to accept the fact that one's lover loves another, and that, even though you are lying side by side in bed, he is far away and will never come back. ("Don't love her," says Florence. "Love me.") The nature of Florence's limits are directly attributable to the culture which produced her: "... As a woman, and your wife, I'm awfully glad you have the job you have at Williams and McElroy, that you're so good at it we can afford a nice home and the help to keep it up, and that I can buy the best books, and when the Broadway shows come to the Biltmore, sit in the best seats, and that Ellen can go to Radcliffe, and feel free to give consideration to other assets in her husband-to-be than whether or not he has a substantial bank account." This is a very honest statement, on its face, and her saying it is not meant to reveal her as the all-American, predatory bitch. She is saying it as a wife and mother, and saying no more than what all wives and mothers have said throughout the ages.

Unless one supposes that it is somehow wrong for women to consider that the safety and security of the nest are paramount, one cannot even quarrel with her assumptions. It is very hard to blame her for the fact that the life she lives is, in brutal truth, a hopeless series of non sequiturs. She is a modern, emancipated woman, but she is appalled by the fact that Eddie sends their daughter out to buy a diaphragm. She is devoted to civil rights, but exhibits a restrained distress when she learns that their daughter is having an affair with a Negro, and is relieved when the affair ends. ("It turned out that Ralph is not the best balanced person in the world. Well, how could you expect him to be?") She believes in the life of the mind and the adventure of the spirit, but is wretchedly dependent on her psychiatrist. She is the book's principal victim, and Kazan never allows us to take any easy attitude toward her. We are confronted with her suffering, in the face of which all judgment is valueless; and, furthermore, she is so placed that, however we judge her, we are, exactly as Eddie is, forced to judge ourselves. She is the book's principal victim because she is one of the principal victims of the way we live now: what, indeed, given the options chosen by men, are *her* options? If Eddie, in the autumn of his life, realizes that he has been a whore, and begins to despise the life he's led and resolves to change it, she is not to be blamed for her panic and pain. *He* became a whore, she did not make him one, and the life his whoring made for her is the only life she knows. Furthermore, Eddie's options, in the land of the free, were not so very great, either, as he discovers when he decides, in effect, like Huck Finn, to "light out for the territory."

As his father lies dying, Eddie-Evangeleh goes to the house where his family had lived for thirty years. In all that great mountain of heirlooms, mementoes of past wealth, photographs of weddings, children, uncles, aunts, cousins, old bills of sale, relics, relics, relics, only one thing seems truly to reflect his father, one thing only, Eddie-Evangeleh concludes, had his father loved: a photograph of the Anatolian mountain in the shadow of which he was born, and to which, now that he is dying, he longs to return. Eddie-Evangeleh thinks:

The mountain represented in that photograph seemed to be demanding some judgment of me, some verdict. What do you think, it seemed to say, what do you really think? And if I had been forced to answer and give a verdict at that moment, I would have had to say that I thought the whole passage of my family to this country had been a failure, not the country's fault perhaps, but the inevitable result of the time, and the spirit in the air in those days. The symbols of affluence gained had been empty even by the standards of the market place. The money they had acquired wasn't worth much; they had found that out in 1929. As for the other acquisitions—the homes, the furniture, the cars, the pianos, the decorations, the clothes, the land—they had meant nothing. These men who had cried, America, America! as the century died had come here looking for freedom and the other human things, and all they had found was the freedom to make as much money as possible . . . They had left that country with its running water, and its orchards of fruit, and all, all that my grandmother never stopped talking about; they had left that to find a better place to live and all they found was a better place to make money.

This is not the official version of American history, but that it very nearly sums it up can scarcely be doubted by anyone with the courage to look into the faces one encounters all over this land: who listens to the voices, hearing incessantly the buried uneasiness, the bewilderment, the unadmitted despair, hearing the arrogant, jaunty, fathomless, utterly astounding ignorance; a cultivated ignorance of all things public, and a terrified ignorance of all things private; translating itself, visibly, hourly, into a hatred of all that is strange or vivid—and what is vivid is always strange; into a hatred, at last, of life. *I don't like my life.* So thinks Eddie-Evangeleh. *How have I become what I've become?*

This is the question, beating, like a muffled drum, through all the American streets, which has become, in this most sinister and preposterous of Edens, of all questions the most forbidden, the most intolerable. *Fire and flood!* thinks Eddie-Evangeleh, while struggling with this question, and he burns down the unloved, loveless, uninhabitable house.

(1967)

A Man's Life: An Autobiography by Roger Wilkins

I NEVER BELIEVED IT—the American Dream—or so I say now. That I didn't believe it, if I didn't, wasn't due to my extraordinary powers of perception. It does not demand perception to realize that you are poor: nor do you need to be gifted in order to realize that you are despised. (But it helps.)

So: the people who hurt me most at the beginning of what we must now, somewhat helplessly, call my professional life—my late teens, when I was aspiring to become a journalist—were not white. They were black. They laughed at me. I stank of the ghetto, this pop-eyed little black boy, who had barely managed high school, could certainly never go further, and was an (undeserved) handicap to the Race.

I put it this way because I hate to put it this way. I'm telling you like it is because that's the way it was; but it is very important to let you know that I can now begin to allow myself to remember that dreadful, distant pain because Roger Wilkins has written *A Man's Life*. Or, in other words: it may still be as it was, but angels have been troubling the waters and Roger Wilkins, praise the Lord, has now accepted that he was born into that same disreputable category.

And, in a way, if life were different, I'd sign off here, and urge you to drop whatever you are doing right now and loot the nearest bookstore.

Life, however, being what it is, and *A Man's Life* being so unprecedented a performance, I am obliged to suggest to you some of the reasons that I consider it to be indispensable reading.

Wilkins has written a most beautiful book, has delivered an impeccable testimony out of that implacable private place where a man either lives or dies.

It says a great deal about this country that, black like each other, legally at least, Roger Wilkins, living on the Hill, and I, born in the Hollow, should have had to undergo so many forms of death in order to realize that our life was the anonymity dictated by the Republic, an institution which could always find a way to use us, though it has yet to find a way to respect us.

What is implicit in this confession—no, this is testimony, far more noble than a mere confession: Mr. Wilkins is not a whining boy—is the extent to which black Americans have been, perhaps still are, the accomplices to our captivity. We both tried to be *white:* he on the Hill, myself in the Hollow. We both tried not to stink. This is because we recognized that the gleaming Republic associated our color and our odor with the color and the odor of shit. We were treated like shit. And we were determined to overcome. Or, in other words, to prove to a people who had to believe, and who, indeed, proclaimed us less than cattle, that we had a title to the tree of life.

And let the record show, we went the route—were much nicer, for example, when the chips were down, to Bobby Kennedy than Bobby Kennedy ever was, or could have dreamed of being, to us. Let us scuttle the Camelot legend. I am weary of Lincoln Memorials, of the American piety, which is nothing less than a Sunday-school apology for genocide.

I have earned the right, from the moment of my own stupendous performance on the auction block, to tell you that this Republic is a total liar and has never contained the remotest possibility, let alone desire, to let my people go. (I know that that offends grammar, but it be's that way sometimes.) The Lincoln Memorial is a pious fraud. Lincoln freed those slaves not because he had the remotest interest in human liberty, still less in the freedom of the slave (a freedom which no one dared, or dares, imagine), but because—to paraphrase him—he was determined to preserve the Union. Which, indeed, for what it's worth, he did.

Blacks have never had a President, in these yet to be United States, who cared whether they lived or died. (Roosevelt didn't dare pass an antilynch bill, as he explained to Walter White of the NAACP, because the Congress would have prevented him from doing "great things" for America and, said the most "liberal" President in American history, "I just can't take that chance.")

And as for Bobby and his brother JFK, they were millionaire sons of a Boston-Irish adventurer, who made his money through one of the American Puritanical convulsions, Prohibition. Well, when Bobby K. decided to channel the black discontent into voter registration, he was doing exactly what Lincoln had done, a century before: he was immobilizing, with the promise of freedom, those slaves he could not buy.

To be a black American is much worse than being in love with, tied to, inexorably, mysteriously, responsible for, someone whom you don't like, don't respect, and don't dare trust.

Read Roger Wilkins's record of how it is. Few documents will, in your lifetime, equal it. Do not read it as a missionary. Do not imagine that anyone is asking you to do anything at all. You have done quite enough already.

Read it, if you have the courage to love your children. This book is an act of love, written by a lover and a father and one of the only friends your children have.

(1982)

FICTION

The Death of a Prophet

"The Death of a Prophet," a story about a young man's reckoning with his father's death, first appeared in *Commentary* in 1950, even as Baldwin continued to work on his first novel, variously titled *In My Father's House* and *Crying Holy*, before its publication as *Go Tell It on the Mountain* in 1953. Some critics imagine the story as anticipating "Notes of a Native Son."

.   .   .

ON THIS SAME AVENUE down which he hurried now, he had once walked with his father on bright Sunday mornings and vibrant Sunday nights. Churchgoers and heretics passed them, dressed in their brightest clothes. On Sunday the sun never failed to shine; on Sunday nights the stars were brighter and the sky was a deeper blue. When they turned the corner that led to the church, they saw the lighted windows and heard, with a fierce excitement, the sound of tambourines and singing and the clapping of hands. Then they hurried to reach the house of God. So had his father lived in the Southern cotton fields; so had his mother lived before him; who, born a slave, and with no knowledge—"as men call knowledge"—yet turned, sobbing, on her final pillow, "A mighty fortress is our God." When Johnnie was very young, though he feared his father and was frightened and troubled at church, he did not doubt that the gospel his father preached, to which the church bore witness, was the truth; that under the shadow of His everlasting wings was all love and all power and the assured redemption of his soul. One wintertime, while his mother was again pregnant and his father had no job, and they lived, his mother and his father and his two brothers and himself, in two cold rooms at the top of a tenement where rats whispered behind the plaster and harlots made love behind the stairs, Johnnie had cursed God. But to curse God is not to doubt Him. His father stripped him naked and beat him until he lay on the splintery floor, in feverish sobbing and in terror of death.

In a hospital in Long Island his father now lay dying. He had been ill a long while, but Johnnie, who no longer lived in Harlem, had never been to see him. And he hurried unwillingly now, only because his mother was ill and had called him at his downtown rooming house to beg him, for her sake, not to let his father die with only strangers at his bedside. By strangers she meant white strangers; she surely knew that Johnnie was a stranger in his father's eyes.

According to the vision of their church, in which, at length, he became a burdened hope, the son of a prophet, all that was in the world was sin. He was not allowed to go to movies or to plays; smoking and drinking were forbidden. It was not thought wise to read more at school than was absolutely necessary, for schools also, it had been revealed, might function as the anteroom to hell. One read the newspapers only to remark how exactly, how relentlessly, the Word of God approached fulfillment. From his pulpit his father warned them of the wrath to come. "Behold, in the last days there shall be wars and rumours of wars; nation shall rise against nation and kingdom against kingdom." Many an ancient throne shall topple and many a king, like Nebuchadnezzar, crawl raving in the dust. But all these things (and Amen! cried the church and once his own heart had cried, Amen!) should bring rejoicing to the hearts of the redeemed. For it meant that their trials on earth were nearly done, their salvation was at hand: in the twinkling of an eye that same power which raised Jesus from the dead would lift them from the guilty earth and, for their reward, they would triumph over death and hell and reign forever with the Father and the Son.

But by this time Johnnie was a child no longer, but an eighteen-year-old about to leave high school, where he had read too much. What he had read undermined his faith and, equally, what his faith had been distorted all that he had read. His faith was nothing but panic and his thoughts were all confusion. Then he hated his father. He fought to be free of his father and his father's God, now so crushingly shapeless and omnipotent, Who had come out of Eden and Jerusalem and Africa to sweeten the cotton field and make endurable the lash, and Who now hovered, like the promise of mercy, above the brutal Northern streets.

He began to backslide as an angel falls: headlong, furious, anxious to discover the utmost joys of hell. The joys of hell are as difficult to discover as the joys of heaven and are even more overrated. He began to smoke, though it made him dizzy, and he began to drink, though it made him sick. He forced his tongue, which had shouted Hallelujah! and Praise the Lord!, to use a more infernal language. The boys he knew then, in his last year at high school, were more civilized than he and more worldly. He listened to their version of the Scriptures. Yet when one of them, a boy named David, one afternoon took him to a movie (he had said very casually, Yes, I'd like to go) he sat in the dark and trembled, waiting for the ceiling to fall, for the awful light of the second coming to fill the theater, and the wrath of God, unloosed, to hurl him into the lake that burned forever with brimstone fire.

David and his father met once, just before Johnnie left home. David called for him one Saturday afternoon to take him downtown somewhere. As David, very hot and uncomfortable in the little living room, rose to leave, his father held out his hand and said, "Are you a Christian?" David reddened and tried to smile. "No," he said. "I'm Jewish." His father dropped his hand and turned away. Johnnie opened the door quickly and pushed David in front of him into the hall. When he pulled the door shut behind him he looked into his father's eyes. His father looked on him with that distant hatred with which one considers Judas; and yet with more than that, for, his father's eyes told him, he was henceforth damned by his own wish, having forsaken the few righteous to make his home in the populous Sodom and entered into an alliance with his father's enemies and the enemies of the Lord.

The conductor called out his station and he walked to the door, waiting for the train to stop. There were trees along the road he took to the hospital and a few neat, characterless houses, with here and there a hedge, clipped into a round shape, as unreal-looking and as fragile as the glittering baubles that hang from Christmas trees. This was a world he might never enter, the world his father had despised. The world had rejected his father as it now rejected him. But "Fear not," his father had preached, "them that are able to kill the body, but are not able to kill the soul; but rather fear Him who is able to destroy both body and soul in hell." When his father spoke from the pulpit one did not ask whether he spoke with the fire of bitterness or the fire of love. In the leaden days, the wintry days, in their several, precarious homes, when they were alone with no singing, and no transfiguring light made his father's head majestic, was he sad? When he wept and trembled on his knees before God in the overwhelming joy of his salvation did he also weep to see that his children grew thin and surly, that he was not always able to provide their bread? Then for the first time he tried to imagine his father lying helpless on white sheets, among strangers, being handled and ruled by strangers, his own will being set at naught.

He passed through the gates and began a half run up the walk, for suddenly he had to look at his father's face again. At the end of the walk stood the great silent building in which his father lay; silence covered these grounds and all the buildings, a silence that frightened him unreasonably.

The nurse considered him with cold, almost hostile detachment. "Yes?"

He realized that his face was wet. He stammered: "Is Gabriel Grimes a patient here?"

"Are you a relative?"

"His son."

Without a word she opened the door so that he could enter and, as he entered, locked it behind him. Then she turned and he followed her. The corridor was much longer than it had seemed when he peered in from the outside and the white pressed on his temples. The floor was white, of some material like marble, slippery and veined with gray. They opened a door and mounted a flight of steps, marble like the floor and whiter. At the top of the staircase was a series of doors, secret, dark-brown, against the pressing white. The thin fall sun crept in through opaque windows; it was like an old house in mourning.

The nurse opened one of the doors and they faced a tall man, nearly bald, who wore a white coat and gray trousers. He was standing in a very small room, which seemed to have no windows and was of a dull, smoke-like color. On the desk, in an ashtray, was a smoking cigar.

.   .   .

"Yes?" said the doctor.

"Grimes," the nurse replied. It was as if some secret signal for his destruction had been exchanged over his head. She left, closing the door behind her.

"Have a seat," the doctor said; very kindly, so that Johnnie knew that the doctor was uncomfortable. He sat down in the soft leather chair, looking about the room for some object which would engage his attention. The doctor sat down behind the desk, facing him; he opened a folder.

"You're his oldest son?"

"Yes."

The gray-green eyes looked at him sharply. He looked away.

"You've never visited your father here before?"

"No." He coughed. It sounded obscene, diseased, in the antiseptic room. "I—I haven't been living at home."

The doctor turned back to the folder. "He was admitted here nearly two years ago. Had you left home then?"

"Yes."

"Did you know he'd been admitted?"

"Yes."

Again the gray-green eyes whipped him lightly, pursuing some conjecture of their own. Johnnie looked down at the smoldering cigar. The string of his loins threatened to snap.

"Do you know what it was your father suffered from?"

"No. I—my mother told me something—it wasn't very clear." He tried to smile; the doctor ignored it.

"It was a kind of paranoia. He was always religious, wasn't he?"

"Yes. He was."

"You're not?"

"No."

The doctor looked at him. "He may have brooded about this. You left very shortly before he was brought here?"

"Yes."

"You and he had quarrelled?"

"Yes."

"Your father stopped working and stopped preaching, stayed at home and read his Bible and prayed. He refused to eat because he said his family was trying to poison him. Your mother has told us that he would steal out of the house and buy a bag of fruit, oranges or the like, and come back and sit in a corner and eat them, rind, pulp, and all."

He said nothing and watched the doctor. The doctor picked up the cigar and put it down.

"We had a great deal of trouble with him here. When he had been here a short while we realized that he was tubercular. We did what we could—" He paused and looked at Johnnie. "He is in a coma now. Would you like to see him?"

"Yes," he said.

The doctor rose from the desk and, standing, crushed the cigar. Automatically, Johnnie rose too, bracing his shaking legs. The doctor moved to the door. "He is just down the hall," the doctor said.

He followed the doctor out of the door. He stared at the doctor's moving back and looked away, for the doctor's jacket was white and the motion made him sick. He felt that he was being slowly, irrevocably trapped.

They entered a small room with curtained windows. There was a shaded bulb high in the ceiling. There was nothing in the room except a bed and a chair and a screen around the bed. The shaded bulb was black-gray in the socket.

"He has been quite ill," the doctor said.

He nodded, but did not move. The doctor looked at him kindly for a moment and motioned for him to follow behind the screen. He moved slowly behind the doctor. At the edge of the screen the doctor stopped; he looked at the doctor, wondering what was wrong, and realized that the doctor was being tactful. He did not feel that he should be present at the last meeting of a son and his father.

So he reluctantly stepped behind the screen. He was overwhelmed by the bed; but he did not look at the bed directly. As though he were wading in deep water he held his head very high and braced his body. He saw the white bedposts, he was aware of a body's outline on the bed; then, with a wrench, as though some strong hand had grasped the back of his head and turned it roughly, as though his father were forcing him to look down on the evidence of some misdemeanor, he forced himself to look down on the bed. There lay his father, black against white sheets.

And his gorge rose. This could not be his father. The heavy skull pressed into the pillow; the deep eye sockets pressed into the skull. The eyes were open, black, and varnished, the straight nose flared and trembled above the purple lips. The mouth was open and foam-flecked. The neck stretched like a phallic column, obscene and secret, with a very slow, indifferent pulsation. The skeleton, beneath the twin, inadequate coverings of the white blankets and the black skin, rose in sharp, sardonic edges, like blunted knives pushing through leather. The wrist was now a polished bone, the fingers were of ebony, with blue nails. From beneath the blanket a wild thigh and ankle showed. The thigh was no thicker than the forearm. All over the room suddenly there was a sick sweet-sour smell.

It was his father that he watched dying; and no more would this violent man possess him; this arm would never be raised again. The ragged edge of sound which now issued from the throat would be silence soon or singing behind the far-flung stars. Now he was the man, the conqueror, alone on the tilting earth.

He felt thrown without mercy into everlasting space; or as though some door on which he had been knocking with all his weight had been, without warning, rudely opened; and now, like a two-year-old, he sprawled on his face and belly and burning knees, into an unfamiliar room, screaming with that unutterably astounded, apocalyptic terror of a child.

He moved nearer to the bed and murmured *Daddy*. And the sound stopped, the skeleton became perfectly still. Then it seemed that there was no sound being made anywhere on earth. Now communication, forgiveness, deliverance, never, the hope was gone. *He's gone to meet the Lord.*

He laughed to himself at the phrase and again he called his father. A voice said, *Here now. Here now.* He felt hands on his shoulders and he tried to break away, screaming for his father. But he knew, in the awful, endless silence at the bottom of his mind, that it was himself who cried and himself who listened, that his cry would never be heard; it would bang forever against the walls of heaven and he would live with his recurring cry, the force of his anguish powerless to defeat the force of time and death. He wanted to run, to hide, to run out of the world and be forever hidden; but hands were holding him, a white face overwhelmed him, shooting out gray-green lights like signals for his destruction. He beat against the whiteness until his arms seemed bleeding in their sockets. Then the hands stapled his arms behind him; he sweated with the pain; and the gray-veined, marble floor opened up and dropped him a long way down.

They made him drink cocoa and rest and they wiped his forehead with an evil-smelling ointment. He took from their hands the brown paper bundle of his father's clothes and walked the long corridor to the door. The door crashed behind him and he ran down the walk to the iron gates which reared and glittered against the black, descending sky.

But the stars were out and the moon, a crescent, hung fanged and evil, gleaming through the passing clouds. He walked the railroad platform, carrying the bundle of his father's clothes, waiting for the train to the city. Far behind him stood the hospital buildings, sprawling and sinister and all the windows dark.

Tomorrow a wagon would arrive from the city to take his father's body away. For three days he would lie in state in a shabby velvet funeral parlor; men and women from the church would come and look down on his father and whisper and leave. They would look on his son, his oldest son, and warn him of the enormity of the danger in which he had placed his soul.

Jesus, thou Son of David, have mercy on me. He paced the platform, carrying the bundle, listening to the sharp crack of his heels on the wood. He lit a cigarette; the brief flare lit up the night around him and he held the match until it burned his fingers and then dropped it and ground it beneath his heel.

A cloud uncovered the moon again. He watched it move slowly across the sky, impossible, eternal, burning, like God hanging over the world.

SOURCES

The material in this book originally appeared in the following publications:

"Mass Culture and the Creative Artist: Some Personal Notes." *Culture for the Millions? Mass Media in Modern Society*, edited by Norman Jacobs. Princeton: Van Nostrand, 1959.

"A Word from Writer Directly to Reader." *Fiction of the Fifties: A Decade of American Writing*, edited by Herbert Gold. New York: Doubleday, 1959.

"From *Nationalism, Colonialism, and the United States: One Minute to Twelve—A Forum.*" Liberation Committee for Africa, first-anniversary celebration, June 2, 1961. New York: Photo-Offset Press, 1961.

"Theater: The Negro In and Out." *Urbanite*, April 1961. Reprinted in *Negro Digest*, April 1966.

"Is *A Raisin in the Sun* a Lemon in the Dark?" *Tone*, April 1961.

"As Much Truth As One Can Bear." *The New York Times Book Review*, January 14, 1962.

"Geraldine Page: Bird of Light." *Show*, February 1962.

"From *What's the Reason Why: A Symposium by Best-Selling Authors*: James Baldwin, *Another Country.*" *The New York Times Book Review*, December 2, 1962.

"The Artist's Struggle for Integrity." *Freedomways*, 1963. Reprinted in *Seeds of Liberation*, edited by Paul Goodman. New York: George Braziller, 1964.

"We Can Change the Country." *Liberation,* October 1963.

"Why I Stopped Hating Shakespeare." *The Observer,* April 19, 1964.

"The Uses of the Blues." *Playboy,* January 1964.

"What Price Freedom?" *Freedomways,* second quarter, 1964.

"The White Problem." *100 Years of Emancipation,* edited by Robert A. Goodwin. Chicago: Rand McNally, 1964.

"Black Power." Originally appeared as "Black Power: James Baldwin in Defense of Stokely Carmichael." *The Guardian,* February 14, 1968.

"The Price May Be Too High." *The New York Times,* February 2, 1969.

"The Nigger We Invent." *Integrated Education,* March–April 1969.

"Speech from the Soledad Rally." *Speeches from the Soledad Brothers Rally, Central Hall, Westminster, 20/4/71.* London: Friends of Soledad, 1974.

"A Challenge to Bicentennial Candidates." Op-ed, *Los Angeles Times,* February 1, 1976. Reprinted as "Looking for the Bicentennial Man" in the *San Francisco Chronicle,* February 15, 1976.

"The News from All the Northern Cities Is, to Understate It, Grim; the State of the Union Is Catastrophic." Op-ed, *The New York Times,* April 5, 1978.

"*Lorraine Hansberry* at the Summit." *Freedomways,* fourth quarter, 1979.

"On Language, Race, and the Black Writer." Op-ed, *Los Angeles Times,* April 29, 1979.

"Of the Sorrow Songs: The Cross of Redemption." *Edinburgh Review,* August 1979.

"Black English: A Dishonest Argument." *Black English and The Education of Black Children and Youth,* a symposium at Wayne State University, Detroit, Michigan, 1980.

"This Far and No Further." *Time Capsule,* summer/fall 1983.

"On Being 'White' . . . and Other Lies." *Essence,* April 1984.

"Blacks and Jews." *Black Scholar,* November–December 1988.

"To Crush a Serpent." *Playboy*, January 1987.

"The Fight: Patterson vs. Liston." *Nugget*, February 1963. Reprinted in *Antaeus*, spring 1989.

"Sidney Poitier." *Look*, July 23, 1968.

"Letters from a Journey." *Harper's*, May 1963.

"The International War Crimes Tribunal." *Freedomways*, third quarter, 1967.

"Anti-Semitism and Black Power." *Freedomways*, first quarter, 1967.

"An Open Letter to My Sister Angela Y. Davis." *The New York Review of Books*, January 7, 1971.

"A Letter to Prisoners." *Inside/Out*, vol. 3, no. 1 (summer 1982).

"The Fire This Time: Letter to the Bishop." *The New Statesman*, August 23, 1985.

"A Quarter-Century of Un-Americana." Originally appeared as the envoi to *A Quarter Century of Un-Americana, 1938–1963: A Tragico-Comical Memorabilia of HUAC*, edited by Charlotte Pomerantz. New York: Manzani & Munsell, 1963.

"*Memoirs of a Bastard Angel: A Fifty-Year Literary and Erotic Odyssey* by Harold Norse." Originally appeared as the preface to *Ole*, no. 5 (1965). Reprinted in *Memoirs of a Bastard Angel*. New York: William Morrow, 1989.

"*The Negro in New York: An Informal Social History, 1626–1940*, edited by Roi Ottley and William J. Weatherby." Originally appeared as the introduction to *The Negro in New York*. New York: Oceana Publications, 1967.

"*Daddy Was a Number Runner* by Louise Meriwether." Originally appeared as the foreward to *Daddy Was a Number Runner*. Englewood Cliffs, N.J.: Prentice-Hall, 1970.

"*A Lonely Rage* by Bobby Seale." Originally appeared as "Stagolee," the foreword to *A Lonely Rage*. New York: Times Books, 1978.

"*Best Short Stories* by Maxim Gorky." Originally appeared as "Maxim Gorki As Artist." *The Nation*, April 12, 1947.

"*Mother* by Maxim Gorky." Originally appeared as "Battle Hymn." *New Leader*, November 29, 1947.

"*The Amboy Dukes* by Irving Shulman." Originally appeared as "When the War Hit Brownsville." *New Leader,* May 17, 1947.

"*The Sure Hand of God* by Erskine Caldwell." Originally appeared as "The Dead Hand of Caldwell." *New Leader,* December 6, 1947.

"*The Sling and the Arrow* by Stuart Engstrand." Originally appeared as "Without Grisly Gaiety." *New Leader,* September 20, 1947.

"*Novels and Stories* by Robert Louis Stevenson, edited by V. S. Pritchett; and *Robert Louis Stevenson* by David Daiches." Originally appeared as "Bright World Darkened." *New Leader,* January 24, 1948.

"*Flood Crest* by Hodding Carter." Originally appeared as "Change Within a Channel." *New Leader,* April 24, 1948.

"*The Moth* by James M. Cain." Originally appeared as "Modern Rover Boys." *New Leader,* August 14, 1948.

"*The Portable Russian Reader,* edited by Bernard Guilbert Guerney." Originally appeared as "Literary Grab-Bag." *New Leader,* February 28, 1948.

"*The Person and the Common Good* by Jacques Maritain." Originally appeared as "Present and Future." *New Leader,* March 13, 1948.

"*The Negro Newspaper* by Vishnu V. Oak; *Jim Crow America* by Earl Conrad; *The High Cost of Prejudice* by Bucklin Moon; *The Protestant Church and the Negro* by Frank S. Loescher; *Color and Conscience* by Buell G. Gallagher; *From Slavery to Freedom* by John Hope Franklin; and *The Negro in America* by Arnold Rose." Originally appeared as "Too Late, Too Late." *Commentary,* January 1949.

"*The Cool World* by Warren Miller." Originally appeared as "War Lord of the Crocodiles." *New York Times Book World,* January 21, 1959.

"*Essays* by Seymour Krim." Originally appeared as "Views of a Near-Sighted Cannoneer." *The Village Voice,* July 13, 1961.

"*The Arrangement* by Elia Kazan." Originally appeared as "God's Country." *New York Review,* March 23, 1967.

"*A Man's Life: An Autobiography* by Roger Wilkins." Originally appeared as "Roger Wilkins: A Black Man's Odyssey in White America." *The Washington Post Book World,* June 6, 1982.

"The Death of a Prophet." *Commentary,* March 1950.

A NOTE ABOUT THE AUTHOR

James Baldwin was born in 1924. He is the author of more than twenty works of fiction and nonfiction. Among the awards he received are a Eugene F. Saxon Memorial Trust Award, a Rosenwald Fellowship, a Guggenheim Fellowship, a *Partisan Review* Fellowship, and a Ford Foundation grant. He was made a Commander of the Legion of Honor in 1986. He died in 1987.

A NOTE ON THE TYPE

This book was set in Monotype Dante, a typeface designed by Giovanni Mardersteig (1892–1977). Its first use was in an edition of Boccaccio's *Trattatello in laude di Dante* that appeared in 1954. Although modeled on the Aldine type used for Pietro Cardinal Bembo's treatise *De Aetna* in 1495, Dante is a thoroughly modern interpretation of the venerable face.

Composed by
North Market Street Graphics, Lancaster, Pennsylvania

Printed and bound by
Berryville Graphics, Berryville, Virginia

Designed by
Maggie Hinders